WEBSTER'S
UNIVERSAL

GRAMMAR
DICTIONARY

WEBSTER'S
UNIVERSAL
GRAMMAR
DICTIONARY

**GEDDES&
GROSSET**

First published in this edition 2007

Copyright © 2004 Geddes & Grosset,
David Dale House, New Lanark, Scotland, ML11 9DJ

ISBN 978-1-84205-630-1

Printed and bound in India

Contents

Grammar

abstract noun a noun which is the name of a thing that cannot be touched but refers to a quality, concept or idea. Examples of abstract nouns include 'anger', 'beauty', 'courage', 'Christianity', 'danger', 'fear', 'greed', 'hospitality', 'ignorance', 'jealousy', 'kudos', 'loyalty', 'Marxism', 'need', 'obstinacy', 'pain', 'quality', 'resistance', 'safety', 'truth', 'unworthiness', 'vanity', 'wisdom', 'xenophobia', 'youth', 'zeal'. *See also* **concrete noun.**

active voice one of the two voices that verbs are divided into, the other being passive voice. In verbs in the active voice, commonly called **active verbs**, the subject of the verb performs the action described by the verb. Thus, in the sentence 'The boy threw the ball', 'throw' is in the active voice since the subject of the verb (the boy) is doing the throwing. Similarly, in the sentence 'Her mother was driving the car', 'driving' is in the active voice since it is the subject of the sentence (her mother) that is doing the driving. Similarly, in the sentence 'We saw the cows in the field', 'saw' is the active voice since it is the subject of the sentence (we) that is doing the seeing.

adjectival clause a kind of subordinate clause that describes or modifies a noun or pronoun. It is better known by the name relative clause.

adjective a word that describes or gives information about a noun or pronoun. It is said to qualify a noun or pronoun since it limits the word it describes in some way, by making it more specific. Thus, adding the adjective 'red' to 'book' limits 'book', since it means we can forget about books of any other colour. Similarly, adding 'large' to 'book' limits it, since it means we can forget about books of any other size.

Adjectives tell us something about the colour, size, number, quality or classification of a noun or pronoun, as in 'purple curtains', 'jet-black hair', 'bluish eyes'; 'tiny baby', 'large houses', 'biggish gardens', 'massive estates'; five children', 'twenty questions', 'seventy-five books'; 'sad people', 'joyful occasions', 'delicious food', 'civil engineering', 'nuclear physics', 'modern languages', 'Elizabethan drama'.

adverb a word that adds to our information about a verb, as in 'work rapidly'; about an adjective, as in 'an extremely beautiful young woman'; or about another adverb, as in 'sleeping very soundly'. Adverbs are said to modify the words to which they apply since they limit the words in some way and make them more specific. Thus, adding 'slowly' to 'walk', as in 'They walked slowly down the hill', limits the verb 'walk' since all other forms of 'walk', such as 'quickly', 'lazily', etc, have been discarded.

adverbial clause a subordinate clause that modifies the main or principal clause by adding information about time, place, concession, condition, manner, purpose and result, as in 'He left after the meal was over', 'They left it where they found it', 'Wherever I went I saw signs of poverty', 'I have to admire his speech, although I disagree with what he said', 'He does his best at school work even though he is not very good at it', 'Whilst I myself do not like him, I can understand why he is popular', 'We cannot go unless we get permission', 'He looked at her as if he hated her', 'They will have to work long hours in order to make that amount of money', 'They started to run so as to get home before it rained', and 'He fell awkwardly so that he broke his leg.' Adverbial clauses usually follow the main clause but most of them can be put in front of the main clause for reasons of emphasis or style.

agent noun a noun that refers to someone who is the 'doer' of the action of a verb. It is usually spelt ending in either *-er*, as 'enquirer', or in *-or*, as in 'investigator' and 'supervisor', but frequently either of these endings is acceptable, as 'adviser/advisor'.

agreement or **concord** the agreeing of two or more elements in a clause or sentence, i.e. they take the same number, person or gender. In English the most common form of agreement is that between subject and verb, and this usually involves **number agreement**. This means that singular nouns are usually accompanied by singular verbs, as in 'She looks well', 'He is working late' and 'The boy has passed the exam', and that plural nouns are usually accompanied by plural verbs, as in 'They look well', 'They are working late' and 'The boys have passed the exam'.

Problems arise when the noun in question can be either singular or plural, for example, 'audience', 'committee', 'crowd', 'family', 'government', 'group'. Such nouns take a singular verb if the user is regarding the people or items referred to by the noun as a group, as in 'The family is moving house', or as individuals, as in 'The family are quarrelling over where to go on holiday'.

Compound subjects, that is two or more nouns acting

as the subject, whether singular or plural, joined with
'and', are used with a plural noun, as in 'My friend and
I are going to the cinema tonight' and 'James and John
are leaving today', unless the two nouns together repre-
sent a single concept, as 'brandy and soda', in which
case the verb is in the singular, as in 'Brandy and soda
is his favourite drink' and 'cheese and pickle' in
'Cheese and pickle is the only sandwich filling available'.

Indefinite pronouns such as 'anyone', 'everyone', 'no
one', 'someone', 'either', 'neither' are singular and
should be followed by a singular verb, as in 'Each of the
flats is self-contained', 'Everyone is welcome', 'No one
is allowed in without a ticket' and 'Neither is quite what
I am looking for'.

Agreement with reference to both number and gender affects pronouns, as in 'She blames herself', 'He
could have kicked himself' and 'They asked themselves
why they had got involved'. Problems arise when the
pronoun is indefinite and so the sex of the person is
unspecified. Formerly in such cases the masculine pronouns were assumed to be neutral and so 'Each of the
pupils was asked to hand in his work' was considered
quite acceptable. The rise of feminism has led to a ques-
tioning of this assumption and alternatives have been
put forward. These include 'Each of the pupils was
asked to hand in his/her (or his or her) work', but some
people feel that this is clumsy. Another alternative is
'Each of the pupils was asked to hand in their work'.
Although it is ungrammatical, this convention is becoming quite acceptable in modern usage. To avoid both
the clumsiness of the former and the ungrammatical

nature of the latter, it is possible to cast the whole sentence in the plural, as in 'All the pupils were asked to hand in their work'.

also an adverb that should not be used as a conjunction instead of 'and'. Thus sentences such as 'Please send me some apples, also some pears' are grammatically incorrect.

although a conjunction that is used to introduce a subordinate adverbial clause of concession, as in 'They are very happy although they are poor', meaning 'Despite the fact they are poor they are happy'. 'Though' or 'even though' can be substituted for 'although', as in 'they are very happy even though they are poor'. *See* **adverbial clause** and **conjunction**.

and a conjunction that is called a coordinating conjunction because it joins elements of language that are of equal status. The elements may be words, as in 'cows and horses', 'John and James', 'provide wine and beer'; phrases, as in 'working hard and playing hard' and 'trying to look after her children and her elderly parents'; clauses, as in 'John has decided to emigrate and his brother has decided to join him' and 'He has lost his job and he now has no money'. When a coordinating conjunction is used, the subject of the second clause can sometimes be omitted if it is the same as the subject of the first clause, as in 'They have been forced to sell the house and are very sad about it'.

The use of and at the beginning of a sentence is disliked by many people. It should be used only for deliberate effect, as in 'And then he saw the monster', or in informal contexts.

Other coordinating conjunctions include 'but', 'or',

'yet', 'both . . . and', 'either . . . or', and 'neither. . . . nor', as in 'poor but honest' and 'the blue dress or the green one'.

antecedent a term that refers to the noun or noun phrase in a main clause to which a relative pronoun in a relative clause refers back. Thus in the sentence 'People who live dangerously frequently get hurt', 'people' is an antecedent. Similarly, in the sentence 'The child identified the old man who attacked her', 'the old man' is the antecedent. *See* **relative clause**.

any a pronoun that may take either a singular or plural verb, depending on the context. When a singular noun is used, a singular verb is used, as in 'Is any of the cloth still usable?' 'Are any of the children coming?' When a plural noun is used, either a plural or a singular verb can be used, the singular verb being more formal, as in 'Did you ask if any of his friends were/was there?'.

anyone a pronoun that should be used with a singular verb, as in 'Has anyone seen my book?' and 'Is anyone coming to the lecture?' To be grammatically correct, anyone should be followed, where relevant, by a singular, not plural, personal pronoun or possessive adjective, but, in order to avoid the sexist 'his', this involves sentences such as 'Has anyone left his/her book?' Because this construction is rather clumsy, there is a growing tendency to use 'their' and be ungrammatical.

apposition a term for a noun or a phrase that provides further information about another noun or phrase. Both nouns and phrases refer to the same person or thing. In the phrase 'Peter Jones, our managing director', ' Peter Jones' and 'our managing director' are said to be in apposition. Similarly, in the phrase 'his cousin, the chairman of the firm', 'his cousin' and 'the chairman of the firm' are in apposition.

as a conjunction that can introduce either a subordinate adverbial clause of time, as in 'I caught sight of him as I was leaving', a subordinate adverbial clause of manner, as in 'He acted as he promised', and a subordinate adverbial clause of reason, as in 'As it's Saturday he doesn't have to work'. it is also used in the as. . . . as construction, as in 'She doesn't play as well as her sister does'.

The construction may be followed by a subject pronoun or an object pronoun, according to sense. In the sentence 'He plays as well as she', which is a slightly shortened form of 'She plays as well as he does', 'he' is a subject pronoun. In informal English the subject pronoun often becomes an object pronoun, as in 'She plays as well as him'. In the sentence 'They hate their father as much as her', 'her' is an object and the sentence means 'They hate their father as much as they hate her', but in the sentence 'They hate their father as much as she', 'she' is a subject and the sentence means 'They hate their father as much as she does'. *See* **adverbial clause** and **conjunction**.

attributive adjective a term for an adjective that is placed immediately before the noun that it qualifies. In the phrases 'a red dress', 'the big house' and 'an enjoyable evening', 'red, 'big' and 'enjoyable' are attributive adjectives.

auxiliary verb a verb that is used in forming tenses, moods and voices of other verbs. These include 'be', 'do' and 'have'.

The verb 'to be' is used as an auxiliary verb with the *-ing* form of the main verb to form the continuous present tense, as in 'They are living abroad just now' and 'We were thinking of going on holiday but we changed our minds'.

The verb 'to be' is used as an auxiliary verb with the past participle of the main verb to form the passive voice, as in 'Her hands were covered in blood' and 'These toys are manufactured in China'.

The verb 'to have' is used as an auxiliary verb along with the past participle of the main verb to form the perfect tenses, as in 'They have filled the post', 'She had realized her mistake' and 'They wished that they had gone earlier'.

The verb 'to be' is used as an auxiliary verb along with the main verb to form negative sentences, as in 'She is not accepting the job'. The verb 'to do' is used as an auxiliary verb along with the main verb to form negative sentences, as in 'he does not believe her'. It is also used along with the main verb to form questions, as in 'Does he know that she's gone?' and to form sentences in which the verb is emphasized, as in 'She *does* want to go'. *See* **modal verb**.

base the basic uninflected form of a verb. It is found as the infinitive form, as in 'to go' and 'to take', and as the imperative form, as in 'Go away!' and 'Take it!' It is also the form that the verb in the present indicative tense takes, except for the third person singular, as in 'I always go there on a Sunday' and 'They go there regularly.'

be *see* **auxiliary verb**.

because a conjunction that introduces a subordinate adverbial clause of reason, as in 'They sold the house because they are going abroad' and 'Because she is shy she never goes to parties'. It is often used incorrectly in such constructions as 'The reason they went away is because they were bored'. This should be rephrased as either 'The reason that they went away is that they were bored' or 'They went away because they were bored'. *See* **adverbial clause**.

before a word that can either be a preposition, an adverb or a conjunction. As a preposition it means either 'coming or going in front of in time', as in 'He was the chairman before this one', or coming or going in front of in place, as in 'She went before him into the restaurant'. As an adverb it means 'at a time previously', as in 'I told you before' and 'He has been married before'. As a conjunction it introduces a subordinate adverbial clause of time, as in 'The guests arrived before she was ready for them' and 'Before I knew it they had arrived'. *See* **adverbial clause**.

both a word that can be used in several ways: as a determiner, as in 'He broke both his arms' and 'He lost both his sons in the war'; as a pronoun, as in 'I don't mind which house we rent, I like them both' and 'Neither of them work here. The boss sacked them both'; as a conjunction, as in 'He both likes and admires her' and 'She is both talented and honest'. Both can sometimes be followed by 'of'. 'Both their children are grown up' and 'Both of their children are grown up' are both acceptable. Care should be taken to avoid using both unnecessarily. In the sentence 'The two items are both identical', 'both' is redundant.

but a conjunction that connects two opposing ideas. It is a coordinating conjunction in that it connects two elements of equal status. The elements may be words, as in 'not James but John'; phrases, as in 'working hard but not getting anywhere' and 'trying to earn a living but not succeeding'; clauses, as in 'He has arrived but his sister is late', 'I know her but I have never met him' and 'He likes reading but she prefers to watch TV'. It should not be used when no element of contrast is present. Thus the following sentence should be rephrased, at least in formal English—'She is not professionally trained but taught herself'. The two clauses are in fact agreeing, not disagreeing, with each other and so, strictly speaking, but should not be used.

The use of but at the beginning of a sentence is disliked by many people. It should be used only for deliberate effect or in informal contexts.

case one of the forms in the declension of a noun, pronoun or adjective in a sentence.

clause a group of words containing a finite verb which forms part of a compound or complex sentence. See main clause, subordinate clauses, adverbial clause, noun clause and relative clause.

commands these are expressed in the imperative mood, as in 'Be quiet!', 'Stop crying!', 'Go away!'

common noun simply the name of an ordinary, everyday non-specific thing or person, as opposed to proper nouns, which refer to the names of particular individuals or specific places. Common nouns include 'baby', 'cat', 'girl', 'hat', 'park', 'sofa' and 'table'.

comparison of adjectives this is achieved in two different ways. Some adjectives form their comparative by adding -*er* to the positive or absolute form, as in 'braver', 'louder', 'madder', 'shorter' and 'taller'. Other adjectives form their comparative by using 'more' in conjunction with them, as in 'more beautiful', 'more realistic', 'more suitable' and 'more tactful'. Which is the correct form is largely a matter of length. One-syllable adjectives, such as 'loud', add *-er*, as 'louder'. Two-syllable adjectives sometimes have both forms as a possibility, as in 'gentler/more gentle', and 'cleverest/most clever'. Adjectives with three or more syllables usually form their comparatives with 'more', as in 'more comfortable', 'more gracious', 'more regular' and 'more understanding'. Some adjectives are irregular in their comparative forms, as in 'good/better', 'bad/worse', 'many/more'. Only if they begin with *un-* are they likely to end in *-er*, as in 'untrustworthier'.

Some adjectives by their very definitions do not normally have a comparative form, for example 'unique'.

complement the equivalent of the object in a clause with a linking verb. In the sentence 'Jack is a policeman', 'a policeman' is the complement. In the sentence 'Jane is a good mother', 'a good mother' is the complement', and in the sentence 'His son is an excellent football player', 'an excellent football player' is the complement.

complex sentence a type of sentence in which there is a main clause and one or more subordinate clauses. The sentence 'We went to visit him although he had been unfriendly to us' is a complex sentence since it is composed of a main clause and one subordinate clause ('although he had been unfriendly to us'). The sentence 'We wondered where he had gone and why he was upset' is a complex sentence since it has a main clause and two subordinate clauses ('where he had gone' and 'why he was upset').

compound sentence a type of sentence with more than

one clause and linked by a coordinating conjunction, such as 'and' or 'but', as in 'He applied for a new job and got it' and 'I went to the cinema but I didn't enjoy the film'.

concord *see* **number agreement**.

concrete noun the name of something that one can touch, as opposed to an abstract noun, which one cannot. Concrete nouns include 'bag', 'glass', 'plate', 'pot', 'clothes', 'field', 'garden', 'flower', 'potato', 'foot' and 'shoe'. *See* **abstract noun**.

conjunction a word that connects words, clauses or sentences. Conjunctions are of two types. A **coordinating conjunction** joins units of equal status, as in 'bread and butter', 'We asked for some food and we got it'. A **subordinating conjunction** joins a dependent or subordinating clause to main verbs: in 'We asked him why he was there', 'why he was there' is a subordinate clause and thus 'why' is a subordinating conjunction.

content words *see* **function word**.

continuous tenses *see* **tense**.

copula *see* **linking verb**.

copular verb *see* **equative** and **linking verb**.

count noun is the same as countable noun.

countable noun is one which can be preceded by 'a' and can take a plural, as in 'hat/hats', 'flower/flowers'. *See also* **uncountable noun**.

dangling participle a participle that has been misplaced in a sentence. A participle is often used to introduce a phrase that is attached to a subject mentioned later in a sentence, as in 'Worn out by the long walk, she fell to the ground in a faint'. 'Worn out' is the participle and 'she' the subject. Another example is 'Laughing in glee at having won, she ordered some champagne'. In this sentence 'laughing' is the participle and 'she' is the subject. It is a common error for such a participle not to be related to any subject, as in 'Imprisoned in the dark basement, it seemed a long time since she had seen the sun'. This participle is said to be 'dangling'. Another example of a dangling participle is contained in 'Living alone, the days seemed long'.

It is also a common error for a participle to be related to the wrong subject in a sentence, as in 'Painting the ceiling, some of the plaster fell on his head', 'Painting' is the participle and should go with a subject 'he'. Instead it goes with 'some of the plaster'. Participles in this situation are more correctly known as **misrelated participles**, although they are also called dangling participles.

declarative mood the same as **indicative mood**.

declarative sentence a sentence that conveys information. The subject precedes the verb in it. Examples include 'They won the battle', 'He has moved to another town', 'Lots of people go there' and 'There is a new person in charge'.

declension the variation of the form of a noun, adjective or pronoun to show different cases, such as nominative and accusative. It also refers to the class into which such words are placed, as in first declension, second declension, etc. The term applies to languages such as Latin but is not applicable to English.

degree a level of comparison of gradable adjectives. The degrees of comparison comprise **absolute** or **positive**, as in 'big', 'calm', 'dark', 'fair', 'hot', 'late', 'short' and 'tall'; **comparative**, as in 'bigger', 'calmer', 'darker', 'fairest', 'hotter', 'late', 'shorter' and 'taller'; **superlative**, as in 'biggest', 'calmest', 'darkest', 'fairest', 'hottest', 'latest', 'shortest' and 'tallest'.

Degree can also refer to adverbs. Adverbs of degree include 'extremely', 'very', 'greatly', 'rather', 'really', 'remarkably', 'terribly', as in 'an extremely rare case', 'a very old man', 'He's remarkably brave' and 'We're terribly pleased'.

demonstrative determiner a determiner that is used to indicate things or people in relationship to the speaker or writer in space or time. 'This' and 'these' indicate nearness to the speaker, as in 'Will you take this book home?' and 'These flowers are for you'. 'That' and 'those' indicate distance from the speaker, as in 'Get that creature out of here!' and 'Aren't those flowers over there beautiful!'

demonstrative pronoun a pronoun that is similar to a demonstrative determiner except that it stands alone in place of a noun rather than preceding a noun, as in 'I'd like to give you this', 'What is that?', 'These are interesting books' and 'Those are not his shoes'.

dependent clause a clause that cannot stand alone and make sense, unlike an independent or main clause. Dependent clauses depend on the main clause. The term is the same as subordinate clause.

determiner a word that is used in front of a noun or pronoun to tell us something about it. Unlike an adjective, it does not, strictly speaking, 'describe' a noun or pronoun. Determiners are divided into the following categories: **articles** (a, an, the) as in 'a cat', 'an eagle', 'the book'; **demonstrative determiners** (this, that, these, those), as in 'this girl', 'that boy' and 'those people';

possessive determiners (my, your, his/her/its, our, their), as in 'my dog', 'her house', 'its colour', 'their responsibility'; **numbers** (one, two, three, four, etc, first, second, third, fourth, etc), as in 'two reasons', 'five ways', 'ten children'; and **indefinite** or **general determiners** (all, another, any, both, each, either, enough, every, few, fewer, less, little, many, most, much, neither, no, other, several, some), as in 'both parents', 'enough food', 'several issues'. Many words used as determiners are also pronouns. *See* **adjective**; **demonstrative determiner**; **number**.

direct object the noun, noun phrase, noun or nominal clause or pronoun that is acted upon by the action of a transitive verb. In the sentence 'She bought milk', 'bought' is a transitive verb and 'milk' is a noun which is the direct object. In the sentence 'She bought loads of clothes', 'bought' is a transitive verb and 'loads of clothes' is the direct object. In the sentence 'He knows what happened', 'knows' is a transitive verb and 'what happened' is a 'noun clause' or 'nominal clause'. A direct object is frequently known just as object. *See* **indirect object**.

direct speech the reporting of speech by repeating exactly the actual words used by the speaker, as in 'Peter said, "I am tired of this." '

distributive pronoun a pronoun that refers to individual members of a class or group. These include 'each', 'either', 'neither', 'none', 'everyone', 'no one'. Such pronouns, where relevant, should be accompanied by singular verbs and singular personal pronouns, as in 'All the men are to be considered for the new posts. Each is to send in his application'. Problems arise when the sex of the noun to which the distributive pronoun refers back is either unknown or unspecified. Formerly it was the convention to treat such nouns as masculine and so to make the distributive pronoun masculine, as in 'All pupils must obey the rule.. Nowadays this convention is frequently considered to be unacceptably sexist and attempts have been made to get round this. One solution is to use 'him/her' (or 'him or her'), etc, as in 'The students have received a directive from the professor. Each is to produce his/her essay by tomorrow.' This convention is considered by many people to be clumsy. They prefer to be ungrammatical and use a plural personal pronoun, as in 'The pupils are being punished. Each is to inform their parents'. This use is becoming increasingly common, even in textbooks. Where possible, it is preferable to rephrase sentences to avoid being either sexist or ungrammatical, as in 'All of the pupils must tell their parents.'

Each, either, etc, in such contexts is fairly formal. In less formal situations 'each of', 'either of', etc, is more usual, as in 'Each of the boys will have to train really hard to win' and 'Either of the dresses is perfectly suitable'.

do an auxiliary verb that is used to form negative forms, as in, 'I do not agree with you', 'They do not always win', 'He does not wish to go' and 'She did not approve of their behaviour'. It is also used to form interrogative forms, as in 'Do you agree?', 'Does she know about it?', 'Did you see that?' and 'I prefer to go by train. Don't you?' Do is also used for emphasis, as in 'I do believe you're right' and 'They do know, don't they?'

double passive a clause that contains two verbs in the

passive, the second of which is an infinitive, as in 'The goods are expected to be dispatched some time this week'. Some examples of double passives are clumsy or ungrammatical and should be avoided, as in 'Redundancy notices are proposed to be issued next week'.

dual gender a category of nouns in which there is no indication of gender. The nouns referred to include a range of words used for people, and occasionally animals, which can be of either gender. Unless the gender is specified we do not know the sex of the person referred to. Such words include 'artist', 'author', 'poet', 'singer', 'child', 'pupil', 'student', 'baby', 'parent', 'teacher', 'dog'. Such words give rise to problems with accompanying singular pronouns. *See* **each**.

dummy subject a subject that has no intrinsic meaning but is inserted to maintain a balanced grammatical structure. In the sentences 'It has started to rain' and 'It is nearly midnight', 'it' is a dummy subject. In the sentences 'There is nothing else to say' and 'There is no reason for his behaviour', 'there' is a dummy subject.

dynamic verb a verb with a meaning that indicates action, as 'work' in 'They work hard', 'play' in 'The boys play football at the weekend' and 'come' in 'The girls come here every Sunday'.

each a word that can be either a determiner or a distributive pronoun. Each as a determiner is used before a singular noun and is accompanied by a singular verb, as in 'Each candidate is to reapply', 'Each athlete has a place in the final', 'Each country is represented by a head of state' and 'Each chair was covered in chintz'.

Each of can sometimes be used instead of each, as in 'each of the candidates'. Again a singular verb is used. If the user wishes to emphasize the fact that something is true about every member of a group, **each one of** should be used and not 'every', as in 'Each one of them feels guilty', 'Each one of us has a part to play.

As a pronoun, each also takes a singular verb, as in 'They hate each other. Each is plotting revenge', 'These exercises are not a waste of time. Each provides valuable experience'.

Each, where relevant, should be accompanied by a singular personal pronoun, as in 'Each girl has to provide her own sports equipment', 'Each of the men is to take a turn at working night shift', 'The boys are all well off and each can afford the cost of the holiday' and 'There are to be no exceptions among the women staff. Each one has to work full time'.

Problems arise when the noun that each refers back to is of unknown or unspecified sex. Formerly nouns in such situations were assumed to be masculine, as in 'Each pupil was required to bring his own tennis racket' and 'Each of the students has to provide himself with a tape recorder'. Nowadays such a convention is regarded as being sexist and the use of 'he/her', 'his/her', etc, is proposed, as in 'Each pupil was required to bring his/her (or 'his or her') own tennis racket' and 'Each student has to provide himself/herself (or 'himself or herself') with a tape recorder'. Even in written English such a convention can be clumsy and it is even more so in spoken English. For this reason many people decide to be ungrammatical and opt for 'Each pupil was required to bring their own tennis racket' and 'Each student has to provide themselves with a tape recorder'. This is becoming increasingly acceptable, even in textbooks.

Both sexism and grammatical error can be avoided by rephrasing such sentences, as in 'All pupils are required to bring their own tennis rackets' and 'All students have to provide themselves with tape recorders'.

either a word that can be used as either a determiner or distributive pronoun. As a determiner it is used with a singular verb, as in 'Either hotel is expensive' and 'In principle they are both against the plan but is either likely to vote for it?'

Either of can be used instead of either. It is used before a plural noun, as in 'either of the applicants' and 'either of the houses'. It is accompanied by a singular verb, as in 'Either of the applicants is suitable' and 'Either of the houses is big enough for their family'.

Either can be used as a distributive pronoun and takes a singular verb, as in 'We have looked at both houses and either is suitable' and 'She cannot decide between the two dresses but either is appropriate for the occasion'. This use is rather formal.

In the **either. . . . or** construction, a singular verb is used if both subjects are singular, as in 'Either Mary or Jane knows what to do' and 'Either my mother or my father plans to be present'. A plural verb is used if both nouns involved are plural, as in 'Either men or women can play' and 'Either houses or flats are available'.

When a combination of singular and plural subjects is involved, the verb traditionally agrees with the subject that is nearer to it, as in 'Either his parents or his sister is going to come' and 'Either his grandmother or his parents are going to come'.

As a pronoun, either should be used only of two possibilities.

emphasizing adjective an adjective that is used for emphasis. 'Very' is an emphasizing adjective in the sentence 'His very mother dislikes him' and 'own' is an emphasizing adjective in 'He likes to think that he is his own master'.

emphasizing adverb an adverb used for emphasis. 'Really' is an emphasizing adverb in the sentence 'She really doesn't care whether she lives or dies', and 'positively' is an emphasizing adverb in the sentence 'He positively does not want to know anything about it'.

emphatic pronoun a reflexive pronoun that is used for emphasis, as in 'He knows himself that he is wrong', 'She admitted herself that she had made a mistake' and 'The teachers themselves say that the headmaster is too strict'.

ending the final part of a word consisting of an inflection that is added to a base or root word. The '-ren' part of 'children' is an ending, the '-er' of 'poorer' is an ending and the '-ing' of 'falling' is an ending.

equative a term that indicates that one thing is equal to, or the same as, another. The verb 'to be' is sometimes known as an **equative verb** because it links a subject and complement that are equal to each other, as in 'He is a rogue' ('he' and 'rogue' refer to the same person) and 'His wife is a journalist' ('his wife' and 'journalist' refer to the same person). Other equative verbs include 'appear', 'become', 'look', 'remain' and 'seem', as in 'She looks a nasty person' and 'He became a rich man'. Such verbs are more usually known as **copular verbs**.

every a word used with a singular noun to indicate that all the members of a group are being referred to. It takes a singular verb, as in 'Every soldier must report for duty', 'Every machine is to be inspected' and 'Every house has a different view'. Every should also be accompanied, where relevant, by a singular pronoun, as in 'Every boy has his job to do', 'Every girl is to wear a dress' and 'Every machine is to be replaced'. Problems arise when the sex of the noun to which every refers is unknown or unspecified. Formerly it was the custom to assume such a noun to be masculine and to use masculine pronouns, as in 'Every pupil is to behave himself properly. This assumption is now regarded as sexist, and to avoid this 'he/she', 'him/her' and 'his/her' can be used. Many people feel that this convention can become clumsy and prefer to be ungrammatical by using 'they', 'them' and 'their', as in 'Every pupil is to behave themselves properly.' This use is becoming increasingly common, even in textbooks. Many sentences of this kind can be rephrased to avoid being either sexist or ungrammatical, as in 'All pupils are to behave themselves properly'. *See* **each**.

everyone a pronoun that takes a singular verb, as in 'Everyone is welcome' and 'Everyone has the right to a decent standard of living'. In order to be grammatically correct, it should be accompanied, where relevant, by a singular personal pronoun but it is subject to the same kind of treatment as every.

feminine the term for the gender that indicates female persons or animals. It is the opposite of 'masculine'. The feminine gender demands the use of the appropriate pronoun, including 'she', 'her', 'hers' and 'herself', as in 'The girl tried to save the dog but *she* was unable to do so', 'The woman hurt *her* leg', 'Mary said that the book is *hers*', and 'The waitress cut *herself*'.

finite clause

The feminine forms of words, formed by adding -*ess*, used to be common but many such forms are now thought to be sexist. Words such as 'author', 'sculptor', 'poet' are now considered to be neutral terms that can be used to refer to a man or a woman. Some -*ess* words are either still being used or are in a state of flux, as in 'actress'. *See* **-ess** in **Affixes** section.

finite clause a clause that contains a finite verb, as in 'when she sees him', 'after she had defeated him', and 'as they were sitting there'.

finite verb a verb that has a tense and has a subject with which it agrees in number and person. For example 'cries' is finite in the sentence 'The child cries most of the time', and 'looks' is finite in the sentence 'The old man looks ill'. However 'go' in the sentence 'He wants to go' is non-finite since it has no variation of tense and does not have a subject. Similarly in the sentence 'Sitting on the river-bank, he was lost in thought', 'sitting' is non-finite.

first person this refers to the person who is speaking or writing when referring to himself or herself. The **first person pronouns** are 'I', 'me', 'myself' and 'mine', with the plural forms being 'we', 'us', 'ourselves' and 'ours'. Examples include 'She said, "*I* am going home"', '"*I* am going shopping," he said', '"*We* have very little money left," she said to her husband' and 'He said, "*We* shall have to leave now if we are to get there on time"'.

The **first person determiners** are 'my' and 'our', as in 'I have forgotten to bring *my* notebook' and 'We must remember to bring *our* books home.'

form word *see* **function word**.

fragmentary sentence *see* **major sentence**.

frequentative a term referring to a verb that expresses frequent repetition of an action. In English the verb endings *-le* and *-el* sometimes indicate the frequentative form, as in 'waddle' from 'wade', 'sparkle' from 'spark', 'crackle' from 'crack' and 'dazzle' from 'daze'. The ending *-er* can also indicate the frequentative form, as in 'stutter', 'spatter' and 'batter'.

function word a word that has very little meaning but is primarily of grammatical significance and merely performs a 'function' in a sentence. Function words include determiners, and prepositions such as in, on and up. Words that are not function words are sometimes known as **content words**.

Function word is also known as **form word** or **structure word**.

future perfect tense the tense of a verb that is formed by 'will' or 'shall' together with the perfect tense, as in 'They will have been married ten years next week', 'You will have finished work by this time tomorrow' and 'By the time Jane arrives here she will have been travelling non-stop for forty-eight hours'.

future tense the tense of a verb that describes actions or states that will occur at some future time. It is marked by 'will' and 'shall'. Traditionally 'shall' was used with subjects in the first person, as in 'I shall see you tomorrow' and 'We shall go there next week', and 'will' was used with subjects in the second and third person, as in 'You will find out next week', 'He will recognize her when he sees her' and 'They will be on the next train'. Formerly 'will' was used with the first person and 'shall' with the second and third person to indicate emphasis or insistence, as in 'I *will* go on my own' and 'We *will* be able to afford it'; 'You *shall* pay what you owe' and 'The children *shall* get a holiday'. In modern usage 'shall' is usually used only for emphasis or insistence, whether with the first, second or third person, except in formal contexts. Otherwise 'will' is used, as in 'I will go tomorrow', 'We will have to see', 'You will be surprised', and 'They will be on their way by now'.

The future tense can also be marked by 'be about to' plus the infinitive of the relevant verb or 'be going to' plus the infinitive of the relevant verb. Examples include 'We are about to leave for work', 'They are about to go on holiday', 'She is going to be late' and 'They are going to demolish the building'.

gemination the doubling of consonants before a suffix.

gender in the English language this usually refers to the natural distinctions of sex (or absence of sex) that exist, and nouns are classified according to these distinctions— masculine, feminine and neuter. Thus, 'man', 'boy', 'king', 'prince', 'emperor', 'duke', 'heir', 'son', 'brother', 'father', 'nephew', 'husband', 'bridegroom', 'widower', 'hero', 'cock', 'drake', 'fox' and 'lion' are masculine nouns. Similarly, 'girl', 'woman', 'queen', 'princess', 'empress', 'duchess', 'heiress', 'daughter', 'sister', 'mother', 'niece', 'wife', 'bride', 'widow', 'heroine', 'hen', 'duck', 'vixen' and 'lioness' are feminine nouns. Similarly, 'table', 'chair', 'desk', 'carpet', 'window', 'lamp', 'car', 'shop', 'dress', 'tie', 'newspaper', 'book', 'building' and 'town' are all neuter.

Some nouns in English can refer either to a man or a woman, unless the sex is indicated in the context. Such neutral nouns are sometimes said to have dual gender. Examples include 'author', 'singer', 'poet', 'sculptor', 'proprietor', 'teacher', 'parent', 'cousin', 'adult' and 'child'. Some words in this category were formerly automatically assumed to be masculine and several of them had feminine forms, such as 'authoress', 'poetess', 'sculptress' and 'proprietrix'. In modern times this was felt to be sexist and many of these feminine forms are now rarely used, for example, 'authoress' and 'poetess'. However some, such as actress and waitress, are still in common use.

genitive case a case that indicates possession or ownership. It is usually marked by *s* and an apostrophe. Many spelling errors centre on the position of the *s* in relation to the apostrophe.

gerund the *-ing* form of a verb when it functions as a noun. It is sometimes known as a **verbal noun**. It has the same form as the present participle but has a different function. For example, in the sentence 'He was jogging down the road', 'jogging' is the present participle in the verb phrase 'was jogging', but in the sentence 'Running is his idea of relaxation', 'running' is a gerund because it acts as a noun as the subject of the sentence. Similarly, in the sentence 'We were smoking when the teacher found us', 'smoking' is the present participle in the verb phrase 'were smoking', but in the sentence 'We were told that smoking is bad for our health', 'smoking' is a gerund since it acts as a noun as the subject of the clause.

get this verb is sometimes used to form the passive voice instead of the verb 'to be'. The use of the verb 'to get' to form the passive, as in 'They get married tomorrow', 'Our team got beaten today' and 'We got swindled by the con man' is sometimes considered to be more informal than the use of 'be'. Often there is more action involved when the get construction is used than when be is used, since get is a more dynamic verb, as in 'She was late leaving the pub because she got involved in an argument' and in 'It was her own fault that she got arrested by the police. She hit one of the constables'.

Get is frequently overused. Such overuse should be avoided, particularly in formal contexts. Get can often be replaced by a synonym such as 'obtain', 'acquire', 'receive', 'get hold of', etc. Thus, 'If you are getting into money difficulties you should get some financial advice. Perhaps you could get a bank loan' could be rephrased as 'If you are in financial difficulty you should obtain some financial help. Perhaps you could receive a bank loan'.

Got, the past tense of get, is often used unnecessarily, as in 'She has got red hair and freckles' and 'We have got enough food to last us the week'. In these sentences 'has' and 'have' are sufficient on their own.

goal this can be used to describe the recipient of the action of a verb, the opposite of 'agent' or 'actor'. Thus, in the sentence 'The boy hit the girl', 'boy' is the 'agent' or 'actor' and 'girl' is the goal. Similarly, in the sentence 'The dog bit the postman', 'dog' is the 'agent' or 'actor' and 'postman' is the goal.

govern a term that is used of a verb or preposition in relation to a noun or pronoun to indicate that the verb or preposition has a noun or pronoun depending on it. Thus, in the phrase 'on the table', 'on' is said to govern 'table'.

gradable a term that is used of adjectives and adverbs to mean that they can take degrees of comparison. Thus 'clean' is a gradable adjective since it has a comparative form (cleaner) and a superlative form (cleanest). 'Soon' is a gradable adverb since it has a comparative form (sooner) and a superlative form (soonest). Such words as 'supreme', which cannot normally have a comparative or superlative form, are called **non-gradable**.

habitual a term used to refer to the action of a verb that occurs regularly and repeatedly. The **habitual present** is found in such sentences as 'He goes to bed at ten every night', 'She always walks to work' and 'The old man sleeps all day'. This is in contrast to the **stative present**, which indicates the action of the verb that occurs at all times, as in 'Cows chew the cud', 'Water becomes ice when it freezes', 'Children grow up' and 'We all die'. Examples of the **habitual past** tense include; 'They travelled by train to work all their lives', 'We worked twelve hours a day on that project' and 'She studied night and day for the exams'.

hanging participle *see* **dangling participle**.

have a verb that has several functions. A major use is its part in forming the 'perfect tense' and 'past perfect tense', or 'pluperfect tense', of other verb tenses. It does this in conjunction with the 'past participle' of the verb in question.

The perfect tense of a verb is formed by the present tense of the verb have and the past participle of the verb. Examples include 'We have acted wisely', 'They have beaten the opposition', 'The police have caught the thieves', 'The old man has died', 'The child has eaten all the food', 'The baby has fallen downstairs', 'They have grabbed all the bargains', 'You have hated him for years' and 'He has indicated that he is going to retire'. The past perfect or pluperfect is formed by the past tense of the verb have and the past participle of the verb in question, as in 'He had jumped over the fence', 'They had kicked in the door', 'The boy had led the other children to safety', 'His mother had made the cake', 'The headmaster had punished the pupils' and 'They had rushed into buying a new house'. Both perfect tenses and past perfect or pluperfect tenses are often contracted in speech or in informal written English, as in 'We've had enough for today', 'You've damaged the suitcase', 'You've missed the bus', 'He's lost his wallet', 'She's arrived too late', 'They'd left before the news came through', 'She'd married without telling her parents', 'He'd packed the goods himself' and 'You'd locked the door without realizing it'.

Have is often used in the phrase **have to** in the sense that something must be done. In the present tense have to can be used instead of 'must', as in 'You have to leave now', 'We have to clear this mess up', 'He has to get the next train' and 'The goods have to be sold today'. If the 'something that must be done' refers to the future the verb **will have to** is used', as in 'He will have to leave now to get there on time', 'The old man will have to go to hospital' and 'They'll have to move out of the house when her parents return'. If the 'something that must be done' refers to the past, **had to** is used, as in 'We had to take the injured man to hospital', 'They had to endure freezing conditions on the mountain', 'They'd to take a reduction in salary' and 'We'd to wait all day for the workman to appear'.

Have is also used in the sense of 'possess' or 'own', as in 'He has a swimming pool behind his house', 'She has a huge wardrobe', 'We have enough food' and 'They have four cars'. In spoken or in informal English 'have got' is often used, as in 'They've got the largest house in the street', 'We've got problems now', 'They haven't got time'. This use should be avoided in formal English.

Have is also used to indicate suffering from an illness or disease, as in 'The child has measles', 'Her father has flu' and 'She has heart disease'. Have can also indicate that an activity is taking place, as in 'She's having a shower', 'We're having a party', 'She is having a baby' and 'They are having a dinner party'.

he a personal pronoun that is used as the subject of a sentence or clause to refer to a man, boy, etc. It is thus said to be a 'masculine' personal pronoun. Since he refers to a third party and does not refer to the speaker or the person being addressed, it is a third-person pronoun. Examples include 'James is quite nice but he can be boring', 'Bob has got a new job and he is very pleased' and 'He is rich now but his parents are still very poor'.

He traditionally was used not only to refer to nouns relating to the masculine sex but also to nouns that are now regarded as being neutral or of dual gender. Such nouns include 'architect', 'artist', 'athlete', 'doctor', 'passenger', 'parent', 'pupil', 'singer', 'student'. Without further information from the context it is impossible to know to which sex such nouns are referring. In modern usage it is regarded as sexist to assume such words to be masculine by using he to refer to one of them unless the context indicates that the noun in question refers to a man or boy. Formerly it was considered acceptable to write or say 'Send a message to the architect who designed the building that he is to attend the meeting'

helping verb

whether or not the writer or speaker knew that the architect was a man. Similarly it was considered acceptable to write or say 'Please tell the doctor that he is to come straight away' whether or not the speaker or writer knew that the doctor was in fact a man. Nowadays this convention is considered sexist. In order to avoid sexism it is possible to use the convention 'he/she', as in 'Every pupil was told that he/she was to be smartly dressed for the occasion', 'Each passenger was informed that he/she was to arrive ten minutes before the coach was due to leave' and 'Tell the doctor that he/she is required urgently'. However this convention is regarded by some people as being clumsy, particularly in spoken English or in informal written English. Some people prefer to be ungrammatical and use the plural personal pronoun 'they' instead of 'he/she' in certain situations, as in 'Every passenger was told that they had to arrive ten minutes before the coach was due to leave' and 'Every student was advised that they should apply for a college place by March' and this use is becoming increasingly common, even in textbooks. In some cases it may be possible to rephrase sentences and avoid being either sexist or ungrammatical, as in 'All the passengers were told that they should arrive ten minutes before the coach was due to leave' and 'All students were advised that they should apply for a college place by March'.

helping verb another name for **auxiliary verb**.

hendiadys a figure of speech in which two nouns joined by 'and' are used to express an idea that would normally be expressed by the use of an adjective and a noun, as in 'through storm and weather' instead of 'through stormy weather'.

her a personal pronoun. It is the third person singular, is feminine in gender and acts as the object in a sentence, as in 'We saw her yesterday', 'I don't know her', 'He hardly ever sees her', 'Please give this book to her', 'Our daughter sometimes plays with her' and 'We do not want her to come to the meeting'. *See* **he**; **she**.

hers a personal pronoun. It is the third person singular, feminine in gender and is in the possessive case. 'The car is not hers', 'I have forgotten my book but I don't want to borrow hers', 'This is my seat and that is hers', and 'These clothes are hers'. *See* **his**; **her** and **possessive**.

him the third person masculine personal pronoun when used as the object of a sentence or clause, as in 'She shot him', 'When the police caught the thief they arrested him' and 'His parents punished him after the boy stole the money'. Traditionally him was used to apply not only to masculine nouns, such as 'man' and 'boy', but also to nouns that are said to be 'of dual gender'. These include 'architect', 'artist', 'parent', 'passenger', 'pupil' and 'student'. Without further information from the context, it is not possible for the speaker or writer to know the sex of the person referred to by one of these words. Formerly it was acceptable to write or say 'The artist must bring an easel with him' and 'Each pupil must bring food with him'. In modern usage this convention is considered sexist and there is a modern convention that 'him/her' should be used instead to avoid sexism, as in 'The artist must bring an easel with him/her' and 'Each pupil must bring food with 'him/her'. This convention is felt by some people to be clumsy, particularly in spoken and informal English, and some people prefer

to be ungrammatical and use the plural personal pronoun 'them' instead, as in 'The artist must bring an easel with them' and 'Each pupil must bring food with
them'. This use has become increasingly, even in textbooks. In some situations it is possible to avoid being
either sexist or ungrammatical by rephrasing the sentence, as in 'All artists must bring easels with them' and
'All pupils must bring food with them'. *See* **he**.

him/her *see* **him**.

his the third personal masculine pronoun when used to
indicate possession, as in 'He has hurt his leg', 'The boy
has taken his books home' and 'Where has your father
left his tools?' Traditionally his was used to refer not
only to masculine nouns, such as 'man', 'boy', etc, but to
what are known as nouns 'of dual gender'. These include 'architect', 'artist', 'parent', 'passenger', 'pupil'
and 'student'. Without further information from the context it is not possible for the speaker or the writer to
know the sex of the person referred to by one of these
words. Formerly it was considered acceptable to use his
in such situations, as in 'Every pupil has to supply his
own sports equipment' and 'Every passenger is responsible for his own luggage'. In modern usage this is now
considered sexist and there is a modern convention that
'his/her' should be used instead to avoid sexism, as in
'Every pupil has to supply his/her own sports equipment' and 'Every passenger is responsible for his/her
own luggage'. This convention is felt by some people to
be clumsy, particularly when used in spoken or informal
written English. Some people prefer to be ungrammatical and use the plural personal pronoun 'their', as in
'Every pupil must supply their own sports equipment'

and 'Every passenger is to be responsible for their own luggage' and this use has become increasingly common, even in textbooks. In some situations it is possible to avoid being sexist, clumsy and ungrammatical by re-phrasing the sentence, as in 'All pupils must supply their own sports equipment' and 'All passengers are to be responsible for their own luggage.

his/her *see* **his**.

hybrid a word that is formed from words or elements derived from different languages, such as 'television'.

if a conjunction that is often used to introduce a subordinate adverbial clause of condition, as in 'If he is talking of leaving he must be unhappy', 'If you tease the dog it will bite you', 'If he had realized that the weather was going to be so bad he would not have gone on the expedition', 'If I had been in charge I would have sacked him' and 'If it were a better organized firm things like that would not happen'.

If can also introduce a 'nominal' or 'noun clause', as in 'He asked if we objected' and 'She inquired if we wanted to go'.

imperative mood the verb mood that expresses commands. The verbs in the following sentences are in the imperative mood: 'Go away!', 'Run faster!', 'Answer me!', 'Sit down!', 'Please get out of here!'. All of these expressions with verbs in the imperative mood sound rather imperious or dictatorial and usually end with an exclamation mark, but this is not true of all expressions with verbs in the imperative mood. For example, the following sentences all have verbs in the imperative mood: 'Have another helping of ice cream', 'Help yourself to more wine', 'Just follow the yellow arrows to the X-ray department', and 'Turn right at the roundabout'. Sentences with verbs in the imperative mood are known as **imperative sentences**.

imperfect a tense that denotes an action in progress but not complete. The term derives from the classification in Latin grammar and was traditionally applied to the 'past imperfect', as in 'They were standing there'. The imperfect has now been largely superseded by the progressive/continuous tense, which is marked by the use of 'be' plus the present participle. Continuous tenses are used when talking about temporary situations at a particular point in time, as in 'They were waiting for the bus'.

impersonal a verb that is used with a formal subject, usually 'it', as in 'It is raining' and 'They say it will snow tomorrow'.

indefinite pronouns these are used refer to people or things without being specific as to exactly who or what they are. They include 'everyone', 'everybody', 'everything', 'anyone', 'anybody', 'anything', 'somebody', 'someone', 'something' and 'nobody', 'no one', 'nothing', as in 'Everyone is to make a contribution', 'Anyone can enter', 'Something will turn up' and 'Nobody cares'.

independent clause a clause that can stand alone and make sense without being dependent on another clause, as in 'The children are safe'. Main clauses are independent clauses. Thus in the sentence 'She is tired and she wants to go home', there are two independent clauses joined by 'and'. In the sentence 'She will be able to rest when she gets home', 'She will be able to rest' is an independent clause and 'when she gets home' is a dependent clause. In the sentence 'Because she is intelligent she thinks for herself', 'she thinks for herself' is an independent clause and 'because she is intelligent' is a dependent clause.

indicative mood the mood of a verb which denotes making a statement. The following sentences have verbs in the indicative mood: 'We go on holiday tomorrow', 'He was waiting for her husband', 'They have lost the match' and 'She will arrive this afternoon'. The indicative mood is sometimes known as the **declarative mood**. The other moods are the imperative mood and subjunctive mood.

indirect object an object that can be preceded by 'to' or 'for'. The indirect object usually refers to the person who benefits from an action or receives something as the result of it. In the sentence 'Her father gave the boy food', 'boy' is the indirect object and 'food' is the direct object. The sentence could be rephrased as 'Her father gave food to the boy'. In the sentence 'He bought his mother flowers', 'his mother' is the indirect object and 'flowers' is the direct object. The sentence could have been rephrased as 'He bought flowers for his mother'. In the sentence 'They offered him a reward', 'him' is the indirect object and 'reward' is the direct object. The sentence could be rephrased as 'They offered a reward to him'.

indirect question a question that is reported in indirect speech, as in 'We asked them where they were going', 'They inquired why we had come' and 'They looked at us curiously and asked where we had come from'. Note that a question mark is not used.

indirect speech also known as **reported speech** a way of reporting what someone has said without using the actual words used by the speaker. There is usually an introductory verb and a subordinate 'that' clause, as in 'He said that he was going away', 'They announced that they were leaving next day' and 'She declared that she had seen him there before'. In direct speech these sentences would become 'He said, "I am going away"', 'They announced, "We are leaving tomorrow"' and 'She declared, "I have seen him there before"'. When the change is made from direct speech to indirect speech, the pronouns, adverbs of time and place and tenses are changed to accord with the viewpoint of the person doing the reporting.

infinitive the base form of a verb when used without any indication of person, number or tense. There are two forms of the infinitive. One is the **to infinitive** form, as in 'They wished to leave', 'I plan to go tomorrow', 'We aim to please' and 'They want to emigrate', 'To know all is to forgive all', 'To err is human', 'Pull the lever to open', 'You should bring a book to read', 'The child has nothing to do', 'She is not very nice to know' and 'It is hard to believe that it happened'. The other form of the infinitive is called the **bare infinitive**. This form consists of the base form of the verb without 'to', as in 'We saw him fall', 'She watched him go', 'They noticed him enter', 'She heard him sigh', 'They let him go', 'I had better leave' and 'Need we return' and 'we dare not go back'. *See* **split infinitive**.

inflect when applied to a word, this means to change form in order to indicate differences of tense, number, gender, case, etc. Nouns inflect for plural, as in 'ships', 'chairs', 'houses' and 'oxen'; nouns inflect for possessive, as in 'boys", 'woman's', 'teachers", and 'parents"; some adjectives inflect for the comparative form, as in 'brighter', 'clearer', 'shorter' and 'taller'; verbs inflect for the third person singular present tense, as in 'hears', 'joins', 'touches' and 'kicks'; verbs inflect for the present participle, as in 'hearing', 'joining', 'touching' and 'kicking'; verbs inflect for the past participle, as in 'heard', 'joined', 'touched' and 'kicked'.

inflection the act of inflecting—*see* **inflect**. It also refers to an inflected form of a word or a suffix or other element used to inflect a word.

-ing form this form of a verb can be either a present participle or a gerund. Present participles are used in the formation of the progressive or continuous tenses, as in 'We were looking at the pictures', 'Children were playing in the snow', 'They are waiting for the bus', 'Parents were showing their anger', 'He has been sitting there for hours'. Present participles can also be used in non-finite clauses or phrases, as in 'Walking along, she did not have a care in the world', 'Lying there, he thought about his life', 'Sighing, he left the room' and 'Smiling broadly he congratulated his friend'.

A large number of adjectives end in -ing. Many of these have the same form as the present participle of a transitive verb and are similar in meaning. Examples include 'an amazing spectacle', 'a boring show', 'an interesting idea', 'a tiring day', 'an exhausting climb' and 'aching limbs'. Some -ing adjectives are related to intransitive verbs, as 'existing problems', 'increasing responsibilities', 'dwindling resources', 'an ageing work force' and 'prevailing circumstances'. Some -ing adjectives are related to the forms of verbs but have different meanings from the verbs, as in 'becoming dress', 'an intensifier

engaging personality', 'a dashing young man' and 'a re-
tiring disposition'. Some -ing adjectives are not related
to verbs at all. These include 'appetizing', 'enterprising',
'impending' and 'balding'. Some -ing adjectives are
used informally for emphasis, as in 'a blithering idiot',
'a stinking cold' and 'a flaming cheek'.

Gerunds act as nouns and are sometimes known as
verbal nouns. Examples include 'Smoking is bad for
one's health', 'Cycling is forbidden in the park' and
'Swimming is his favourite sport'.

intensifier the term for an adverb that affects the degree
of intensity of another word. Intensifiers include 'thoroughly' in 'We were thoroughly shocked by the news',
'scarcely' in 'We scarcely recognized them' and 'totally' in 'She was totally amazed'.

interjection a kind of exclamation. Sometimes they are
formed by actual words and sometimes they simply
consist of sounds indicating emotional noises. Examples
of interjections include 'Oh! I am quite shocked', 'Gosh!
I'm surprised to hear that!', 'Phew! It's hot!', 'Ouch!
That was my foot!', 'Tut-tut! He shouldn't have done
that!' and 'Alas! She is dead.'

interrogative adjective or **determiner** an adjective or
determiner that asks for information in relation to the
nouns which it qualifies, as in 'What dress did you
choose in the end?', 'What kind of book are you looking
for?', 'Which house do you like best?', 'Which pupil
won the prize?', 'Whose bike was stolen?' and 'Whose
dog is that?'

interrogative adverb an adverb that asks a question, as
in 'When did they leave?', 'When does the meeting
start?', 'Where do they live?', 'Where was the stolen car

found?', 'Where did you last see her?', 'Why was she crying?', 'Why have they been asked to leave?', 'How is the invalid?', 'How do you know that she has gone?' and 'Wherever did you find that?'

interrogative pronoun a pronoun that asks a question, as in 'Who asked you to do that?', 'Who broke the vase?', 'What did he say?, 'What happened next?', 'Whose are those books?', 'Whose is that old car?', 'To whom was that remark addressed?' and 'To whom did you address the package?'

interrogative sentence a sentence that asks a question, as in 'Who is that?', 'Where is he?', 'Why have they appeared?', 'What did they take away?, 'Which do you prefer?' and 'Whose baby is that?'. Sentences that take the form of an interrogative question do not always seek information. Sometimes they are exclamations, as in 'Did you ever see anything so beautiful?', 'Isn't she sweet?' and 'Aren't they lovely?'. Sentences that take the form of questions may really be commands or directives, as in 'Could you turn down that radio?', 'Would you make less noise?' and 'Could you get her a chair?'. Sentences that take the form of questions may function as statements, as in 'Isn't there always a reason?' and 'Haven't we all experienced disappointment?'. Some interrogative sentences are what are known as rhetorical questions, which are asked purely for effect and require no answer, as in 'Do you think I am a fool?', 'What is the point of life?' and 'What is the world coming to?'.

intransitive verb a verb that does not take a direct object, as in 'Snow fell yesterday', 'The children played in the sand', 'The path climbed steeply', 'Time will tell', 'The situation worsened', 'Things improved' and 'Prices increased'. Many verbs can be either transitive or intransitive, according to the context. Thus 'play' is intransitive in the sentence 'The children played in the sand' but transitive in the sentence 'The boy plays the piano'. Similarly 'climb' is intransitive in the sentence 'The path climbs steeply' but transitive in the sentence 'The mountaineers climbed Everest'. Similarly 'tell' is intransitive in the sentence 'Time will tell' but transitive in the sentence 'He will tell his life story'.

introductory it the use of 'it' as the subject of a sentence in the absence of a meaningful subject. It is used particularly in sentences about time and the weather, as in 'It is midnight', 'It is dawn', 'It is five o'clock', 'It is twelve noon', 'It is raining', 'It was snowing', 'It was windy' and 'It was blowing a gale'.

invariable a word whose form does not vary by inflection. Such words include 'sheep' and 'but'.

inversion the reversal of the usual word order. It particularly refers to subjects and verbs. Inversion is used in questions, in some negative sentences, and for literary effect. In questions, an auxiliary verb is usually put in front of the subject and the rest of the verb group is put after the subject, as in 'Are you going to see her?' and 'Have they inspected the goods yet?'. The verb 'to do' is frequently used in inversion, as in 'Did he commit the crime?' and 'Do they still believe that?'. Examples of the use of inversion in negative sentences include 'Seldom have I witnessed such an act of selfishness', 'Never had she experienced such pain' and 'Rarely do we have time to admire the beauty of the countryside'. This use in negative sentences is rather formal.

Inversion frequently involves adverbial phrases of

place, as in 'Beyond the town stretched field after field', 'Above them soared the eagle' and 'Along the driveway grew multitudes of daffodils'.

Inversion is also found in conditional clauses that are not introduced by conjunction, as in 'Had you arrived earlier you would have got a meal' and 'Had we some more money we could do more for the refugees'.

irregular adjective an adjective that does not conform to the usual rules of forming the comparative and super- lative (*see* **comparison of adjectives**). Many adjec- tives either add *-er* for the comparative and *-est* for the superlative, as in 'taller', 'shorter' and 'tallest', 'short- est' from 'tall' and 'short'. Some adjectives form their comparatives with 'more' and their superlatives with 'most', as in 'more beautiful', 'more practical' and 'most beautiful', 'most practical'. Irregular adjectives do not form their comparatives and superlatives in either of these ways. Irregular adjectives include:

positive	*comparative*	*superlative*
good	better	best
bad	worse	worst
little	less	least
many	more	most

irregular sentence *see* **major sentence**.

irregular verb a verb that does not conform to the usual pattern of verbs in that some of its forms deviate from what one would expect if the pattern of regular verbs was being followed. There are four main forms of a **regular verb**: the infinitive or base form, as in 'hint', 'halt', 'hate' and 'haul'; the third-person singular form, as 'hints', 'halts', 'hates' and 'hauls'; the -ing form or present participle, as 'hinting', halting', 'hating' and 'hauling'; the *-ed* form or 'past tense' or 'past participle', as 'hinted', halted', 'hated' and 'hauled.

Irregular verbs deviate in some way from that pattern, in particular from the pattern of adding *-ed* to the past tense and past participle. They fall into several categories.

One category concerns those that have the same form in the past tense and past participle forms as the infinitive and do not end in *-ed*, like regular verbs.

Some irregular verbs have two past tenses and two past participles which are the same.

Some irregular verbs have past tenses that do not end in *-ed* and have the same form as the past participle.

Some irregular verbs have regular past tense forms but two possible past participles, one of which is regular.

Some irregular verbs have past tenses and past participles that are different from each other and different from the infinitive.

jussive a type of clause or sentence that expresses a command, as in 'Do be quiet! I'm trying to study', 'Let's not bother going to the party. I'm too tired', 'Would you pass me that book' and 'Look at that everybody! The river has broken its banks'.

linking adverbs and **linking adverbials** words and phrases that indicate some kind of connection between one clause or sentence and another. Examples include 'however', as in 'The award had no effect on their financial situation. It did, however, have a marked effect on their morale'; 'moreover', as in 'He is an unruly pupil. Moreover, he is a bad influence on the other pupils';

'then again', as in 'She does not have very good qualifications. Then again, most of the other candidates have even fewer'; 'in the meantime', as in 'We will not know the planning committee's decision until next week. In the meantime we can only hope'; 'instead', as in 'I thought he would have reigned. Instead he seems determined to stay'.

linking verb a verb that 'links' a subject with its complement. Unlike other verbs, linking verbs do not denote an action but indicate a state. Examples of linking verbs include 'He is a fool', 'She appears calm', 'He appeared a sensible man', 'You seemed to become anxious', 'They became Buddhists', 'The child feels unwell', 'It is getting rather warm', 'It is growing colder', 'You look well', 'She remained loyal to her friend', 'She lived in America but remained a British citizen' and 'You seem thoughtful' and 'She seems a nice person'. Linking verbs are also called **copula** or **copular verbs**.

main clause the principal clause in a sentence on which any subordinate clauses depend for their sense. The main clause can stand alone and make some sense but the subordinate clauses cannot. In the sentence 'I left early because I wanted to catch the 6 o'clock train', 'I left early' is the principal clause and 'because I wanted to catch the 6 o'clock train' is the subordinate clause. In the sentence 'When we saw the strange man we were afraid', the main clause is 'we were afraid' and the subordinate clause is 'when we saw the strange man'. In the sentence 'Because it was late we decided to start out for home as soon as we could', the main clause is 'we decided to start out for home' and the subordinate clauses are 'because it was late' and 'as soon as we could'. A main clause can also be known as a **principal clause** or an independent clause.

major sentence a sentence that contains at least one subject and a finite verb, as in 'We are going' and 'They won'. They frequently have more elements than this, as in 'They bought a car', 'We lost the match', 'They arrived yesterday' and 'We are going away next week'. They are sometimes described as **regular** because they divide into certain structural patterns: a subject, finite verb, adverb or adverbial clause, etc. The opposite of a major sentence is called a **minor sentence**, **irregular sentence** or **fragmentary sentence**. These include interjections such as 'Ouch!' and 'How terrible'; formula expressions, such as 'Good morning' and 'Well done'; and short forms of longer expressions, as in 'Traffic diverted', 'Shop closed', 'No dogs' and 'Flooding ahead'. Such short forms could be rephrased to become major sentences, as in 'Traffic has been diverted because of roadworks', 'The shop is closed on Sundays', 'The owner does not allow dogs in her shop' and 'There was flooding ahead on the motorway'.

masculine in grammatical terms, one of the genders that nouns are divided into. Nouns in the masculine gender include words that obviously belong to the male sex, as in 'man', 'boy', 'king', 'prince' 'bridegroom', 'schoolboy' and 'salesman'. Many words now considered to be of dual gender formerly were assumed to be masculine. These include such words as 'author', 'sculptor' and 'engineer'. Gender also applies to personal pronouns, and the third personal singular pronoun masculine is 'he' (subject), 'him' (object) and 'his' (possessive). For further information *see* **he**; **she**.

mass noun the same as **uncountable noun**.

minor sentence *see* **major sentence**.

misrelated participle *see* **dangling participle**.

modal verb a type of auxiliary verb that 'helps' the main verb to express a range of meanings including, for example, such meanings as possibility, probability, wants, wishes, necessity, permission, suggestions, etc. The main modal verbs are 'can', 'could'; 'may', 'might'; 'will', 'would'; 'shall', 'should'; 'must'. Modal verbs have only one form. They have no *-s* form in the third person singular, no infinitive and no participles. Examples of modal verbs include 'He cannot read and write', 'She could go if she wanted to' (expressing ability); 'You can have another biscuit', 'You may answer the question' (expressing permission); 'We may see her on the way to the station', 'We might get there by nightfall' (expressing possibility); 'Will you have some wine?', 'Would you take a seat?' (expressing an offer or invitation); 'We should arrive by dawn', 'That must be a record' (expressing probability and certainty); 'You may prefer to wait', 'You might like to leave instructions' (expressing suggestion); 'Can you find the time to phone him for me?', 'Could you give him a message?' (expressing instructions and requests); 'They must leave at once', 'We must get there on time' (expressing necessity).

modifier a word, or group of words, that 'modifies' or affects the meaning of another word in some way, usually by adding more information about it. Modifiers are frequently used with nouns. They can be adjectives, as in 'He works in the *main* building' and 'They need a *larger* house'. Modifiers of nouns can be nouns themselves, as in 'the *theatre* profession', 'the *publishing* industry' and

mood

'*singing* tuition'. They can also be place names, as in 'the *Edinburgh* train', a *Paris* café' and 'the *London* underground', or adverbs of place and direction, as in 'a *downstairs* cloakroom' and 'an *upstairs* sitting room'.

Adverbs, adjectives and pronouns can be accompanied by modifiers. Examples of modifiers with adverbs include 'walking *amazingly* quickly' and 'stopping *incredibly* abruptly'. Examples of modifiers with adjectives include 'a *really* warm day' and 'a *deliriously* happy child'. Examples of modifiers with pronouns include '*almost* no one there' and '*practically* everyone present'.

The examples given above are all premodifiers. *See also* **postmodifier**.

mood one of the categories into which verbs are divided. The verb moods are indicative, imperative and subjunctive. The **indicative** makes a statement, as in 'He lives in France', 'They have two children' and 'It's starting to rain'. The **imperative** is used for giving orders or making requests, as in 'Shut that door!', 'Sit quietly until the teacher arrives' and 'Please bring me some coffee'. The **subjunctive** was originally a term in Latin grammar and expressed a wish, supposition, doubt, improbability or other non-factual statement. It is used in English for hypothetical statements and certain formal 'that' clauses, as in 'If I were you I would have nothing to do with it', 'If you were to go now you would arrive on time', 'Someone suggested that we ask for more money' and 'It was his solicitor who suggested that he sue the firm'. The word 'mood' arose because it was said to indicate the verb's attitude or viewpoint.

more an adverb that is added to some adjectives to make

the comparative form (*see* **comparison of adjectives**). In general it is the longer adjectives that have more as part of their comparative form, as in 'more abundant', 'more beautiful', 'more catastrophic', 'more dangerous', 'more elegant', 'more frantic', 'more graceful', 'more handsome', 'more intelligent', 'more luxurious', 'more manageable', 'more opulent', 'more precious', 'more ravishing', 'more satisfactory', 'more talented', 'more unusual', 'more valuable'. Examples of adverbs with more in their comparative form include 'more elegantly', 'more gracefully', 'more energetically', 'more dangerously' and 'more determinedly'.

most an adverb added to some adjectives and adverbs to make the superlative form. In general it is the longer adjectives that have most as part of their superlative form, as in 'most abundant', 'most beautiful', 'most catastrophic', 'most dangerous', 'most elegant', 'most frantic', 'most graceful', 'most handsome', 'most intelligent', 'most luxurious', 'most manageable', 'most noteworthy', 'most opulent', 'most precious', most ravishing', 'most satisfactory', 'most talented', 'most unusual', 'most valuable'. Examples of adverbs with most in their superlative form include 'most elegantly', 'most gracefully', 'most energetically', 'most dangerously' and 'most determinedly'.

multi-sentence a sentence with more than one clause, as in 'She tripped over a rock and broke her ankle' and 'She was afraid when she saw the strange man'.

negative sentence a sentence that is the opposite of a **positive sentence**. 'She has a dog' is an example of a positive sentence. 'She does not have a dog' is an example of a negative sentence. The negative concept is expressed by an auxiliary verb accompanied by 'not' or 'n't'. Other words used in negative sentences include 'never', 'nothing' and 'by no means', as in 'She has never been here' and 'We heard nothing'.

neither an adjective or a pronoun that takes a singular verb, as in 'Neither parent will come' and 'Neither of them wishes to come'. In the **neither . . . nor** construction, a singular verb is used if both parts of the construction are singular, as in 'Neither Jane nor Mary was present'. If both parts are plural the verb is plural, as in 'Neither their parents nor their grandparents are willing to look after them'. If the construction involves a mixture of singular and plural, the verb traditionally agrees with the subject that is nearest it, as in 'Neither her mother nor her grandparents are going to come' and 'Neither her grandparents nor her mother is going to come'. If pronouns are used, the nearer one governs the verb as in 'Neither they nor he is at fault' and 'Neither he nor they are at fault'.

neuter one of the grammatical genders. The other two grammatical genders are masculine and feminine. Inanimate objects are members of the neuter gender. Examples include 'table', 'desk', 'garden', 'spade', 'flower' and 'bottle'.

nominal clause *see* **noun clause**.

non-finite clause a clause which contains a non-finite verb. Thus in the sentence 'He works hard to earn a living', 'to earn a living' is a non-finite clause since 'to earn' is an infinitive and so a non-finite verb. Similarly in the sentence 'Getting there was a problem', 'getting there' is a non-finite clause, 'getting' being a present participle and so a non-finite verb.

non-finite verb a verb that shows no variation in tense and has no subject. The non-finite verb forms include the infinitive form, as in 'go', the present participle and gerund, as in 'going', and the past participle, as in 'gone'.

non-gradable *see* **gradable**.

noun the name of something or someone. Thus 'anchor', 'baker', 'cat', 'elephant', 'foot', 'gate', 'lake', 'pear', 'shoe', 'trunk' and 'wallet' are all nouns. There are various categories of nouns. *See* **abstract noun, common noun, concrete noun, countable noun, proper noun** and **uncountable noun**.

noun clause a subordinate clause that performs a function in a sentence similar to a noun or noun phrase. It can act as the subject, object or complement of a main clause. In the sentence 'Where he goes is his own business', 'where he goes' is a noun clause. In the sentence 'They asked why he objected', 'why he objected' is a noun clause. A noun clause is also known as a **nominal clause**.

noun phrase a group of words containing a noun as its main word and functioning like a noun in a sentence. Thus it can function as the subject, object or complement of a sentence. In the sentence 'The large black dog bit him', 'the large black dog' is a noun phrase, and in the sentence 'They bought a house with a garden', 'with a garden' is a noun phrase. In the sentence 'She is a complete fool', 'a complete fool' is a noun phrase.

number in grammar this is a classification consisting of 'singular' and 'plural'. Thus the number of the pronoun 'they' is 'plural' and the number of the verb 'carries' is singular. *See* **number agreement**.

number agreement or **concord** the agreement of grammatical units in terms of number. Thus a singular subject is followed by a singular verb, as in 'The girl likes flowers', 'He hates work' and 'She was carrying a suitcase'. Similarly a plural subject should be followed by a plural verb, as in 'They have many problems', 'The men work hard' and 'The girls are training hard'.

object the part of a sentence that is acted upon or is affected by the verb. It usually follows the verb to which it relates. There are two forms of object—the direct object and indirect object. A direct object can be a noun, and in the sentence 'The girl hit the ball', 'ball' is a noun and the object. In the sentence 'They bought a house', 'house' is a noun and the object. In the sentence 'They made an error', 'error' is a noun and the object. A direct object can be a noun phrase, and in the sentence 'He has bought a large house', 'a large house' is a noun phrase and the object. In the sentence 'She loves the little girl', 'the little girl' is a noun phrase and the object. In the sentence 'They both wear black clothes', 'black clothes' is a noun phrase and the object'. A direct object can be a noun clause, and in the sentence 'I know what he means', 'what he means' is a noun phrase and the object. In the sentence 'He denied that he had been involved', 'that he had been involved' is a noun phrase and the object. In the sentence 'I asked when he would return', 'when he would return' is a noun phrase and the object. A direct object can also be a pronoun, and in the sentence 'She hit him', 'him' is a pronoun and the object. In the sentence 'They had a car but they sold it', 'it' is a pronoun and the object. In the sentence 'She loves them', 'them' is a pronoun and the object.

objective case the case expressing the object. In Latin it is known as the accusative case.

part of speech each of the categories (e.g. verb, noun, adjective, etc) into which words are divided according to their grammatical and semantic functions.

participle a part of speech, so called because, although a verb, it has the character both of verb and adjective and is also used in the formation of some compound tenses. *See also* **-ing form** and **past participle**.

passive voice the voice of a verb whereby the subject is the recipient of the action of the verb. Thus, in the sentence 'Mary was kicked by her brother', 'Mary' is the receiver of the 'kick' and so 'kick' is in the passive voice. Had it been in the active voice it would have been 'Her brother kicked Mary'. Thus 'the brother' is the subject and not the receiver of the action.

past participle this is formed by adding *-ed* or *-d* to the base words of regular verbs, as in 'acted', ' alluded', 'boarded', 'dashed', 'flouted', 'handed', 'loathed', 'tended' and 'wanted', or in various other ways for irregular verbs.

past tense this tense of a verb is formed by adding *-ed* or *-d* to the base form of the verb in regular verbs, as in 'added', 'crashed', 'graded', 'smiled', 'rested' and 'yielded', and in various ways for irregular verbs.

perfect tense *see* **tense**.

personal pronoun a pronoun that is used to refer back to someone or something that has already been mentioned. The personal pronouns are divided into subject pronouns, object pronouns and possessive pronouns. They are also categorized according to 'person'. *See* **first person**, **second person** and **third person**.

phrasal verb a usually simple verb that combines with a preposition or adverb, or both, to convey a meaning more than the sum of its parts, e.g. to phase out, to come out, to look forward to.

phrase two or more words, usually not containing a finite verb, that form a complete expression by themselves or constitute a portion of a sentence.

positive sentence *see* **negative sentence**.

possessive *see* **genitive**.

possessive pronoun *see* **personal pronoun**; **first person**; **second person** and **third person**.

postmodifier a modifier that comes after the main word of a noun phrase, as in 'of stone' in 'tablets of stone'.

predicate all the parts of a clause or sentence that are not contained in the subject. Thus in the sentence 'The little girl was exhausted and hungry', 'exhausted and hungry' is the predicate. Similarly, in the sentence 'The tired old man slept like a top', 'slept like a top' is the predicate.

predicative adjective an adjective that helps to form the predicate and so comes after the verb, as 'tired' in 'She was very tired' and 'mournful' in 'The music was very mournful'.

premodifier a modifier that comes before the main word of a noun phrase, as 'green' in 'green dress' and 'pretty' in 'pretty houses'.

preposition a word that relates two elements of a sentence, clause or phrase together. Prepositions show how the elements relate in time or space and generally precede the words that they 'govern'. Words governed by prepositions are nouns or pronouns. Prepositions are often very short words, as 'at', 'in', 'on', 'to', 'before' and 'after'. Some complex prepositions consist of two words, as 'ahead of', 'instead of', 'apart from', and some consist of three, as 'with reference to', 'in accordance with' and 'in addition to'. Examples of prepositions in sentences include 'The cat sat on the mat', 'We were at a concert', 'They are in shock', 'We are going to France', 'She arrived before me', 'Apart from you she has no friends' and 'We acted in accordance with your instructions'.

present continuous *see* **tense**.

present participle *see* **-ing words**.

present tense *see* **tense**.

principal clause *see* **main clause**.

progressive present *see* **tense**.

pronoun a word that takes the place of a noun or a noun phrase. *See* **personal pronouns**, **he**, **her**, **him** and **his**, **reciprocal pronouns**, **reflexive pronouns**, **demonstrative pronouns**, **relative pronouns**, **distributive pronouns**, **indefinite pronouns** and **interrogative pronouns**.

proper noun a noun that refers to a particular individual or a specific thing. It is the 'name' of someone or something', as in Australia, Vesuvius, John Brown, River Thames, Rome and Atlantic Ocean.

question tag a phrase that is interrogative in form but is not really asking a question. It is added to a statement to seek agreement, etc. Examples include 'That was a lovely meal, wasn't it?', 'You will be able to go, won't you?', 'He's not going to move house, is he?' and 'She doesn't drive, does she?' Sentences containing question tags have question marks at the end.

reciprocal pronoun a pronoun used to convey the idea of reciprocity or a two-way relationship. The reciprocal

reciprocal verb

pronouns are 'each other' and 'one another'. Examples include 'They don't love each other any more', 'They seem to hate each other', 'We must try to help each other', 'The children were calling one another names', 'The two families were always criticizing one another' and 'The members of the family blame one another for their mother's death'.

reciprocal verb a verb such as 'consult', 'embrace', 'marry', 'meet', etc, that expresses a mutual relationship, as in 'They met at the conference', 'She married him in June'.

reflexive pronoun a pronoun that ends in '-self' or '-selves' and refers back to a noun or pronoun that has occurred earlier in the same sentence. The reflexive pronouns include 'myself', 'ourselves'; 'yourself', 'yourselves'; 'himself', 'herself', 'itself', 'themselves'. Examples include 'The children washed themselves', 'He cut himself shaving', 'Have you hurt yourself?' and 'She has cured herself of the habit'.

Reflexive pronouns are sometimes used for emphasis, as in 'The town itself was not very interesting' and 'The headmaster himself punished the boys'. They can also be used indicate that something has been done by somebody by his/her own efforts without any help, as in 'He built the house himself', 'We converted the attic ourselves'. They can also indicate that someone or something is alone, as in 'She lives by herself' and 'The house stands by itself'.

reflexive verb a verb that has as its direct object a reflexive pronoun, e.g. 'They pride themselves on their skill as a team'.

regular sentence *see* **major sentence**.

regular verb *see* **irregular verb**.

relative clause a subordinate clause that has the function of an adjective. It is introduced by a relative pronoun.

relative pronoun a pronoun that introduces a relative clause. The relative pronouns are 'who', 'whom', 'whose', 'which' and 'that'. Examples of relative clauses introduced by relative pronouns include 'There is the man who stole the money', 'She is the person to whom I gave the money', 'This is the man whose wife won the prize', 'They criticized the work which he had done' and 'That's the house that I would like to buy'. Relative pronouns refer back to a noun or noun phrase in the main clause. These nouns and noun phrases are known as antecedents. The antecedents in the example sentences are respectively 'man', 'person', 'man', 'work' and 'house'.

Sometimes the relative clause divides the parts of the main clause, as in 'The woman whose daughter is ill is very upset', 'The people whom we met on holiday were French' and 'The house that we liked best was too expensive'.

reported speech *same as* **indirect speech**

rhetorical question a question that is asked to achieve some kind of effect and requires no answer. Examples include 'What's this country coming to?', 'Did you ever see the like', 'Why do these things happen to me?', 'Where did youth go?', 'Death, where is thy sting?' and 'Where does time go?'. *See also* **interrogative sentence**.

second person the term used for the person or thing to whom one is talking. The term is applied to personal sentence

pronouns. The second person singular whether acting as the subject of a sentence is 'you', as in 'I told you so', 'We informed you of our decision' and 'They might have asked you sooner'. The second person personal pronoun does not alter its form in the plural in English, unlike in some languages. The possessive form of the second person pronoun is 'yours' whether singular or plural, as in 'These books are not yours' and 'This pen must be yours'.

sentence is at the head of the hierarchy of grammar. All the other elements, such as words, phrases and clauses, go to make up sentences. It is difficult to define a sentence. In terms of recognizing a sentence visually it can be described as beginning with a capital letter and ending with a full stop, or with an equivalent to the full stop, such as an exclamation mark. It is a unit of grammar that can stand alone and make sense and obeys certain grammatical rules, such as usually having a subject and a predicate, as in 'The girl banged the door', where 'the girl' is the subject and 'the door' is the predicate. *See* **major sentence**, **simple sentence**, **complex sentence**.

simple sentence a sentence that cannot be broken down into other clauses. It generally contains a finite verb. Simple sentences include 'The man stole the car', 'She nudged him' and 'He kicked the ball'. *See* **complex sentence** and **compound sentence**.

singular noun a noun that refers to 'one' rather than 'more than one', which is the plural form. *See also* **irregular plural**.

split infinitive an infinitive that has had another word in the form of an adverb placed between itself and 'to', as in 'to rudely push' and 'to quietly leave'. This was once considered a great grammatical sin but the split infinitive is becoming acceptable in modern usage. In any case it sometimes makes for a clumsy sentence if one slavishly adheres to the correct form.

stative present *see* **habitual** and **tense**.

strong verb the more common term for **irregular verb**.

structure word *see* **function word**.

subject that which is spoken of in a sentence or clause and is usually either a noun, as in 'Birds fly' (birds is the noun as subject); a noun phrase, as in 'The people in the town dislike him' (the people in the town' is the subject); a pronoun, as in 'She hit the child' (she is the pronoun as subject); a proper noun, as in 'Paris is the capital of France'. *See* **dummy subject**.

subjunctive *see* **mood**.

subordinate clause a clause that is dependent on another clause, namely the main clause. Unlike the main clause, it cannot stand alone and make sense. Subordinate clauses are introduced by conjunctions. Examples of conjunctions that introduce subordinate clauses include 'after', 'before', 'when', 'if', 'because' and 'since'. *See* **adverbial clause**; **noun clause**.

subordinating conjunction *see* **conjunction**.

suffix *see* **Affix** section.

superlative form the form of an adjective or adverb that expresses the highest or utmost degree of the quality or manner of the word. The superlative forms follow the same rules as comparative forms except that they end in -*est* instead of -*er* and the longer ones use 'most' instead of 'more'. *See also* **comparison of adjectives**.

tense the form of a verb that is used to show the time at which the action of the verb takes place. One of the tenses in English is the **present tense**. It is used to indicate an action now going on or a state now existing. A distinction can be made between the **habitual present**, which marks habitual or repeated actions or recurring events, and the **stative present**, which indicates something that is true at all times. Examples of habitual present include 'He works long hours' and 'She walks to work'. Examples of the stative tense include 'The world is round' and 'Everyone must die eventually'.

The **progressive present** or **continuous present** is formed with the verb 'to be' and the present participle, as in, 'He is walking to the next village', 'She was driving along the road when she saw him' and 'They were worrying about the state of the economy'.

The **past tense** refers to an action or state that has taken place before the present time. In the case of regular verbs it is formed by adding *-ed* to the base form of the verb, as in 'fear/feared', 'look/looked', and 'turn/turned'. *See also* **irregular verbs**.

The **future tense** refers to an action or state that will take place at some time in the future. It is formed with 'will' and 'shall'. Traditionally 'will' was used with the second and third person pronouns ('you', 'he/she/it', 'they') and 'shall' with the first person ('I' and 'we'), as in 'You will be bored', 'He will soon be home', 'They will leave tomorrow', 'I shall buy some bread' and 'We shall go by train'. Also traditionally 'shall' was used with the second and third persons to indicate emphasis, insistence, determination, refusal, etc, as in 'You shall go to the ball' and 'He shall not be admitted'. 'Will' was used with the first person in the same way, as in 'I will get even with him'.

In modern usage 'will' is generally used for the first person as well as for second and third, as in 'I will see you tomorrow' and 'We will be there soon' and 'shall' is used for emphasis, insistence, etc, for first, second and third persons.

The future tense can also be formed with the use of 'be about to' or 'be going to', as in 'We were about to leave' and 'They were going to look for a house'.

Other tenses include the **perfect tense**, which is formed using the verb 'to have' and the past participle. In the case of regular verbs the past participle is formed by adding *ed* to the base form of the verb. *See also* **irregular verbs**. Examples of the perfect tense include 'He has played his last match', 'We have travelled all day' and 'They have thought a lot about it'.

The **past perfect tense** or **pluperfect tense** is formed using the verb 'to have' and the past participle, as in 'She had no idea that he was dead' and 'They had felt unhappy about the situation'.

The **future perfect** is formed using the verb 'to have' and the past participle, as in 'He will have arrived by now'.

they *see* **him** and **third person**.

third person a third party, not the speaker or the person or thing being spoken to. Note that 'person' in this context can refer to things as well as people. 'Person' in this sense applies to personal pronouns. The third person singular forms are 'he', 'she' and 'it' when the subject of a sentence or clause, as in 'She will win' and 'It will be fine'. The third person singular forms are 'him', 'her',

to-infinitive

'it' when the object, as in 'His behaviour hurt her' and 'She meant it'. The third person plural is 'they' when the subject, as in 'They have left' and 'They were angry' and 'them' when the object, as in 'His words made them angry' and 'We accompanied them'.

The possessive forms of the singular are 'his', 'hers' and 'its', as in 'he played his guitar' and 'The dog hurt its leg', and the possessive form of the plural is theirs, as in 'That car is theirs' and 'They say that the book is theirs'. *See* **he**.

to-infinitive the infinitive form of the verb when it is accompanied by 'to' rather than when it is the bare infinitive without 'to'. Examples of the to-infinitive include 'We were told to go', 'I didn't want to stay' and 'To get there on time we'll have to leave now'.

transitive verb a verb that takes a direct object. In the sentence 'The boy broke the window', 'window' is a direct object and so 'broke' (past tense of break) is a transitive verb. In the sentence 'She eats fruit', 'fruit' is a direct object and so 'eat' is a transitive verb. In the sentence 'They kill enemy soldiers' 'enemy soldiers' is a direct object and so 'kill' is a transitive verb. *See* **intransitive verb**.

uncountable noun or **uncount noun** a noun that is not usually pluralized or 'counted'. Such a noun is usually preceded by 'some', rather than 'a'. Uncountable nouns often refer to substances or commodities or qualities, processes and states. Examples of uncountable nouns include butter, china, luggage, petrol, sugar, heat, information, poverty, richness and warmth. In some situations it is possible to have a countable version of what is usually an uncountable noun. Thus 'sugar' is usually considered to be an uncountable noun but it can be used in a countable form in contexts such as 'I take two sugars in my coffee please'. Some nouns exist in an uncountable and countable form. Examples include 'cake', as in 'Have some cake' and 'She ate three cakes' and 'She could not paint for lack of light' and 'the lights went out'.

verb the part of speech often known as a 'doing' word. Although this is rather restrictive, since it tends to preclude auxiliary verbs, modal verbs, etc, the verb is the word in a sentence that is most concerned with the action and is usually essential to the structure of the sentence. Verbs 'inflect' and indicate tense, voice, mood, number, and person. Most of the information on verbs has been placed under related entries. *See* **active voice, auxiliary verb, finite verb, -ing form, intransitive verb, irregular verbs, linking verb, modal verb, mood, non-finite verb, passive voice** and **transitive verb**.

verb phrase a group of verb forms that have the same function as a single verb. Examples include 'have been raining', 'must have been lying', 'should not have been doing' and 'has been seen doing'.

verbal noun *see* **gerund** and **-ing form**.

vocative case a case that is relevant mainly to languages such as Latin which are based on cases and inflections. In English the vocative is expressed by addressing someone, as 'John, could I see you for a minute', or by some form of greeting, endearment or exclamation.

voice one of the categories that describes verbs. It involves two ways of looking at the action of verbs. It is divided into active voice and passive voice.

weak verb a less common term for a regular verb, in which inflection is effected by adding a letter or syllable (dawn, dawned) rather than a change of vowel (rise, rose). *See* **irregular verb**.

Usage

a, an the indefinite article. *See* **Spelling.**

-abled is a suffix meaning 'able-bodied'. It is most usually found in such phrases as 'differently abled', a 'politically correct', more positive way of referring to people with some form of disability, as in 'provide access to the club building for differently abled members'.

ableism or **ablism** means discrimination in favour of able-bodied people as in 'people in wheelchairs unable to get jobs because of ableism'. Note that the suffix '-ism' is often used to indicate discrimination against the group to which it refers, as in 'ageism'.

Aboriginal rather than **Aborigine** is now the preferred term for an original inhabitant of Australia, especially where the word is in the singular.

abuse and **misuse** both mean wrong or improper use or treatment. However, **abuse** tends to be a more condemnatory term, suggesting that the wrong use or treatment is morally wrong or illegal. Thus we find 'misuse of the equipment' or 'misuse of one's talents', but 'abuse of a privileged position' or 'abuse of children'. 'Child abuse' is usually used to indicate physical violence or sexual assault. **Abuse** is also frequently applied to the use of substances that are dangerous or injurious to health, as 'drug abuse', or 'alcohol abuse'. In addition, it is used to describe insulting or offensive language, as in 'shout abuse at the referee'.

academic is used to describe scholarly or educational matters, as 'a child with academic rather than sporting interests'. From this use it has come to mean theoretical rather than actual or practical, as in 'wasting time discussing matters of purely academic concern'. In modern use it is frequently used to mean irrelevant, as in 'Whether you vote for him or not is academic. He is certain of a majority of votes'.

access is usually a noun meaning 'entry or admission', as in 'try to gain access to the building', or 'the opportunity to use something', as in 'have access to confidential information'. It is also used to refer to the right of a parent to spend time with his or her children, as in 'Father was allowed access to the children at weekends'.

However **access** can also be used as a verb. It is most commonly found in computing, meaning obtaining information from, as in 'accessing details from the computer file relating to the accounts'. In modern usage many technical words become used, and indeed overused, in the general language. Thus the verb **access** can now be found meaning to obtain information not on a computer, as in 'access the information in the filing cabinet'. It can also be found in the sense of gaining entry to a building, as in 'Their attempts to access the building at night were unsuccessful'.

accessory and **accessary** are interchangeable as regards only one meaning of **accessory**. A person who helps another person to commit a crime is known either as an **accessory** or an **accessary**, although the former is the more modern term. However, only **accessory** is used to describe a useful or decorative extra that is not strictly necessary, as in 'Seat covers are accessories that are included in the price of the car' and 'She wore a red dress with black accessories' ('accessories' in the second example being handbag, shoes and gloves).

accompany can be followed either by the preposition 'with' or 'by'. When it means 'to go somewhere with someone', 'by' is used, as in 'She was accompanied by her parents to church' Similarly, 'by' is used when **accompany** is used in a musical context, as in 'The singer was accompanied on the piano by her brother'. When **accompany** means 'to go along with something' or 'supplement something', either 'by' or 'with' may be used, as in 'The roast turkey was accompanied by all the trimmings', 'His words were accompanied by/with a gesture of dismissal', and 'The speaker accompanied his words with expressive gestures'.

acoustics can take either a singular or plural verb. When it is being thought of as a branch of science it is treated as being singular, as in 'Acoustics deals with the study of sound', but when it is used to describe the qualities of a hall, etc, with regard to its sound-carrying properties, it is treated as being plural, as in 'The acoustics in the school hall are very poor'.

activate and **actuate** both mean 'make active' but are commonly used in different senses. **Activate** refers to physical or chemical action, as in 'The terrorists activated the explosive device'. **Actuate** means 'to move to action' and 'to serve as a motive', as in 'The murderer was actuated by jealousy'.

actress is still widely used as a term for a woman who acts in plays or films, although many people prefer the term 'actor', regarding this as a neutral term rather than simply the masculine form. The **-ess** suffix, used to indicate the feminine form of a word, is generally becoming less common as these forms are regarded as sexist or belittling.

acute and **chronic** both refer to disease. **Acute** is used of a disease that is sudden in onset and lasts a relatively short time, as in 'flu is an acute illness'. **Chronic** is used of a disease that may be slow to develop and lasts a long time, possibly over several years, as in 'Asthma is a chronic condition'.

AD and BC are abbreviations that accompany year numbers. AD stands for 'Anno Domini', meaning 'in the year of our Lord' and indicates that the year concerned is one occurring after Jesus Christ was born. Traditionally AD is placed before the year number concerned, as in 'Their great-grandfather was born in AD 1801', but in modern usage it sometimes follows the year number, as in 'The house was built in 1780 AD.' BC stands for 'Before Christ' and indicates that the year concerned is one occurring before Jesus Christ was born. It follows the year number, as in 'The event took place in Rome in 55 BC'.

adapter and **adaptor** can be used interchangeably, but commonly **adapter** is used to refer to a person who adapts, as in 'the adapter of the stage play for television and **adaptor** is used to refer to a thing that adapts, specifically a type of electrical plug.

admission and **admittance** both mean 'permission or right to enter'. **Admission** is the more common term, as in 'They refused him admission to their house', and, unlike **admittance**, it can also mean 'the price or fee charged for entry' as in 'Admission to the football match is £3'. **Admittance** is largely used in formal or official situations, as in 'They ignored the notice saying "No

Admittance"'. **Admission** also means 'confession' or 'acknowledgement of responsibility', as in 'On her own admission she was the thief'.

admit may be followed either by the preposition 'to' or the preposition 'of', depending on the sense. In the sense of 'to confess', **admit** is usually not followed by a preposition at all, as in 'He admitted his mistake' and 'She admitted stealing the brooch'. However, in this sense **admit** is sometimes followed by 'to', as in 'They have admitted to their error' and 'They have admitted to their part in the theft'.

In the sense of 'to allow to enter', **admit** is followed by 'to', as in 'The doorman admitted the guest to the club'. Also in the rather formal sense of 'give access or entrance to', **admit** is followed by 'to', as in 'the rear door admits straight to the garden'. In the sense of 'to be open to' or 'leave room for', **admit** is followed by 'of', as in 'The situation admits of no other explanation'.

admittance *see* **admission**.

adopted and **adoptive** are liable to be confused. **Adopted** is applied to children who have been adopted, as in 'The couple have two adopted daughters'. **Adoptive** is applied to a person or people who adopt a child, as in 'Her biological parents tried to get the girl back from her adoptive parents'.

aeroplane is commonly abbreviated to **plane** in modern usage. In American English **aeroplane** becomes **airplane.**

affinity may be followed by the preposition 'with' or 'between', and means 'close relationship', 'mutual attraction' or similarity, as in 'the affinity which twins have with each other' and 'There was an affinity between the two families who had lost children'. In modern usage it is sometimes followed by 'for' or 'towards', and means 'liking', as in 'She has an affinity for fair-haired men'.

ageism means discrimination on the grounds of age, as in 'By giving an age range in their job advert the firm were guilty of ageism'. Usually it refers to discrimination against older or elderly people, but it also refers to discrimination against young people.

agenda in modern usage is a singular noun having the plural **agendas**. It means 'a list of things to be attended to', as in 'The financial situation was the first item on the committee's agenda'. Originally it was a plural noun, derived from Latin, meaning 'things to be done'.

aggravate literally means 'to make worse', as in 'Her remarks simply aggravated the situation'. In modern usage it is frequently found meaning 'to irritate or annoy', as in 'The children were aggravating their mother when she was trying to read'. It is often labelled as 'informal' in dictionaries and is best avoided in formal situations.

agnostic and **atheist** are both words meaning 'disbeliever in God', but there are differences in sense between the two words. **Agnostics** believe that it is not possible to know whether God exists or not. **Atheists** believe that there is no God.

alcohol abuse is a modern term for alcoholism. *See* **abuse**.

alibi is derived from the Latin word for 'elsewhere'. It is used to refer to a legal plea that a person accused or under suspicion was somewhere other than the scene of the crime at the time the crime was committed. In modern usage **alibi** is frequently used to mean simply 'excuse' or 'pretext', as in 'He had the perfect alibi for not going to the party—he was ill in hospital'.

all together and **altogether** are not interchangeable. **All together** means 'at the same time' or 'in the same place', as in 'The guests arrived all together' and 'They kept their personal papers all together in a filing cabinet'. **Altogether** means 'in all, in total' or 'completely', as in "We collected £500 altogether' and 'The work was altogether too much for him'.

alternate and **alternative** are liable to be confused. **Alternate** means 'every other' or 'occurring by turns', as in 'They visit her mother on alternate weekends' and 'between alternate layers of meat and cheese sauce'. **Alternative** means 'offering a choice' or 'being an alternative', as in 'If the motorway is busy there is an alternative route'. **Alternative** is found in some cases in modern usage to mean 'not conventional, not traditional', as in 'alternative medicine' and 'alternative comedy'.

Alternative as a noun refers to the choice between two possibilities, as in 'The alternatives are to go by train or by plane'. In modern usage, however, it is becoming common to use it to refer also to the choice among two or more possibilities, as in 'He has to use a college from five alternatives'.

although and **though** are largely interchangeable but **though** is slightly less formal, as in 'We arrived on time although/though we left late'.

amiable and **amicable** both refer to friendliness and goodwill. **Amiable** means 'friendly' or 'agreeable and pleasant', and is mostly used of people or their moods, as in 'amiable neighbours', 'amiable travelling companions', 'of an amiable temperament' and 'be in an amiable mood'. **Amicable** means 'characterized by friendliness and goodwill' and is applied mainly to relationships, agreements, documents, etc, as in 'an amicable working relationship', 'reach an amicable settlement at the end of the war' and 'send an amicable letter to his former rival'.

among and **amongst** are interchangeable, as in 'We searched among/amongst the bushes for the ball,' 'Divide the chocolate among/amongst you', and 'You must choose among/amongst the various possibilities'.

among and **between** may be used interchangeably in most contexts. Formerly **between** was used only when referring to the relationship of two things, as in 'Share the chocolate between you and your brother', and **among** was used when referring to the relationship of three or more things, as in 'Share the chocolate among all your friends'. In modern usage **between** may be used when referring to more than two things, as in 'There is agreement between all the countries of the EU' and 'Share the chocolate between all of you'. However, **among** is still used only to describe more than two things.

amoral and **immoral** are not interchangeable. **Amoral** means 'lacking moral standards, devoid of moral sense', indicating that the person so described has no concern with morals, as in 'The child was completely amoral and did not know the difference between right and wrong'. **Immoral** means 'against or breaking moral standards, bad'. 'He knows he's doing wrong but he goes on being completely immoral' and 'commit immoral acts'. Note the spelling of both words. **Amoral** has only one *m* but **immoral** has double *m*.

anaesthetic and **analgesic** are liable to be confused. As an adjective, **anaesthetic** means 'producing a loss of feeling', as in 'inject the patient with an anaesthetic substance', and as a noun it means 'a substance that produces a loss of feeling', as in 'administer an anaesthetic to the patient on the operating table'. A local anaesthetic produces a loss of feeling in only part of the body, as in 'remove the rotten tooth under local anaesthetic'. A **general anaesthetic** produces loss of feeling in the whole body and induces unconsciousness, as in 'The operation on his leg will have to be performed under general anaesthetic'. As an adjective **analgesic** means 'producing a lack of or reduction in, sensitivity to pain, pain-killing', as in 'aspirin has an analgesic effect'. As a noun **analgesic** means 'a substance that produces a lack of, or reduction in, sensitivity to pain', as in 'aspirin, paracetamol, and other analgesics'.

arbiter and **arbitrator**, although similar in meaning, are not totally interchangeable. **Arbiter** means 'a person who has absolute power to judge or make decisions', as in 'Parisian designers used to be total arbiters of fashion'. **Arbitrator** is 'a person appointed to settle differences in a dispute', as in 'act as arbitrator between management and workers in the wages dispute'. **Arbiter** is occasionally used with the latter meaning also.

artist and **artiste** are liable to be confused. **Artist** refers to 'a person who paints or draws,' as in 'Renoir was a great artist'. The word may also refer to 'a person who is skilled in something', as in 'The mechanic is a real artist with an engine'. **Artiste** refers to 'an entertainer, such as a singer or a dancer', as in 'a list of the artistes in the musical performances'. The word is becoming a little old-fashioned.

at this moment in time is an overused phrase meaning simply 'now'. In modern usage there is a tendency to use what are thought to be grander-sounding alternatives for simple words. It is best to avoid such overworked phrases and use the simpler form.

atheist *see* **agnostic**.

au fait is French in origin but it is commonly used in English to mean 'familiar with' or 'informed about', as in 'not completely au fait with the new office system'. It is pronounced *o* fay.

authoress is not used in modern usage since it is considered sexist. **Author** is regarded as a neutral term to describe both male and female authors.

avoid *see* **evade**.

avoidance *see* **evasion**.

baited *see* **bated**.

barmaid is disliked by many people on the grounds that it sounds a belittling term and is thus sexist. It is also disliked by people who are interested in political correctness. However the word continues to be quite common, along with **barman**, and efforts to insist on **bar assistant** or **barperson** have not yet succeeded.

basically means literally 'referring to a base or basis, fundamentally', as in 'The scientist's theory is basically unsound', but it is frequently used almost meaninglessly as a fill-up word at the beginning of a sentence, as in 'Basically he just wants more money'. Overuse of this word should be avoided.

basis, meaning 'something on which something is founded', as in 'The cost of the project was the basis of his argument against it', has the plural form **bases** although it is not commonly used. It would be more usual to say 'arguments without a firm basis' than 'arguments without firm bases'.

bated as in 'with bated breath' meaning 'tense and anxious with excitement', is frequently misspelt **baited**. Care should be taken not to confuse the two words.

bathroom *see* **toilet**.

BC *see* **AD**.

because means 'for the reason that', as in 'He left because he was bored', and is sometimes misused. It is wrong to use it in a sentence that also contains 'the reason that', as in 'The reason she doesn't say much is that she is shy'. The correct form of this is 'She doesn't say much because she is shy' or 'The reason she doesn't say much is that she is shy'.

because of *see* **due to**.

beg the question is often used wrongly. It means 'to take for granted the very point that has to be proved', as in 'To say that God must exist because we can see all his wonderful creations in the world around us begs the question'. The statement assumes that these creations have been made by God although this has not been proved and yet this fact is being used as evidence that there is a God. **Beg the question** is often used wrongly to mean 'to evade the question', as in 'The police tried to get him to say where he had been but he begged the question and changed the subject'.

benign means 'kindly, well-disposed' when applied to people, as in 'fortunate enough to have a benign ruler'. This meaning may also be used of things, as in 'give a benign smile' and 'live in a benign climate'. As a medical

bête noire

term **benign** means 'nonmalignant, non-cancerous'. **Innocent** is another word for **benign** in this sense.

bête noire refers to 'something that one detests or fears', as in 'Loud pop music is her father's bête noire, although she sings with a pop group'. Note the spelling, particularly the accent (circumflex) on **bête** and the *e* at the end of **noire.** The phrase is French in origin and the plural form is **bêtes noires**, as in 'A bearded man is one of her many bêtes noires'.

better should be preceded by 'had' when it means 'ought to' or 'should', as in 'You had better leave now if you want to arrive there by nightfall' and 'We had better apologize for upsetting her'. In informal contexts, especially in informal speech as in 'Hey Joe, Mum says you better come now', the 'had' is often omitted but it should be retained in formal contexts. The negative form is 'had better not', as in 'He had better not try to deceive her'.

between is often found in the phrase 'between you and me' as in 'Between you and me I think he stole the money'. Note that 'me' is correct and that 'I' is wrong. This is because prepositions like 'between' are followed by an object, not a subject. 'I' acts as the subject of a sentence, as in 'I know her', and 'me' as the object, as in 'She knows me'.

between *see* **among**.

bi- of the words beginning with the prefix bi-, biannual and biennial are liable to be confused. **Biannual** means 'twice a year' and **biennial** means 'every two years'. **Bicentenary** and **bicentennial** both mean 'a 200th anniversary', as in 'celebrating the bicentenary/bicentennial of the firm'. **Bicentenary** is, however, the more common expression in British English, although **bicentennial** is more common in American English.

Biweekly is a confusing word as it has two different meanings. It means both 'twice a week' and 'once every two weeks'. Thus there is no means of knowing without other information whether 'a bi-weekly publication' comes out once a week or every two weeks. The confusion arises because the prefix 'bi-', which means 'two', can refer both to doubling, as in 'bicycle', and halving, as in 'bisection'.

biannual *see* **bi-**.

bicentenary and **bicentennial** *see* **bi-**.

biennial *see* **bi-**.

billion traditionally meant 'one million million' in British English, but in modern usage it has increasingly taken on the American English meaning of 'one thousand million'. When the number of million pounds, etc, is specified, the number immediately precedes the word 'million' without the word 'of', as in 'The firm is worth five billion dollars', but if no number is present then 'of' precedes 'dollars, etc', ' as in 'The research project cost the country millions of dollars'. The word **billion** may also be used loosely to mean 'a great but unspecified number', as in 'Billions of people in the world live in poverty'.

birth name is a suggested alternative for **maiden name**, a woman's surname before she married and took the name of her husband. **Maiden name** is considered by some to be inappropriate since maiden in one of its senses is another name for 'virgin' and it is now not at all usual for women to be virgins when they marry. Another possible name alternative is **family name.**

biweekly *see* **bi-**.

black is the word now usually applied to dark-skinned people of Afro-Caribbean origins and is the term preferred by most black-skinned people themselves. **Coloured** is considered by many to be offensive since it groups all non-Caucasians together. In America, African-American is becoming increasingly common as a substitute for **black.**

blond and **blonde** are both used to mean 'a fair-haired person', but they are not interchangeable. **Blond** is used to describe a man or boy, **blonde** is used to describe a woman or girl. They are derived from the French adjective, which changes endings according to the gender of the noun.

boat and **ship** are often used interchangeably, but usually **boat** refers to a smaller vessel than a ship.

bona fide is an expression of Latin origin meaning literally 'of good faith'. It means 'genuine, sincere' or 'authentic', as in 'a bona fide member of the group', 'a bona fide excuse for not going', or 'a bona fide agreement'.

bottom line is an expression from accountancy that has become commonly used in the general language. In accountancy it refers to the final line of a set of company accounts, which indicates whether the company has made a profit or a loss, obviously a very important line. In general English, **bottom line** has a range of meanings, from 'the final outcome or result', as in 'The bottom line of their discussion was that they decided to sell the company', through 'the most important point of something', as in 'The bottom line was whether they could get there on time or not', to 'the last straw', as in 'His affair with another woman was the bottom line of their stormy relationship and she left him'.

can and **may** both mean in one of their senses 'to be permitted'. In this sense **can** is much less formal than **may** and is best restricted to informal contexts, as in ' "Can I go to the park now?" asked the child.' **May** is used in more formal contexts, as in 'May I please have your name?' Both **can** and **may** have other meanings. **Can** has the meaning 'to be able', as in 'They thought his legs were permanently damaged but he can still walk'. **May** has the additional meaning 'to be likely', as in 'You may well be right'.

The past tense of **can** is **could**, as in 'The children asked if they could (= be permitted to) go to the park'. 'The old man could (= be unable to) not walk upstairs'. The past tense of **may** is **might**, as in 'The child asked if he might have a piece of cake (= be permitted to)'. 'They might (= be likely to) well get here tonight'.

cannot, can not, and **can't** all mean the same thing but they are used in different contexts. **Cannot** is the most usual form, as in 'The children have been told that they cannot go' and 'We cannot get there by public transport'. **Cannot** is written as two words only for emphasis, as in 'No, you can not have any more' and 'The invalid certainly can not walk to the ambulance'. **Can't** is used in less formal contexts and often in speech, as in 'I can't be bothered going out' and 'They can't bear to be apart'.

cardigan, jersey, jumper and **sweater** all refer to knitted garments for the top part of the body. **Cardigan** refers to a jacket-like garment with buttons down the front. **Jersey, jumper** and **sweater** refer to a knitted garment pulled over the head to get it on and off.

cardinal and **ordinal** numbers refer to different aspects of numbers. **Cardinal** is applied to those numbers that refer to quantity or value without referring to their place in the set, as in 'one', 'two', 'fifty' 'one hundred'. **Ordinal** is applied to numbers that refer to their order in a series, as in 'first', 'second', 'fortieth', 'hundredth'.

carer has recently taken on the meaning of 'a person who looks after a sick, handicapped or old relative or friend', as in 'carers requiring a break from their responsibilities'.

carpet and **rug** both refer to forms of floor covering. Generally a rug is smaller than a carpet, and the fitted variety of fabric floor covering is always known as carpet.

caster and **castor** are mainly interchangeable. Both forms can be applied to 'a swivelling wheel attached to the base of a piece of furniture to enable it to be moved easily' and 'a container with a perforated top from which sugar is sprinkled'. The kind of sugar known as **caster** can also be called **castor**, although this is less usual. The lubricating or medicinal oil known as **castor oil** is never spelt **caster**.

Catholic and **catholic** have different meanings. **Catholic** as an adjective refers to the Roman Catholic Church, as in 'The Pope is head of the Catholic Church', or to the universal body of Christians. As a noun it means 'a member of the Catholic Church', as in 'She is a Catholic but he is a Protestant'. Catholic with a lower-case initial letter means 'general, wide-ranging', as in 'a catholic selection of essays', and ' broad-minded, liberal', as in 'a catholic attitude to the tastes of others'.

celibate means 'unmarried' or 'remaining unmarried and chaste, especially for religious reasons', as in 'Roman Catholic priests have to be celibate'. In modern usage, because of its connection with chastity, **celibate** has come to mean 'abstaining from sexual intercourse', as in 'The threat of Aids has made many people celibate'. The word is frequently misspelt. Note the *i* after *l*.

Celsius, centigrade and **Fahrenheit** are all scales of temperature. **Celsius** and **centigrade** mean the same and refer to a scale on which water freezes at 0° and boils at 100°. This scale is now the principal unit of temperature. **Celsius** is now the more acceptable term. **Fahrenheit** refers to a scale on which water freezes at 32° and boils at 212°. It is still used, informally at least, of the weather, and statements such as 'The temperature reached the nineties today' are still common.

Note the initial capital letters in **Celsius** and **Fahrenheit**. This is because they are named after people, namely the scientists who devised them.

centenary and **centennial** are both used to refer to a 'one-hundredth anniversary'. **Centenary** is the more common term in British English, as in 'celebrate the town's centenary', whereas **centennial** is more common in American English. **Centennial** may be used as an adjective, as in 'organize the town's centennial celebrations'.

centigrade *see* **Celsius**.

centre and **middle** mean much the same, but **centre** is used more precisely than **middle** in some cases, as in 'a line through the centre of the circle' and 'She felt faint in the middle of the crowd'.

centre on and **centre around** are often used interchangeably, as in 'Her world centres on/around her children'.

Centre around is objected to by some people on the grounds that **centre** is too specific to be used with something as vague as **around**. When it is used as a verb with place names, **centre** is used with 'at', as in 'Their business operation is centred at London'.

centuries are calculated from 1001, 1501, 1901, etc, not 1000, 1500, 1900, etc. This is because the years are counted from AD 1, there being no year 0.

chair is often used to mean 'a person in charge of a meeting, committee, etc', as in 'The committee has a new chair this year'. Formerly **chairman** was always used in this context, as in 'He was appointed chairman of the fund-raising committee' but this is disapproved of on the grounds that it is sexist. Formerly, **chairman** was sometimes used even if the person in charge of the meeting or committee was a woman, and sometimes **chairwoman** was used in this situation. **Chairperson**, which also avoids sexism, is frequently used instead of **chair**. **Chair** is also a verb meaning 'to be in charge of a meeting, committee, etc'.

-challenged is a modern suffix that is very much part of politically correct language. It is used to convey a disadvantage, problem or disorder in a more positive light. For example, 'visually challenged' is used in politically correct language instead of 'blind' or 'partially sighted', and 'aurally challenged' is used instead of 'deaf' or 'hard of hearing'. **-Challenged** is often used in humorous coinages, as in 'financially challenged', meaning 'penniless', and 'intellectually challenged', meaning 'stupid'.

charisma was formerly a theological word used to mean

'a spiritual gift', such as the gift of healing, etc. In modern usage it is used to describe 'a special quality or power that influences, inspires or stimulates other people, personal magnetism', as in 'The president was elected because of his charisma'. The adjective from **charisma** is **charismatic**, as in 'his charismatic style of leadership'.

chauvinism originally meant 'excessive patriotism', being derived from the name of Nicolas Chauvin, a soldier in the army of Napoleon Bonaparte, who was noted for his excessive patriotism. In modern usage **chauvinism** has come to mean 'excessive enthusiasm or devotion to a cause' or, more particularly, 'an irrational and prejudiced belief in the superiority of one's own cause'. When preceded by 'male', it refers specifically to attitudes and actions that assume the superiority of the male sex and thus the inferiority of women, as in 'accused of not giving her the job because of male chauvinism'. **Chauvinism** is frequently used to mean **male chauvinism**, as in 'He shows his chauvinism towards his female staff by never giving any of them senior jobs'. The adjective formed from **chauvinism** is **chauvinistic**.

chemist and **pharmacist** have the same meaning in one sense of **chemist** only. **Chemist** and **pharmacist** are both words for 'one who prepares drugs ordered by medical prescription'. **Chemist** has the additional meaning of 'a scientist who works in the field of chemistry', as in 'He works as an industrial chemist'.

childish and **childlike** both refer to someone being like a child but they are used in completely different contexts. **Childish** is used in a derogatory way about someone to indicate that he or she is acting like a child in an immature way, as in 'Even though she is 20 years old she has childish tantrums when she does not get her own way' and 'childish handwriting for an adult'. **Childlike** is a term of approval or a complimentary term used to describe something that has some of the attractive qualities of childhood, as in 'She has a childlike enthusiasm for picnics' and 'He has a childlike trust in others'.

Christian name is used to mean someone's first name as opposed to someone's **surname**. It is increasingly being replaced by **first name** or **forename** since Britain has become a multicultural society where there are several religions as well as Christianity.

chronic *see* **acute**.

city and **town** in modern usage are usually distinguished on grounds of size and status, a city being larger and more important than a town. Originally in Britain a **city** was a town which had special rights conferred on it by royal charter and which usually had a cathedral.

clean and **cleanse** as verbs both mean 'to clean', as in 'clean the house' and 'cleanse the wound'. However, **cleanse** tends to indicate a more thorough cleaning than **clean** and sometimes carries the suggestion of 'to purify', as in 'prayer cleansing the soul'.

client and **customer**, although closely related in meaning, are not interchangeable. **Client** refers to 'a person who pays for the advice or services of a professional person', as in 'They are both clients of the same lawyer', 'a client waiting to see the bank manager' and 'hairdressers who keep their clients waiting'. **Customer** refers to 'a person who purchases goods from a shop, etc', as in 'customers complaining to shopkeepers about faulty goods' and 'a regular customer at the local supermarket'. **Client** is used in the sense of 'customer' by shops who regard it as a more superior word, as in ' clients of an exclusive dress boutique'.

climate no longer refers just to weather, as in 'go to live in a hot climate', 'Britain has a temperate climate'. It has extended its meaning to refer to 'atmosphere', as in 'live in a climate of despair' and to 'the present situation', as in 'businessmen nervous about the financial climate'.

clone originally was a technical word meaning 'one of a group of offspring that are asexually produced and which are genetically identical to the parent and to other members of the group'. In modern usage **clone** is frequently used loosely to mean 'something that is very similar to something else', as in 'In the sixties there were many Beatles' clones', and 'grey-suited businessmen looking like clones of each other'.

collaborate and **cooperate** are not interchangeable in all contexts. They both mean 'to work together for a common purpose', as in 'The two scientists are collaborating/cooperating on cancer research' and 'The rival building firms are collaborating/cooperating on the new shopping complex'. When the work concerned is of an artistic or creative nature **collaborate** is the more commonly used word, as in 'The two directors are collaborating on the film' and 'The composers collaborated on the theme music'. **Collaborate** also has the meaning of 'to work with an enemy, especially an enemy that is occupying one's country', as in 'a Frenchman

coloured

who collaborated with the Germans when they installed a German government in France'.

coloured *see* **black**.

commence, begin, and **start** mean the same, but **commence** is used in a more formal context than the other two words, as in 'The legal proceedings will commence tomorrow' and 'The memorial service will commence with a hymn'. **Begin** and **start** are used less formally, as 'The match begins at 2 p.m.' and 'The film has already started'.

commensurate is followed by 'with' to form a phrase meaning 'proportionate to, appropriate to', as in 'a salary commensurate with her qualifications' and 'a price commensurate with the quality of the goods'.

comparatively means 'relatively, in comparison with a standard', as in 'The house was comparatively inexpensive for that area of the city' and 'In an area of extreme poverty they are comparatively well off'. In modern usage it is often used loosely to mean 'rather' or 'fairly' without any suggestion of reference to a standard, as in 'She has comparatively few friends' and 'It is a comparatively quiet resort'.

compare may take either the preposition 'to' or 'with'. 'To' is used when two things or people are being likened to each other or being declared similar, as in 'He compared her hair to silk' and 'He compared his wife to Helen of Troy'. 'With' is used when two things or people are being considered from the point of view of both similarities and differences, as in 'If you compare the new pupil's work with that of the present class you will find it brilliant', and 'If you compare the prices in the two stores you will find that the local one is the cheaper'.

In modern usage the distinction is becoming blurred because the difference is rather subtle.

comparison is usually followed by the preposition 'with', as in 'In comparison with hers his work is brilliant'. However, when it means 'the action of likening something or someone to something or someone else', it is followed by 'to', as in 'the comparison of her beauty to that of Garbo'.

complementary medicine is a term applied to the treatment of illness or disorders by techniques other than conventional medicine. These include homeopathy, osteopathy, acupuncture, acupressure, iridology, etc. The word **complementary** suggests that the said techniques complement and work alongside conventional medical techniques. **Alternative medicine** means the same as **complementary medicine**, but the term suggests that they are used instead of the techniques of conventional medicine rather than alongside them.

complex in one of its senses is used rather loosely in modern usage. It refers technically to 'an abnormal state caused by unconscious repressed desires or past experiences', as in 'an inferiority complex'. In modern usage it is used loosely to describe 'any obsessive concern or fear', as in 'She has a complex about her weight', 'He has a complex about his poor background'. **Complex** is also used to refer to 'a group of connected or similar things'. It is now used mainly of a group of buildings or units connected in some way, as in 'a shopping complex' or 'a sports complex'.

Complex is also an adjective meaning 'complicated', as in 'His motives in carrying out the crime were

compose

complex' and 'The argument was too complex for most people to understand'.

compose, comprise and **constitute** are all similar in meaning but are used differently. **Compose** means 'to come together to make a whole, to make up'. It is most commonly found in the passive, as in 'The team was composed of young players' and 'The group was composed largely of elderly people'. It can be used in the active voice, as in 'the tribes which composed the nation' and 'the members which composed the committee', but this use is rarer. **Constitute** means the same as **compose** but it is usually used in the active voice, as in 'the foodstuffs that constitute a healthy diet' and 'the factors that constitute a healthy environment'. **Comprise** means 'to consist of, to be made up of'.

concave and **convex** are liable to be confused. **Concave** means 'curved inwards', as in 'The inside of a spoon would be described as concave'. **Convex** means 'curved outwards, bulging', as in 'The outside or bottom of a spoon would be described as convex'.

conducive, meaning 'leading to, contributing to', is followed by the preposition 'to', as in 'conditions conducive to health growth'.

conform may be followed by the preposition 'to' or the preposition 'with'. It is followed by 'to' when it means 'to keep to or comply with', as in 'conform to the conventions' and 'refuse to conform to the company regulations', and with 'with' when it means 'to agree with, to go along with', as in 'His ideas do not conform with those of the rest of the committee'.

connection and **connexion** are different forms of the

same word, meaning 'a relationship between two things'. In modern usage **connection** is much the commoner spelling, as in 'no connection between the events' and 'a fire caused by a faulty connection'.

connote and **denote** are liable to be confused. **Connote** means 'to suggest something in addition to the main, basic meaning of something', as in 'the fear that the word cancer connotes' and 'The word 'home' connotes security and love'. **Denote** means 'to mean or indicate', as in 'The word cancer denotes a malignant illness' and 'The word "home" denotes the place where one lives'.

consist can be followed either by the preposition 'of' or by the preposition 'in', depending on the meaning. **Consist of** means 'to be made up of, to comprise', as in 'The team consists of eleven players and two reserve players'. **Consist in** means 'to have as the chief or only element or feature, to lie in', as in 'The charm of the village consists in its isolation' and 'The effectiveness of the plan consisted in its simplicity'.

constitute *see* **compose**.

contagious and **infectious** both refer to diseases that can be passed on to other people but they do not mean the same. **Contagious** means 'passed on by physical contact', as in 'He caught a contagious skin disease while working in the clinic' and 'Venereal diseases are contagious'. **Infectious** means 'caused by airborne or water-borne microorganisms', as in 'The common cold is highly infectious and is spread by people sneezing and coughing'.

contemporary originally meant 'living or happening at the same time', as in 'Shakespeare and Marlowe were

convex

contemporary playwrights' and 'Marlowe was contemporary with Shakespeare'. Later it came to mean also 'happening at the present time, current', as in 'What is your impression of the contemporary literary scene?' and 'Contemporary moral values are often compared unfavourably with those of the past'. These two uses of **contemporary** can cause ambiguity. In modern usage it is also used to mean 'modern, up-to-date', as in 'extremely contemporary designs'.

convex *see* **concave**.

cooperate *see* **collaborate**.

co-respondent *see* **correspondent**.

correspondent and **co-respondent** are liable to be confused. **Correspondent** refers either to 'a person who communicates by letter', as in 'They were correspondents for years but had never met', or to 'a person who contributes news items to a newspaper or radio or television programme', as in 'the foreign correspondent of the *Times*'. A **co-respondent** is 'a person who has been cited in a divorce case as having committed adultery with one of the partners'.

cousin can cause confusion. The children of brothers and sisters are **first cousins** to each other. The children of **first cousins** are **second cousins** to each other. The child of one's **first cousin** and the **first cousin** of one's parents is one's **first cousin first removed**. The grandchild of one's **first cousin** or the **first cousin** of one's grandparent is one's **second cousin twice removed**.

crisis literally means 'turning point' and should be used to refer to 'a turning point in an illness', as in 'The fever reached a crisis and she survived' and 'a decisive or crucial moment in a situation, whose outcome will make a definite difference or change for better or worse', as in 'The financial situation has reached a crisis—the firm will either survive or go bankrupt'. In modern usage **crisis** is becoming increasingly used loosely for 'any worrying or troublesome situation', as in 'There's a crisis in the kitchen. The cooker's broken down'. The plural is **crises**.

criterion, meaning 'a standard by which something or someone is judged or evaluated', as 'What criterion is used for deciding which pupils will gain entrance to the school?' and 'The standard of play was the only criterion for entrance to the golf club'. It is a singular noun of which **criteria** is the plural, as in 'They must satisfy all the criteria for entrance to the club or they will be refused'.

critical has two main meanings. It means 'finding fault', as in 'His report on her work was very critical'. It also means 'at a crisis, at a decisive moment, crucial', as in 'It was a critical point in their relationship'. This meaning is often applied to the decisive stage of an illness, as in 'the critical hours after a serious operation', and is used also to describe an ill person who is at a crucial stage of an illness or dangerously ill. **Critical** also means 'involved in making judgements or assessments of artistic or creative works', as in 'give a critical evaluation of the author's latest novel'.

crucial means 'decisive, critical', as in 'His vote is crucial since the rest of the committee is split down the middle'. In modern usage it is used loosely to mean

curriculum

'very important', as in 'It is crucial that you leave now'.
Crucial is derived from crux, meaning 'a decisive
point', as in 'the crux of the situation'.

curriculum is derived from Latin and originally took the
plural form **curricula**, but in modern usage the plural
form **curriculums** is becoming common.

curriculum vitae refers to 'a brief account of a person's
qualifications and career to date'. It is often requested by
an employer when a candidate is applying for a job. **Vitae** is pronounced *vee*-ti, the second syllable rhyming
with my.

data was formerly used mainly in a scientific or technical
context and was always treated as a plural noun, taking a
plural verb, as in 'compare the data which were provided
by the two research projects'. The singular form was
datum, which is now rare. In modern usage the word
data became used in computing as a collective noun
meaning 'body of information' and is frequently used
with a singular verb, as in 'The data is essential for our
research'. This use has spread into the general language.

dates these are usually written in figures, as in 1956,
rather than in words, as in nineteen fifty-six, except in
formal contexts, such as legal documents. There are
various ways of writing dates. The standard form in
Britain is becoming day followed by month followed by
year, as in '24 February 1970'. In North America the
standard form of this is 'February 24, 1970', and that is
a possibility in Britain also. Alternatively, some people
write '24th February 1970'. Care should be taken with
the writing of dates entirely in numbers, especially if
one is corresponding with someone in North America.
In Britain the day of the month is put first, the month

second and the year third, as in '2/3/50', '2 March 1950'. In North America the month is put first, followed by the day of the month and the year. Thus in North America '2/3/50' would be '3 February 1950'.

Centuries may be written either in figures, as in 'the 19th century', or in words, as in 'the nineteenth century'

Decades and centuries are now usually written without apostrophes, as in '1980s' and '1990s'.

datum *see* **data**.

deadly and **deathly** both refer to death but they have different meanings. **Deadly** means 'likely to cause death, fatal', as in 'His enemy dealt him a deadly blow with his sword' and 'He contracted a deadly disease in the jungle'. **Deathly** means 'referring to death, resembling death', as in 'She was deathly pale with fear'.

decimate literally means 'to kill one in ten' and is derived from the practice in ancient Rome of killing every tenth soldier as a punishment for mutiny. In modern usage it has come to mean 'to kill or destroy a large part of', as in 'Disease has decimated the population'. It has also come to mean 'to reduce considerably', as in 'the recession has decimated the jobs in the area'.

defective and **deficient** are similar in meaning but are not interchangeable. **Defective** means 'having a fault, not working properly', as in 'return the defective vacuum cleaner to the shop', 'The second-hand car proved to be defective' and 'He cannot be a pilot as his eyesight is defective'. **Deficient** means 'having a lack, lacking in', as in 'The athlete is very fast but he is deficient in strength' and 'Her diet is deficient in vitamin C'.

deficient *see* **defective**.

definite article *see* **the**.

delusion and **illusion** in modern usage are often used interchangeably but they are not quite the same. **Delusion** means 'a false or mistaken idea or belief', as in 'He is under the delusion that he is brilliant' and 'suffer from delusions of grandeur'. It can be part of a mental disorder, as in 'He suffers from the delusion that he is Napoleon'. **Illusion** means 'a false or misleading impression', as in 'There was no well in the desert—it was an optical illusion', 'The conjurer's tricks were based on illusion' and 'the happy childhood illusions that everyone lived happy ever after'.

demise is a formal word for death, as in 'He never recovered from the demise of his wife'. In modern usage it applies to the ending of an activity, as in 'The last decade saw the demise of coal-mining in the area'. In modern usage it has come to mean also 'the decline or failure of an activity', as in 'the gradual demise of his business'.

dénouement means 'the final outcome', as in 'The novel had a unexpected denouement'. It is pronounced day-*noo*-mon.

derisive and **derisory** are both adjectives connected with the noun 'derision' but they have different meanings. **Derisive** means 'expressing derision, scornful, mocking' as in 'give a derisive smile' and 'His efforts were met with derisive laughter'. Derisory means 'deserving derision, ridiculous' as in 'Their attempts at playing the game were derisory'. **Derisory** is frequently used to mean 'ridiculously small or inadequate', as in 'The salary offered was derisory'.

despatch and **dispatch** are interchangeable. It is most common as a verb meaning 'to send', as in 'despatch/

dispatch an invitation'. It is rarer as a noun. It means 'a message or report, often official', as in 'receive a despatch/dispatch that the soldiers were to move on'. It also means 'rapidity, speed', as in 'carry out the orders with despatch/dispatch'.

dessert, **pudding**, **sweet** and **afters** all mean the same thing. They refer to the last and sweet course of a meal. **Dessert** has relatively recently become the most widespread of these terms. **Pudding** was previously regarded by the upper and middle classes as the most acceptable word of these, but it is now thought of by many as being rather old-fashioned or as being more suited to certain types of dessert than others—thus syrup sponge would be a pudding, but not fresh fruit salad. **Sweet** is a less formal word and is regarded by some people as being lower-class or regional. **Afters** is common only in very informal English.

devil's advocate is a phrase that is often misunderstood. It means 'someone who points out the possible flaws or faults in an argument etc', as in 'He played the devil's advocate and showed her the weakness in her argument so that she was able to perfect it before presenting it to the committee'. The phrase is sometimes wrongly thought of as meaning 'someone who defends an unpopular point of view or person'.

diagnosis and **prognosis** are liable to be confused. Both are used with reference to disease but have different meanings. **Diagnosis** refers to 'the identification of a disease or disorder', as in 'She had cancer but the doctor failed to make the correct diagnosis until it was too late'. **Prognosis** refers to 'the prediction of the likely course of a disease or disorder', as in 'According to the

dice

___

doctor's prognosis, the patient will be dead in six
months'.

dice was originally the plural form of the singular noun
die, but **die** is now rarely used. Instead, **dice** is used
as both a singular and a plural noun, as in 'throw a
wooden dice' and 'use three different dice in the same
game'.

different is most usually followed by the preposition
'from', as in 'Their style of living is different from ours'.
Different from is considered to be the most correct
construction, particularly in formal English. **Different
to** is used in informal situations, as in 'His idea of a
good time is different to ours'. **Different than** is used
in American English.

dilemma is frequently used wrongly. It refers to 'a situation in which one is faced with two or more equally un-
desirable possibilities', as in 'I can't decide which of the
offers to accept. It's a real dilemma'.

dinner, lunch, supper and **tea** are terms that can cause
confusion. Their use can vary according to class, region
of the country and personal preference. Generally
speaking, people who have their main meal in the evening call it **dinner**. However, people who have their
main meal in the middle of the day frequently call this
meal **dinner**. People who have **dinner** in the evening
usually refer to their midday meal, usually a lighter
meal, as **lunch**. A more formal version of this word is
luncheon, which is now quite a rare word. **Supper**
has two meanings, again partly dependent on class and
region. It can refer either to the main meal of the day if
it is eaten in the evening—when it is virtually a synonym for **dinner**. Alternatively, it can refer to a light

snack, such as cocoa and toasted cheese, eaten late in
the evening before going to bed. **Tea** again has two
meanings when applied to a meal. It either means a light
snack-type meal of tea, sandwiches and cakes eaten in
the late afternoon. Alternatively, it can refer to a cooked
meal, sometimes taken with tea, and also referred to as
high tea, eaten in the early evening, rather than **dinner** later in the evening.

disabled is objected to by some people on the grounds
that it is a negative term, but it is difficult to find an acceptable alternative. In politically correct language
physically challenged has been suggested as has
differently abled, but neither of these has gained
widespread use. It should be noted that the use of 'the
disabled' should be avoided. 'Disabled people' should
be used instead.

disablism and **disableism** mean 'discrimination against
disabled people', as in 'He felt his failure to get a job was
because of disablism'. **Disablist** and **disableist** are
adjectives meaning 'showing or practising disablism', as
in 'guilty of disablist attitudes'. They also refer to 'a person who discriminates on the grounds of disability', as in
'That employer is a disablist'.

disassociate and **dissociate** are used interchangeably,
as in 'She wished to disassociate/dissociate herself from
the statement issued by her colleagues', but **dissociate**
is the more usual.

discover and **invent** are not interchangeable. **Discover**
means 'to find something that is already in existence but
is generally unknown', as in 'discover a new route to
China' and 'discover the perfect place for a holiday'.
Invent means 'to create something that has never before

disempowered

existed', as in 'invent the telephone' and 'invent a new form of heating system'.

disempowered in modern usage does not mean only 'having one's power removed', as in 'The king was disempowered by the invading general', but also means the same as 'powerless', as in 'We are disempowered to give you any more money'. **Disempowered** is seen in politically correct language as a more positive way of saying **powerless**.

disinterested and **uninterested** are often used inter-changeably in modern usage to mean 'not interested, indifferent', as in 'pupils totally disinterested/uninter-ested in school work'. Many people dislike **disinter-ested** being used in this way and regard it as a wrong use, but it is becoming increasingly common. **Disin-terested** also means 'impartial, unbiased', as in 'ask a disinterested party to settle the dispute between them'.

disorient and **disorientate** are used interchangeably. 'The town had changed so much since his last visit that he was completely disoriented/disorientated' and 'After the blow to her head she was slightly disoriented/disori-entated'.

divorcee refers to 'a divorced person', as in 'a club for divorcees'. **Divorcé** refers to 'a divorced man', and **di-vorcée** to 'a divorced woman'.

double negative the occurrence of two negative words in a single sentence or clause, as in 'He didn't say noth-ing' and 'We never had no quarrel'. This is usually con-sidered incorrect in standard English, although it is a feature of some social or regional dialects. The use of the double negative, if taken literally, often has the opposite meaning to the one intended. Thus 'He didn't say nothing' conveys the idea that 'He said something'.

Some double negatives are considered acceptable, as in 'I wouldn't be surprised if they don't turn up', although it is better to restrict such constructions to informal contexts. The sentence quoted conveys the impression that the speaker will be quite surprised if 'they' do 'turn up'. Another example of an acceptable double negative is 'I can't not worry about the children. Anything could have happened to them'. Again this type of construction is best restricted to informal contexts.

It is the semi-negative forms, such as 'hardly' and 'scarcely', that cause most problems with regard to double negatives, as in 'We didn't have hardly any money to buy food' and 'They didn't have barely enough time to catch the bus'. Such sentences are incorrect.

doubtful and **dubious** can be used interchangeably in the sense of 'giving rise to doubt, uncertain', as in 'The future of the project is dubious/doubtful', and in the sense of 'having doubts, unsure', as in 'I am doubtful/dubious about the wisdom of going'. **Dubious** also means 'possibly dishonest or bad', as in 'of dubious morals'.

draughtsman/woman and **draftsman/woman** are not the same. **Draughtsman/woman** refers to 'a person who draws detailed plans of a building, etc', as in 'study the plans of the bridge prepared by the draughtsman'. **Draftsman/woman** refers to 'a person who prepares a preliminary version of plans, etc', as in 'several draftswomen working on the draft parliamentary bills'.

drawing room *see* **sitting room**.

dreamed and **dreamt** are interchangeable both as the

past tense and the past participle of the verb 'dream', as in 'She dreamed/dreamt about living in the country' and in 'He has dreamed/dreamt the same dream for several nights'.

drier and **dryer** can both be used to describe 'a machine or appliance that dries', as in 'hair-drier/hair-dryer' and 'tumbler drier/dryer'. As an adjective meaning 'more dry', **drier** is the usual word, as in 'a drier summer than last year'.

dubious *see* **doubtful**.

due to, owing to and **because of** should not be used interchangeably. Strictly speaking, **due to** should be used only adjectivally, as in 'His poor memory is due to brain damage' and 'cancellations due to bad weather'. When a prepositional use is required **owing to** and **because of** should be used, as in 'the firm was forced to close owing to a lack of capital' and 'The train was cancelled because of snow on the line'. In modern usage it is quite common for **due to** to be used instead of **owing to** or **because of** because the distinction is rather difficult to comprehend.

e.g. means 'for example' and is an abbreviation of the Latin phrase *exempli gratia*. It is used before examples of something just previously mentioned, as in 'He cannot eat dairy products, e.g. milk, butter and cream'. A comma is usually placed just before it and, unlike some abbreviations, it has full stops.

each other and **one another** used not to be used interchangeably. It was taught that **each other** should be used when only two people are involved and that **one another** should be used when more than two people are involved, as in 'John and Mary really love each other' and 'All the members of the family love one another'. In modern use this restriction is often ignored.

EC and **EEC** both refer to the same thing, but **EC**, the abbreviation for **Economic Community** replaced **EEC**, the abbreviation for **European Economic Community.**

Both have now been replaced by **EU**, for **European Union**.

effeminate *see* **female**.

egoist and **egotist** are frequently used interchangeably in modern usage. Although they are not, strictly speaking, the same, the differences between them are rather subtle. **Egoist** refers to 'a person intent on self-interest, a selfish person', as in 'an egoist who never gave a thought to the needs of others'. **Egotist** refers to 'a person who is totally self-centred and obsessed with his/her own concerns', as in 'a real egotist who was always talking about herself'".

eke out originally meant 'to make something more adequate by adding to it or supplementing it', as in 'The poor mother eked out the small amount of meat with a lot of vegetables to feed her large family'. It can now also mean 'to make something last longer by using it sparingly', as in 'try to eke out our water supply until we reach a town', and 'to succeed or make with a great deal of effort', as in 'eke out a meagre living from their small farm'.

elder and **older** are not interchangeable. **Elder** is used only of people, as in 'The smaller boy is the elder of the two'. It is frequently used of family relationships, as in 'His elder brother died before him'. **Older** can be used of things as well as people, as in 'The church looks ancient but the castle is the older of the buildings' and 'The smaller girl is the older of the two'. It also can be used of family relationships, as in 'It was his older brother who helped him'. **Elder** used as a noun suggests experience or worthiness as well as age, as in 'Important issues used to be decided by the village elders' and 'Children should respect their elders and betters'.

elderly, as well as meaning 'quite or rather old', as in 'a town full of middle-aged and elderly people', is a more polite term than 'old', no matter how old the person referred to is, as in 'a residential home for elderly people'. **Elderly** is used only of people, except when used humorously, as in 'this cheese is getting rather elderly'.

eldest and **oldest** follow the same pattern as **elder** and **older**, as in 'The smallest boy is the eldest of the three', 'His eldest brother lived longer than any of them', 'The castle is the oldest building in the town' and 'He has four brothers but the oldest one is dead'.

empathy and **sympathy** are liable to be confused although they are not interchangeable. **Empathy** means 'the ability to imagine and share another's feelings, experiences, etc', as in 'As a single parent herself, the journalist has a real empathy with women bringing up children on their own' and 'The writer felt a certain empathy with the subject of his biography since they both came from a poverty-stricken childhood'. **Sympathy** means 'a feeling of compassion, pity or sorrow towards someone', as in 'feel sympathy for homeless children' and 'show sympathy towards the widow'.

endemic is usually used to describe a disease and means 'occurring in a particular area', as in 'a disease endemic to the coastal areas of the country' and 'difficult to clear the area of endemic disease'.

enervate is a word that is frequently misused. It means 'to weaken, to lessen in vitality', as in 'she was enervated by the extreme heat' and 'Absence of funding had totally enervated the society'. It is often wrongly used as though it meant the opposite.

enquiry and **inquiry** are frequently used interchangeably, as in 'make enquiries/inquiries about her health'. However some people see a distinction between them and use **enquiry** for ordinary requests for information, as in 'make enquiries about the times of trains'. They use **inquiry** only for 'investigation', as in 'The police have begun a murder inquiry' and 'launch an inquiry into the hygiene standards of the food firm'.

equal can be followed either by the preposition 'with' or the preposition 'to', but the two constructions are not interchangeable. **Equal to** is used in such sentences as 'He wished to climb the hill but his strength was not equal to the task'. **Equal with** is used in such sentences as 'After many hours of playing the two players remained equal with each other' and 'The women in the factory are seeking a pay scale equal with that of men'.

equally should not be followed by 'as'. Examples of it used correctly include 'Her brother is an expert player but she is equally talented' and 'He is trying hard but his competitors are trying equally hard'. These should not read 'but she is equally as talented' nor 'but his competitors are trying equally as hard'.

Esq. a word that can be used instead of 'Mr' when addressing an envelope to a man, as in 'John Jones, Esq.'.

It is mostly used in formal contexts. Note that Esq. is used instead of 'Mr', not as well as it. It is usually spelt with a full stop.

etc the abbreviation of a Latin phrase *et cetera*, meaning 'and the rest, and other things'. It is used at the end of lists to indicate that there exist other examples of the kind of thing that has just been named, as in 'He grows potatoes, carrots, turnips, etc', 'The girls can play tennis, hockey, squash, etc', 'The main branch of the bank can supply francs, marks, lire, kroner, etc'. Etc is preceded by a comma and can be spelt with or without a full stop.

ethnic is a word that causes some confusion. It means 'of a group of people classified according to race, nationality, culture, etc', as in 'a cosmopolitan country with a wide variety of ethnic groups'. It is frequently used loosely to mean 'relating to race', as in 'violent clashes thought to be ethnic in origin', or 'foreign' as in 'prefer ethnic foods to British foods'.

EU the abbreviation for European Union, the term which has replaced European Community and European Economic Community.

evade and **avoid** are similar in meaning but not identical. **Evade** means 'to keep away from by cunning or deceit', as in 'The criminal evaded the police by getting his friend to impersonate him'. **Avoid** means simply 'to keep away from', as in 'Women avoid that area of town at night'.

evasion and **avoidance** are frequently applied to the non-payment of income tax but they are not interchangeable. Tax **avoidance** refers to 'the legal nonpayment of tax by clever means'. Tax **evasion** refers to 'the illegal means of avoiding tax by cunning and dishonest means'.

even should be placed carefully in a sentence since its position can influence the meaning. Compare 'He didn't even acknowledge her' and 'He didn't acknowledge even her', and 'He doesn't even like Jane, let alone love her' and 'He hates the whole family—he doesn't like even Jane'. This shows that **even** should be placed immediately before the word it refers to in order to avoid ambiguity. In spoken English people often place it where it feels most natural, before the verb as in 'He even finds it difficult to relax on holiday'. To be absolutely correct this should be 'He finds it difficult to relax even on holiday' or 'Even on holiday he finds it difficult to relax'.

except is commoner than **except for**. **Except** is used in such sentences as 'They are all dead except his father', 'He goes every day except Sunday'. **Except for** is used at the beginning of sentences, as in 'Except for Fred, all the workers were present', and where **except** applies to a longish phrase, as in 'There was no one present except for the maid cleaning the stairs' and 'The house was silent except for the occasional purring of the cat'. When followed by a pronoun, this should be in the accusative or objective, as in 'There was no one there except *him*' and 'Everyone stayed late except *me*'.

explicit and **implicit** are liable to be confused although they are virtually opposites. **Explicit** means 'direct, clear', as in 'The instructions were not explicit enough' and 'Give explicit reasons for your decision'. **Explicit** is often used in modern usage to mean 'with nothing hidden or implied', as in 'explicit sex scenes'. **Implicit**

means 'implied, not directly expressed', as in 'There was an implicit threat in their warning' and 'an implicit criticism in his comments on their actions'. **Implicit** also means 'absolute and unquestioning', as in 'an implicit faith in his ability to succeed' and 'an implicit confidence in her talents'.

extrovert and **introvert** are liable to be confused although they are opposites. **Extrovert** refers to 'a person who is more interested in what is going on around him/her than in his/her own thoughts and feelings, such a person usually being outgoing and sociable', as in 'She is a real extrovert who loves to entertain the guests at parties'. **Introvert** refers to 'a person who is more concerned with his/her own thoughts and feelings than with what is going around him/her, such a person usually being shy and reserved', as in 'an introvert who hates having to speak in public' and 'introverts who prefer to stay at home than go to parties'. Both **extrovert** and **introvert** can be adjectives as well as nouns, as in 'extrovert behaviour' and 'introvert personality'. Note the spelling of **extrovert.** It was formerly spelt with an *a* instead of an *o*.

fahrenheit *see* **Celsius**.

family name is used in politically correct language instead of **maiden name** since this is thought to imply that all women are virgins before they are married. Thus 'Her family name was Jones' would be used instead of 'Her maiden name was Jones'. Another politically correct term is **birth name**, as in 'Her birth name was Jones'.

fantastic literally means 'relating to fantasy, fanciful, strange', as in 'fantastic dreams' and 'tales of fantastic events'. In modern usage it is often used informally to mean 'exceptionally good, excellent', as in 'have a fantastic holiday' and 'be a fantastic piano player'. It can also mean in informal usage 'very large', as in 'pay a fantastic sum of money'.

farther and **further** are not used interchangeably in all situations in modern usage. **Farther** is mainly restricted to sentences where physical distance is involved, as in 'It is farther to Glasgow from here than it is to Edinburgh'. **Further** can also be used in this sense, as in 'It is further to the sea than I thought'. When referring to time or extent, **further** is used, as in 'Further time is required to complete the task' and 'The police have ordered further investigations'. It can also mean 'additional', as in 'We shall require further supplies'. **Further**, unlike **farther**, can be used as a verb to mean 'to help the progress or development about', as in 'further the cause of freedom'.

faux pas is a French phrase that has been adopted into the English language. It means 'a social blunder, an indiscreet or embarrassing remark or deed', as in 'The hostess made a faux pas when she asked after her guest's wife, not knowing that they had divorced last year'. **Faux** is pronounced to rhyme with *foe*, and **pas** is pronounced *pa*.

fax is an abbreviation of 'facsimile' and refers to 'an electronic system for transmitting documents using telephone lines'. As a noun **fax** can refer to the machine transmitting the documents, as in 'the fax has broken down again'; to the system used in the transmission, as in 'send the report by fax'; and the document or documents so transmitted, as in 'He replied to my fax at once'.

female, feminine and **feminist** all relate to women but they are by no means interchangeable. **Female** refers to the sex of a person, animal or plant, as in 'the female members of the group', 'the female wolf and her cubs' and 'the female reproductive cells'. It refers to the child-bearing sex and contrasts with 'male'. **Feminine** means 'having qualities that are considered typical of women or are traditionally associated with women', as in 'wear feminine clothes', 'take part in supposedly feminine pursuits, such as cooking and sewing' and 'feminine hairstyles'. It is the opposite of 'masculine'. It can be used of men as well as women, when it is usually derogatory, as in 'He has a very feminine voice' and 'He walks in a very feminine way'. When applied in a derogatory way to a man, **feminine** means much the same as **effeminate**. **Feminine** also applies to the gender of words, as in 'Lioness is the feminine form of lion'. **Feminist** means 'referring to feminism', 'feminism' being 'a movement based on the belief that women should have the same rights, opportunities, etc', as in 'management trying to avoid appointing anyone with feminist ideas' and 'Equal opportunities is one of the aims of the feminist movement'.

ferment and **foment** can both mean 'to excite, to stir up', as in 'Troublemakers out to ferment discontent' and 'People out to foment trouble in the crowd'. Both words have other meanings that do not relate to each other. **Ferment** means 'to undergo the chemical process known as fermentation', as in 'home-made wine fermenting in the basement'. **Foment** means 'to apply warmth and moisture to in order to lessen pain or discomfort', as in 'foment the old man's injured hip'.

few and **a few** do not convey exactly the same meaning. **Few** is used to mean the opposite of 'many', as in 'We expected a good many people to come but few did' and 'Many people entered the competition but few won a prize'. The phrase **a few** is used to mean the opposite of 'none', as in 'We didn't expect anyone to turn up but a few did' and 'We thought that none of the students would get a job but a few did'.

fewer *see* **less**.

fictional and **fictitious** are both derived from the noun 'fiction' and are interchangeable in the sense of 'imagined, invented', as in 'a fictional character based on an old man whom he used to know' and 'The events in the novel are entirely fictitious'. However, **fictitious** only is used in the sense of 'invented, false', as in 'an entirely fictitious account of the accident' and 'think up fictitious reasons for being late'.

fill in and **fill out** are both used to mean 'to complete a form, etc, by adding the required details', as in 'fill in/ fill out an application form for a passport'. In British English **fill in** is the more common term, although **fill out** is the accepted term in American English.

first and **firstly** are now both considered acceptable in lists, although formerly **firstly** was considered unacceptable. Originally the acceptable form of such a list was as in 'There are several reasons for staying here. First, we like the house, secondly we have pleasant neighbours, thirdly we hate moving house'. Some users now prefer to use the adjectival forms of 'second' and 'third' when using **first**, as in 'He has stated his reasons for going to another job. First, he has been offered a higher salary, second, he has more opportunities for promotion, third, he will have a company car'. As indicated, **firstly** is now quite acceptable and is the form preferred by many people, as in 'They have several reasons for not having a car. Firstly they have very little money, secondly, they live right next to the bus-stop, thirdly, they feel cars are not environmentally friendly'.

first name *see* **Christian name**.

fish and **fishes** are both found as plural forms of 'fish', but **fish** is by far the more widely used form, as in 'He keeps tropical fish', 'Some fish live in fresh water and some in the sea' and 'there are now only three fish in the tank'. **Fishes** is rarely used but when it is, it is usually used to refer to different species of fish, as in 'He is comparing the fishes of the Pacific Ocean with those of the Indian Ocean'. **Fish** can also be used in this case.

flak originally referred to 'gunfire aimed at enemy aircraft', as in 'Pilots returning across the English Channel encountered heavy flak'. In modern usage it is also applied to 'severe criticism', as in 'the government receiving flak for raising taxes'.

flammable and **inflammable** both mean 'easily set on fire, burning easily', as in 'Children's nightclothes should not be made of flammable/inflammable material' and 'The chemical is highly flammable/inflammable'. **Inflammable** is frequently misused because some people wrongly regard it as meaning 'not burning easily', thinking that it is like such words as 'incredible', 'inconceivable' and 'intolerant' where the prefix 'in' means 'not'.

flotsam and **jetsam** are often used together to refer to 'miscellaneous objects, odds and ends', as in 'We have moved most of the furniture to the new house—there's just the flotsam and jetsam left', and 'vagrants, tramps', as in 'people with no pity in their hearts for the flotsam and jetsam of society'. In the phrase **flotsam and jetsam** they are used as though they meant the same thing but this is not the case. Both words relate to the remains of a wrecked ship, but **flotsam** refers to 'the wreckage of the ship found floating in the water', as in 'The coastguards knew the ship must have broken up when they saw bits of flotsam near the rocks', while **jetsam** refers to 'goods and equipment thrown overboard from a ship in distress in order to lighten it', as in 'The coastguards were unable to find the ship although they found the jetsam'.

forbear and **forebear** are interchangeable in one meaning of **forbear** only. **Forbear** is a verb meaning 'to refrain from', as in 'I hope she can forbear from pointing out that she was right' and this cannot be spelt **forebear**. However, **forebear** meaning 'ancestor' can also be spelt **forbear**, as in 'One of his *forebears/forbears* received a gift of land from Henry VIII'.

The verb **forbear** is pronounced with the emphasis on the second syllable as for-*bair*. The nouns **forbear** and **forebear** are pronounced alike with the emphasis on the first syllable as *for*-bair. The past tense of the verb **forbear** is **forbore**, as in 'He forbore to mention that he was responsible for the mistake'.

forever can be spelt as two words when it means 'eternally, for all time', as in 'doomed to separate forever/for ever' and 'have faith in the fact that they would dwell forever/for ever with Christ'. In the sense of 'constantly or persistently', only **forever** is used, as in 'His wife was forever nagging' and 'the child was forever asking for sweets'.

former and **latter** are opposites. **Former** refers to 'the first of two people or things mentioned' while **latter** refers to 'the second of two people or things mentioned', as in 'He was given two options, either to stay in his present post but accept less money or to be transferred to another branch of the company. He decided to accept the former/latter option'. **Former** also means 'previous, at an earlier time', as in 'He is a former chairman of the company' and 'She is a former holder of the championship title'.

further *see* **farther**.

gaol *see* **jail**.

gay originally meant 'merry, light-hearted', as in 'the gay laughter of children playing' and 'everyone feeling gay at the sight of the sunshine'. Although this meaning still exists in modern usage, it is rarely used since **gay** has come to be an accepted word for 'homosexual', as in 'gay rights' and 'gay bars'. Although the term can be applied to men or women it is most commonly applied to men, the corresponding word for women being **lesbian**. There is a growing tendency among homosexuals to describe themselves as **queer**, a term that was formerly regarded as being offensive.

geriatric is frequently found in medical contexts to mean 'elderly' or 'old', as in 'an ever-increasing number of geriatric patients' and 'a shortage of geriatric wards'. In such contexts **geriatric** is not used in a belittling or derogatory way, **geriatrics** being the name given to the branch of medicine concerned with the health and diseases of elderly people. However, **geriatric** is often used in the general language to refer to old people in a derogatory or scornful way, as in 'geriatric shoppers getting in the way' or 'geriatric drivers holding up the traffic'.

gibe and **jibe** both mean 'to jeer at, mock, make fun of', as in 'rich children gibing/jibing at the poor children for wearing out-of-date clothes'. **Gibe** and **jibe** are nouns as well as verbs as in 'politicians tired of the gibes/jibes of the press'.

Gipsy and **Gypsy** are both acceptable spellings, as in 'Gipsies/Gypsies travelling through the country in their caravans'. Some people object to the word **Gipsy** or **Gypsy**, preferring the word traveller, as in 'councils being asked to build sites for travellers'. The term **traveller** is used to apply to a wider range of people who travel the country, as in 'New Age travellers', and not just to Gipsies, who are Romany in origin.

girl means 'a female child or adolescent', as in 'separate schools for girls and boys' and 'Girls tend to mature more quickly than boys'. However it is often applied to a young woman, or indeed to a woman of any age, as in 'He asked his wife if she was going to have a night out with the girls from the office'. Many women object to this use, regarding it as patronizing, although the user of the term does not always intend to convey this impression.

gourmand and **gourmet** and **glutton** all have reference to food but they do not mean quite the same thing. **Gourmand** refers to 'a person who likes food and eats a lot of it', as in 'Gourmands tucking into huge helpings of the local food'. It means much the same as **glutton**, but **glutton** is a more condemnatory term, as in 'gluttons stuffing food into their mouths'. **Gourmet** is a more refined term, being used to refer to 'a person who enjoys food and who is discriminating and knowledgeable about it', as in 'gourmets who spend their holidays seeking out good local restaurants and produce'. In modern usage **gourmet** is often used as an adjective to mean 'high-class, elaborate, expensive', as in 'gourmet restaurants' and 'gourmet foods'.

graffiti Italian in origin and actually the plural form of **graffito**, meaning a single piece of writing or drawing, but this is now hardly ever used in English.

green is used to mean 'concerned with the conservation of the environment', as in 'a political party concerned with green issues' and 'buy as many green products as possible'. The word is derived from German *grün*, the political environmental lobby having started in West Germany, as it was then called.

grey and **gray** are both acceptable spellings. In British English, however, **grey** is the more common, as in 'different shades of grey' and 'grey hair', but **gray** is the standard form in American English.

gypsy *see* **gipsy**.

handicapped is disliked by some people because they feel it is too negative a term. There is as yet no widespread alternative apart from **disabled**, although various suggestions have been made as part of the politically correct language movement, such as **physically challenged** and **differently abled**.

hard and **soft** are both terms applied to drugs. **Hard drugs** refer to 'strong drugs that are likely to be addictive', as in 'Heroin and cocaine are hard drugs'. **Soft drugs** refer to 'drugs that are considered unlikely to cause addiction', as in 'cannabis and other soft drugs'.

hardly is used to indicate a negative idea. Therefore a sentence or clause containing it does not require another negative. Sentences, such as 'I couldn't hardly see him' and 'He left without hardly a word' are *wrong*. They should read 'I could hardly see him' and 'He left with hardly a word'. **Hardly** is followed by 'when', not 'than', as in 'Hardly had he entered the house when he collapsed', although the 'than' construction is very common.

he/she is a convention used to avoid sexism. Before the rise of feminism anyone referred to, whose sex was not specified, was assumed to be male, as in 'Each pupil must take his book home' and 'Every driver there parked his car illegally'. The only exception to this occurred in situations that were thought to be particularly appropriate to women, as in 'The cook should make her own stock' and 'The nurse has left her book behind'. In modern usage where attempts are made to avoid sexism either **he/she** or 'he or she' is frequently used, as in 'Each manager is responsible for his/her department' or 'It is a doctor's duty to explain the nature of the treatment to his or her patient'. People who regard this convention as being clumsy should consider restructuring the sentence or putting it in the plural, as in 'All managers are responsible for their departments'. Some users prefer to be ungrammatical and use a plural pronoun with a singular noun, as in 'Every pupil should take their books home' and this use is becoming increasingly common, even in textbooks.

heterosexism refers to discrimination and prejudice by a heterosexual person against a homosexual one, as in 'He was convinced that he had not got the job because he was gay—that the employer had been guilty of heterosexism'.

historic and **historical** are both adjectives formed from the noun 'history' but they are not interchangeable. **Historic** refers to events that are important enough to earn, or have earned, a place in history, as in 'Nelson's historic victory at Trafalgar' and 'the astronaut's historic landing on the moon'. It can be used loosely to mean 'extremely memorable', as in 'attend a historic party'. **Historical** means 'concerning past events', as in 'historical studies', or 'based on the study of history'.

hopefully has two meanings. The older meaning is 'with hope', as in 'The child looked hopefully at the sweet shop window' and 'It is better to travel hopefully than to arrive'. A more recent meaning, which is disliked by some people, means 'it is to be hoped that', as in 'Hopefully we shall soon be there'.

humanism and **humanitarianism** are liable to be confused. **Humanism** is a philosophy that values greatly human beings and their rôle, and rejects the need for religion, as in 'She was brought up as a Christian but she decided to embrace humanism in later life'. **Humanitarianism** refers to the philosophy and actions of people who wish to improve the lot of their fellow human beings and help them, as in 'humanitarians trying to help the refugees by taking them food and clothes'.

hyper- and **hypo-** are liable to be confused. They sound rather similar but they are opposites. **Hyper-** means 'above, excessively', as in 'hyperactive', 'hyperexcitable'. **Hypo-** means 'under, beneath', as in 'hypothermia'.

I and **me** are liable to be confused. I should be used as the subject of a sentence, as in 'You and I have both been invited', 'May Jane and I play?' and me as the object, as in 'The cake was made by Mary and me' and 'My brother and father played against my mother and me'. People often assume wrongly that me is less 'polite' than I. This is probably because they have been taught that in answer to such questions as 'Who is there?' the grammatically correct reply is 'It is I'. In fact, except in formal contexts, 'It is me' is frequently found in modern usage, especially in spoken contexts. Confusion arises as to whether to use I or me after 'between'. Since 'between' is followed by an object, me is the correct form. Thus it is correct to say 'Just between you and me, I think he is dishonest'.

i.e. is the abbreviation of a Latin phrase *id est*, meaning 'that is', as in 'He is a lexicographer, i.e. a person who edits dictionaries'. It is mostly used in written, rather than formal contexts.

identical in modern usage can be followed by either 'with' or 'to'. Formerly only 'with' was considered correct, as in 'His new suit is identical with the one he bought last year'. Now 'to' is also considered acceptable, as in 'a brooch identical to one which he bought for his wife'.

illegible and **unreadable** are not totally interchangeable. **Illegible** refers to something that is impossible to make out or decipher, as in 'her handwriting is practically illegible'. **Unreadable** can also mean this, as in 'unreadable handwriting', but it can also mean 'unable to be read with understanding or enjoyment', as in 'His writing is so full of jargon that it is unreadable'.

imbroglio means 'a confused, complicated or embarrassing situation', as in 'politicians getting involved in an international imbroglio during the summit conference'. It is liable to be misspelt and mispronounced. Note the *g* which is liable to be omitted erroneously as it is not pronounced. It is pronounced im-*bro*-lio with emphasis on the second syllable which rhymes with 'foe'. **Imbroglio** is used only in formal or literary contexts.

impasse causes problems with reference to meaning, spelling and pronunciation. It means 'a difficult position or situation from which there is no way out, deadlock', as in 'The negotiations between management and workers have reached an impasse with neither side being willing to compromise'. Note the final *e* in the spelling. The first syllable can be pronounced 'am', or 'om' in an attempt at following the original French pronunciation, although in modern usage it is frequently totally anglicized as 'im'.

implicit *see* **explicit**.

imply and **infer** are often used interchangeably but they in fact are different in meaning. **Imply** means 'to suggest, to hint at', as in 'We felt that she was implying that he was lying' and 'She did not actually say that there was going to be a delay but she implied it'. **Infer** means 'to deduce, to conclude', as in 'From what the employer said we inferred that there would be some redundancies' and 'From the annual financial reports observers inferred the company was about to go bankrupt'. Note that **infer** doubles the *r* when adding '-ed' or '-ing' to form the past tense, past participle or present participle as **inferred** and **inferring**.

impracticable and **impractical** are liable to be confused. **Impracticable** means 'impossible to put into practice, not workable', as in 'In theory the plan is fine

but it is impracticable in terms of costs'. **Impractical**
means 'not sensible or realistic', as in 'It is impractical
to think that you will get there and back in a day'; 'not
skilled at doing or making things', as in 'He is a brilliant
academic but he is hopelessly impractical'.

indefinite article *see* **a, an.**

in lieu, which means 'instead of', as in 'receive extra pay
in lieu of holidays', causes problems with pronunciation.
It may be pronounced in lew or in loo.

indexes and **indices** are both plural forms of 'index'. In
modern usage **indexes** is the more common form in
general language, as in 'Indexes are essential in large
reference books'. An **index** in this sense is 'an alpha-
betical list given at the back of a book as a guide to its
contents'. The form **indices** is mostly restricted to
technical contexts, such as mathematical information.
Indices is pronounced in-dis-is and is the Latin form
of the plural.

individual refers to 'a single person as opposed to a
group', as in 'The rights of the community matter but so
do the rights of the individual'. **Individual** is also sometimes used instead of 'person', but in such cases it is often used in a disapproving or belittling way, as in 'What
an unpleasant individual she is!' and 'The individual
who designed that building should be shot'.

indoor and **indoors** are not interchangeable. **Indoor** is
an adjective, as in 'have an indoor match' and 'indoor
games'. **Indoors** is an adverb, as in 'children playing
outdoors instead of watching television indoors' and
'sleep outdoors on warm evenings instead of indoors'.

infer *see* **imply.**

infinite and **infinitesimal** are similar in meaning but are not interchangeable. **Infinite** means 'without limit', as in 'infinite space', or 'very great', as in 'have infinite patience' and 'He seems to have an infinite capacity for hard work'. **Infinitesimal** means 'very small, negligible', as in 'an infinitesimal difference in size' and 'an infinitesimal increase'. **Infinitesimal** is pronounced with the emphasis on the fourth syllable in-fin-it-*es*-im-il.

informer and **informant** both refer to 'a person who provides information' but they are used in different contexts. **Informer** is used to refer to 'a person who gives information to the police or authorities about a criminal, fugitive, etc', as in 'The local police have a group of informers who tell them what is going on in the criminal underworld' and 'The resistance worker was caught by the enemy soldier when an informer told them about his activities'. An **informant** provides more general information, as in 'My informant keeps me up-to-date with changes in personnel'.

in-law is usually found in compounds such as 'mother-in-law' and 'father-in-law'. When these compounds are in the plural the *s* should be added to the first word of the compound, not to **in-law**, as in 'mothers-in-law' and 'fathers-in-law'.

input used to be a technical term with particular application to computers. This meaning still exists and **input** can refer to the data, power, etc, put into a computer. As a verb it means 'to enter data into a computer', as in 'input the details of all the travel resorts in the area'. In modern usage it is frequently used in general language to mean 'contribution', as in 'Everyone is expected to provide some input for tomorrow's conference'. It is even found in this sense as a verb, as in 'input a great deal to the meeting'.

inquiry *see* **enquiry**.

install and **instal** are now both considered acceptable spellings. **Install** was formerly considered to be the only correct spelling and it is still the more common. The *l* is doubled in **instal** in the past participle, past tense and present participle as **installed**, **installing**. It means 'to put in', as in 'he installed a new television set'. The noun is spelt **instalment**.

instantaneously and **instantly** are interchangeable. Both mean 'immediately, at once', as in 'They obeyed instantaneously/instantly' and 'The accident victims were killed instantly/instantaneously'.

intense and **intensive** are not interchangeable. Intense means 'very strong, extreme', as in 'an intense desire to scream' and 'unable to tolerate the intense cold on the icy slopes'. **Intensive** means 'thorough', as in 'conduct an intensive search', and 'concentrated', as in 'an intensive course in first aid' and 'intensive bombing'.

invalid refers to two different words. If it is pronounced with the emphasis on the second syllable, as in-*val*-id it means 'not valid, no longer valid', as in 'This visa becomes invalid after six months'. If it is pronounced with the emphasis on the first syllable, as *in*-val-id, it means 'a person who is ill', as in 'The doctor has arrived to see the invalid'.

invent *see* **discover**.

inward and **inwards** are not used interchangeably. **Inward** is an adjective, as in 'an inward curve' and 'No one could guess her inward feelings'. **Inwards** is an adverb, as in 'toes turning inwards' and 'thoughts turning inwards'. **Inward** can be used as an adverb in the same way as **inwards.**

IQ is the abbreviation of 'intelligence quotient', as in 'He has a high IQ'. It is always written in capital letters and is sometimes written with full stops and sometimes not, according to preference.

irrespective is followed by the preposition 'of'. The phrase means 'not taking account of, not taking into consideration', as in 'All can go on the trip, irrespective of age'.

irrevocable is frequently misspelt and mispronounced. Note the double *r* and the *-able* ending. It is pronounced with the emphasis on the second syllable, as ir-*rev*-ok-ibl. When applied to legal judgements, etc, it is sometimes pronounced with the emphasis on the third syllable, as ir-rev-*ok*-ibl. The word means 'unable to be changed or revoked', as in 'Their decision to get divorced is irrevocable' and 'The jury's decision is irrevocable'.

its and **it's** are liable to be confused. **Its** is an adjective meaning 'belonging to it', as in 'The house has lost its charm' and 'The dog does not like its kennel'. **It's** means 'it is', as in 'Do you know if it's raining?' and 'It's not fair to expect her to do all the chores'.

jail and **gaol** are both acceptable spellings although jail is the more common. They mean 'prison' and can be both nouns and verbs, as in 'sent to jail/gaol for killing his wife' and 'jail/gaol him for his part in the bank robbery'.

jersey *see* **cardigan**.

jetsam *see* **flotsam**.

just is liable to be put in the wrong place in a sentence. It should be placed before the word it refers to, as in 'He has just one book left to sell', not 'He just has one book left to sell'. **Just** in the sense of 'in the very recent past' is used with the perfect tense, as in 'They have just finished the job', not 'They just finished the job'.

kind should be used with a singular noun, as 'This kind of accident can be avoided'. This should not read 'These kind of accidents can be avoided'. Similarly 'The children do not like that kind of film' is correct, not 'The children do not like those kind of films'. A plural noun can be used if the sentence is rephrased as 'Films of that kind are not liked by children'.

kindly can be either an adjective or adverb. The adjective means 'kind, friendly, sympathetic', as in 'A kindly lady took pity on the children and lent them some money to get home' and 'She gave them a kindly smile'. The adverb means 'in a kind manner', as in 'We were treated kindly by the local people' and 'They will not look kindly on his actions'.

kind of, meaning 'rather', as in 'That restaurant's kind of dear' and 'She's kind of tired of him', is informal and should be avoided in formal contexts.

knit in modern usage is becoming increasingly used as a noun to mean 'a knitted garment', as in 'a shop selling beautifully coloured knits'.

lady and **woman** cause controversy. **Lady** is objected to by many people when it is used instead of **woman**. Formerly, and still in some circles, it was regarded as a polite form of **woman**, as in " 'Please get up and give that lady a seat", said the mother to her son'. Indeed, **woman** was thought to be rather insulting. For many people **woman** is now the preferred term and **lady** is seen as classist, because it is associated with nobility, privilege, etc, or condescending. However, **lady** is still quite commonly used, particularly when women are being addressed in a group, as in ' "Ladies, I hope we can reach our sales target", said the manager' and 'Come along, ladies the bus is about to leave'. Phrases, such as **dinner lady** and **cleaning lady** are thought by some to be condescending but others still find **woman** rather insulting.

last is liable to cause confusion because it is not always clear which meaning is meant. **Last** as an adjective has several meanings. It can mean 'final', as in 'That was the musician's last public appearance—he died shortly after'; 'coming after all others in time or order', as in 'December is the last month in the year', 'The last of the runners reached the finishing tape'; 'latest, most recent', as in 'Her last novel is not as good as her earlier ones'; 'previous, preceding', as in 'This chapter is interesting but the last one was boring'. In order to avoid confusion it is best to use a word other than **last** where ambiguity is likely to arise. An example of a sentence which could cause confusion is 'I cannot remember the title of his last book', which could mean either 'his latest book' or 'his final book'.

latter *see* **former**.

lavatory *see* **toilet**.

lay and **lie** are liable to be confused. They are related but are used in different contexts. **Lay** means 'to put or place' and is a transitive verb, i.e. it takes an object. It is found in such sentences as 'Ask them to lay the books carefully on the table' and 'They are going to lay a new carpet in the bedroom'. **Lie**, meaning 'to rest in a horizontal position', is an intransitive verb, i.e. it does not take an object. It is found in such sentences as 'They were told to lie on the ground' and 'Snow is apt to lie on the mountain tops for a long time'. The confusion between the two words arises from the fact that **lay** is also the past tense of **lie**, as in 'He lay still on the ground' and 'Snow lay on the mountain tops'. The past tense of **lay** is **laid**, as in 'They laid the books on the table'. There is another verb **lie**, meaning 'to tell falsehoods, not to tell the truth', as in 'He was told to lie to the police'. The past tense of **lie** in this sense is **lied**, as in 'We suspect that he lied but we cannot prove it'.

leading question is often used wrongly. It should be used to mean 'a question that is so worded as to invite (or lead to) a particular answer desired by the questioner', as in 'The judge refused to allow the barrister to ask the witness the question on the grounds that it was a leading question'. However, it is often used wrongly to mean 'a question that is difficult, unfair or embarrassing'.

learn and **teach** are liable to be confused. **Learn** means 'to gain information or knowledge about', as in 'She learnt Spanish as a child', or 'to gain the skill of', as in 'She is learning to drive'. **Teach** means 'to give instruction in, to cause to know something or be able to do something', as in 'She taught her son French' and 'She taught her son to swim'. **Learn** is frequently used wrongly instead of **teach**, as in 'She learnt us to drive'.

learned and **learnt** are both acceptable forms of the past participle and past tense of the verb 'to learn', as in 'She has now learned/learnt to drive' and 'They learned/learnt

French at school'. **Learned** in this sense can be pronounced either lernd or lernt. However, **learned** can also be an adjective, meaning 'having much knowledge, erudite', as in 'an learned professor', or 'academic', as in 'learned journals'. It is pronounced *ler*-ned.

leave and **let** are not interchangeable. **Leave go** should not be substituted for **let go** in such sentences as 'Do not let go of the rope'. 'Do not leave go of the rope' is considered to be incorrect. However both **leave alone** and **let alone** can be used in the sense of 'to stop disturbing or interfering with', as in 'Leave/let the dog alone or it will bite you' and 'leave/let your mother alone—she is not feeling well'. **Leave alone** can also mean 'leave on one's own, cause to be alone', as in 'Her husband went away and left her alone', but **let alone** cannot be used in this sense. **Let alone** can also mean 'not to mention, without considering', as in 'They cannot afford proper food, let alone a holiday', but **leave alone** should not be used in this sense.

legible and **readable** are not interchangeable. **Legible** means 'able to be deciphered or made out', as in 'His writing is scarcely legible'. **Readable** can also be used in this sense, as in 'His handwriting is just not readable'. However **readable** is also used to mean 'able to be read with interest or enjoyment', as in 'He is an expert on the subject but I think his books are simply not readable' and 'I find her novels very readable but my friend does not like her style'.

lend and **loan** can cause confusion. **Lend** is used as a verb in British English to mean 'to allow someone the use of temporarily', as in 'Can you lend me a pen?' and

'His father refused to lend him any money'. **Loan** is a noun meaning 'something lent, the temporary use of', as in 'They thanked her for the loan of her car'. In American English **loan** is used as a verb to mean **lend**, and this use is becoming common in Britain although it is still regarded as not quite acceptable.

lengthways and **lengthwise** are used interchangeably, as in 'fold the tablecloth lengthways/lengthwise' and 'measure the room lengthwise/lengthways'.

lengthy and **long** are not interchangeable. **Lengthy** means 'excessively long', as in 'We had a lengthy wait before we saw the doctor' and 'It was such a lengthy speech that most of the audience got bored'. **Lengthy** is frequently misspelt. Note the *g*.

less and **fewer** are often confused. Less means 'a smaller amount or quantity of' and is the comparative form of 'little'. It is found in sentences such as 'less milk', 'less responsibility' and 'less noise'. **Fewer** means 'a smaller number of' and is the comparative of 'few'. It is found in sentences such as 'buy fewer bottles of milk', 'have fewer responsibilities', 'have fewer opportunities' and 'hear fewer noises'. **Less** is commonly wrongly used where **fewer** is correct. It is common but ungrammatical to say or write 'less bottles of milk' and 'less queues in the shops during the week'.

liable to and **likely to** both express probability. They mean much the same except that **liable to** suggests that the probability is based on past experience or habit. 'He is liable to lose his temper' suggests that he has been in the habit of doing so in the past. 'He is likely to lose his temper' suggests that he will probably lose his temper, given the situation, but that the probability is not based on how he has reacted in the past. This distinction is not always adhered to, and some people use the terms interchangeably.

libel and **slander** both refer to defamatory statements against someone but they are not interchangeable. **Libel** refers to defamation that is written down, printed or drawn, as in 'The politician sued the newspaper for libel when it falsely accused him of fraud'. **Slander** refers to defamation in spoken form, as in 'She heard that one of her neighbours was spreading slander about her'. Both **libel** and **slander** can act as verbs, as in 'bring a suit against the newspaper for libelling him' and 'think that one of her neighbours was slandering her'. Note that the verb **libel** doubles the *l* in the past participle, past tense and present participle, as **libelled** and **libelling**.

licence and **license** are liable to cause confusion in British English. **Licence** is a noun meaning 'an official document showing that permission has been given to do, use or own something', as in 'require a licence to have a stall in the market', 'have a licence to drive a car', and 'apply for a pilot's licence'. **License** is a verb meaning 'to provide someone with a licence', as in 'The council have licensed him as a street trader', 'The restaurant has been licensed to sell alcohol'. Note **licensed grocer** and **licensing laws** but **off-licence**. In American English both the noun and verb are spelt **license**.

lie *see* **lay**.

light years are a measure of distance, not time. A **light year** is the distance travelled by light in one year (about six million, million miles) and is a term used in astronomy. **Light years** are often referred to in an informal context when time, not distance, is involved, as in 'Owning their own house seemed light years away' and 'It seems light years since we had a holiday'.

like tends to cause confusion. It is a preposition meaning 'resembling, similar to', as in 'houses like castles', gardens like jungles', 'actors like Olivier', 'She looks like her mother', 'She plays like an expert', 'The child swims like a fish' and 'Like you, he cannot stand cruelty to animals'. To be grammatically correct **like** should not be used as a conjunction. Thus 'The house looks like it has been deserted' is incorrect. It should read 'The house looks as though/if it has been deserted'. Similarly, 'Like his mother said, he has had to go to hospital' should read 'As his mother said, he has had to go to hospital'.

likeable and **likable** are both acceptable spellings. The word means 'pleasant, agreeable, friendly', as in 'He is a likeable/likable young man'.

likely to *see* **liable to**.

literally is frequently used simply to add emphasis to an idea rather than to indicate that the word, phrase, etc, used is to be interpreted word for word. Thus, 'She was literally tearing her hair out' does not mean that she was pulling her hair out by the handful but that she was very angry, anxious, frustrated, etc.

livid and **lurid** are liable to be confused although they mean different things. **Livid** means 'discoloured, of a greyish tinge', as in 'a livid bruise on her face', and 'furious', as in 'When he saw his damaged car he was livid'. **Lurid** means 'sensational, shocking', as in 'give the lurid details about finding the body', and 'garish, glaringly bright', as in 'wear a lurid shade of green'.

living room *see* **sitting room**.

loo *see* **toilet**.

lots of and **a lot of**, meaning 'many' and 'much', should be used only in informal contexts', as in " 'I've got lots of toys," said the child' and 'You're talking a lot of rubbish'. They should be avoided in formal prose.

lounge *see* **sitting room**.

low and **lowly** are not interchangeable. **Low** means 'not high', as in 'a low fence', 'a low level of income', 'speak in a low voice' and 'her low status in the firm'. It can also mean 'despicable, contemptible', as in 'That was a low trick' or 'He's a low creature'. **Lowly** means 'humble', as in 'of lowly birth' and 'the peasant's lowly abode'.

lunch and **luncheon** both refer to a meal eaten in the middle of the day. **Lunch**, as in 'a business lunch' and 'have just a snack for lunch', is by far the more usual term. **Luncheon**, as in 'give a luncheon party for the visiting celebrity', is a very formal word and is becoming increasingly uncommon. *See also* **dinner**.

lurid *see* **livid**.

madam and **madame** are liable to be confused. **Madam** is the English-language form of the French **madame**. It is a form of formal of address for a woman, as in 'Please come this way, madam'. It is used in formal letters when the name of the woman being written to is not known, as in 'Dear Madam'. **Madam** can be written either with a capital letter or a lower-case letter. **Madam** is pronounced *mad*-am, with the emphasis on the first syllable. **Madame**, which is the French equivalent of 'Mrs', is occasionally found in English, as in Madame Tussaud's, and is pronounced in the same way as **madam**. In French **madame** is pronounced ma-*dam*.

majority and **minority** are opposites. **Majority** means 'more than half the total number of', as in 'The majority of the pupils live locally' and 'the younger candidate received the majority of the votes'. **Minority** means less than half the total number of', as in 'A small minority of the football fans caused trouble' and 'Only a minority of the committee voted against the motion'. **Majority** and **minority** should not be used to describe the greater or lesser part of a single thing. Thus it is wrong to say 'The majority of the book is uninteresting'.

male, masculine and **mannish** all refer to the sex that is not female but the words are used in different ways. **Male** is the opposite of 'female' and refers to the sex of a person or animal, as in 'no male person may enter', 'a male nurse', 'a male elephant' and 'the male reproductive system'. **Masculine** is the opposite of 'feminine' and refers to people or their characteristics. It refers to characteristics, etc, that are traditionally considered to be typically **male**. Examples of its use include 'a very masculine young man', 'a deep, masculine voice'. It can be used of women, as in 'She has a masculine walk' and 'She wears masculine clothes'. When used of women it is often derogatory and is sometimes replaced with **mannish**, which is derogatory, as in 'women with mannish haircuts'. **Male** can also be used as a noun, as in 'the male of the species' 'of the robins, the male is more colourful' and 'the title can be held only by males'.

man

man causes a great deal of controversy. To avoid being sexist it should be avoided when it really means 'person'. 'We must find the right man for the job' should read 'We must find the right person for the job'. Similarly, 'All men have a right to a reasonable standard of living' should read 'All people have a right to a reasonable standard of living' or 'Everyone has a right to a reasonable standard of living'. Problems also arise with compounds, such as 'chairman'. In such situations 'person' is often used, as in 'chairperson'. Man is also used to mean 'mankind, humankind', as in 'Man is mortal' and 'Man has the power of thought'. Some people also object to this usage and consider it sexist. They advocate using 'humankind' or 'the human race'.

many is used in more formal contexts rather than 'a lot of' or 'lots of', as in 'The judge said the accused had had many previous convictions'. **Many** is often used in the negative in both formal and informal contexts, as in 'They don't have many friends' and 'She won't find many apples on the trees now'.

masculine *see* **male**.

may *see* **can**.

maybe and **may be** are liable to be confused although they have different meanings. **Maybe** means 'perhaps', as in 'Maybe they lost their way' and 'He said, "Maybe" when I asked him if he was going'. It is used in more informal contexts than 'perhaps'. **May be** is used in such sentences as 'He may be poor but he is very generous' and 'They may be a little late'.

mayoress means 'the wife or partner of a male mayor', as in 'an official dinner for the mayor and mayoress'. A mayor who is a woman is called either 'mayor' or 'lady mayor'.

me *see* **I**.

meaningful originally meant 'full of meaning', as in 'make very few meaningful statements' and 'There was a meaningful silence'. In modern usage it has come to mean 'important, significant, serious', as in 'not interested in a meaningful relationship' and 'seeking a meaningful career'. The word now tends to be very much over-used.

means in the sense of 'way, method' can be either a singular or plural noun, as in 'The means of defeating them is in our hands' and 'Many different means of financing the project have been investigated'. **Means** in the sense of 'wealth' and 'resources' is plural, as in 'His means are not sufficient to support two families'.

media gives rise to confusion. In the form of **the media** it is commonly applied to the press, to newspapers, television and radio, as in 'The politician claimed that he was being harassed by the media'. **Media** is a plural form of 'medium', meaning 'means of communication', as in 'television is a powerful medium'. In modern usage **media** is beginning to be used as a singular noun, as in 'The politician blamed a hostile media for his misfortunes', but this is still regarded as being an incorrect use.

middle *see* **centre**.

mileage and **milage** are both acceptable spellings for 'the distance travelled or measured in miles', as in 'The car is a bargain, given the low mileage'. However **mileage** is much more common than **milage**. The word also means informally 'benefit, advantage', as in 'The politician got a lot of mileage from the scandal surrounding his opponent' and 'There's not much mileage in pursuing that particular line of inquiry'.

militate and **mitigate** are liable to be confused. **Militate** means 'to have or serve as a strong influence against', as in 'Their lack of facts militated against the success of their application' and 'His previous record will militate against his chances of going free'. **Mitigate** means 'to alleviate', as in 'try to mitigate the suffering of the refugees', or 'moderate', as in 'mitigate the severity of the punishment'.

millennium is liable to be misspelt. Note the double *n* which is frequently omitted in error. The plural form is **millennia**. **Millennium** refers to 'a period of 1000 years', as in 'rock changes taking place over several millennia'. In religious terms it refers to 'the thousand-year reign of Christ prophesied in the Bible'.

minority *see* **majority**.

Miss *see* **Ms**.

misuse *see* **abuse**.

mitigate *see* **militate**.

mnemonic refers to 'something that aids the memory'. For example, some people use a **mnemonic** in the form of a verse to remind them how to spell a word or to recall a date. The word is liable to be misspelt and mispronounced. Note the initial *m*, which is silent. **Mnemonic** is pronounced nim-*on*-ik, with the emphasis on the second syllable.

modern and **modernistic** are not quite the same. **Modern** means 'referring to the present time or recent times', as in 'the politics of modern times' and 'a production of

Shakespeare's *Twelfth Night* in modern dress'. It also means 'using the newest techniques, equipment, buildings, etc, as in 'a modern shopping centre' and 'a modern office complex'. **Modernistic** means 'characteristic of modern ideas, fashions, etc', and is often used in a derogatory way, as in 'She says she hates that modernistic furniture'.

modus vivendi refers to 'a practical, sometimes temporary, arrangement or compromise by which people who are in conflict can live or work together', as in 'The two opposing parties on the committee will have to reach a modus vivendi if any progress is to be made'. It is a Latin phrase that literally means 'a way of living' and is pronounced *mo*-dus viv-*en*-di.

more is used to form the comparative of adjectives and adverbs that do not form the comparative by adding -*er*. This usually applies to longer adjectives, as in 'more beautiful', 'more gracious', 'more useful', and 'more flattering'. **More** should not be used with adjectives that have a comparative ending already. Thus it is wrong to write 'more happier'. **Most** is used in the same way to form the superlative of adjectives and adverbs, as in 'most beautiful', 'most gracious' etc.

Moslem *see* **Muslim**.

most *see* **more**.

movable and **moveable** are both possible spellings but **movable** is the more common, as in 'movable possessions' and 'machines with movable parts'.

Ms, Mrs and **Miss** are all used before the names of women in addressing them and in letter-writing. Formerly **Mrs** was used before the name of a married woman and **Miss**

before the name of an unmarried woman or girl. In modern usage **Ms** is often used instead of **Miss** or **Mrs**. This is sometimes because the marital status of the woman is not known and sometimes from a personal preference. Many people feel that since no distinction is made between married and unmarried men when they are being addressed, no distinction should be made between married and unmarried women. On the other hand some people, particularly older women, object to the use of **Ms**.

much, except in negative sentences, is used mainly in rather formal contexts, as in 'They own much property'. 'A great deal of' is often used instead, as in 'They own a great deal of property'. In informal contexts 'a lot of' is often used instead of **much**, as in 'a lot of rubbish' not 'much rubbish'. **Much** is used in negative sentences, as in 'They do not have much money'.

Muslim and **Moslem** refer to 'a follower of the Islamic faith'. In modern usage **Muslim** is the preferred term rather than the older spelling **Moslem**.

naught and **nought** are not totally interchangeable. **Naught** means 'nothing', as in 'All his projects came to naught', and is rather a formal or literary word in this sense. **Naught** is also a less usual spelling of **nought**, which means 'zero' when it is regarded as a number, as in 'nought point one (0.1)'.

nearby and **near by** can cause problems. **Nearby** can be either an adjective, as in 'the nearby village', or an adverb, as in 'Her mother lives nearby'. **Near by** is an adverb, as in 'He doesn't have far to go—he lives near by'. In other words, the adverbial sense can be spelt either **nearby** or **near by**.

née is used to indicate the maiden or family name of a

married woman, as in 'Jane Jones, née Smith'. It is derived from French, being the feminine form of the French word for 'born'. It can be spelt either with an acute accent or not—**née** or **nee**.

never in the sense of 'did not', as in 'He never saw the other car before he hit it', should be used in only very informal contexts. **Never** means 'at no time, on no occasion', as in 'He will never agree to their demands' and 'She has never been poor'. It is also used as a negative for the sake of emphasis, as in 'He never so much as smiled'.

nevertheless and **none the less** mean the same thing, as in 'He has very little money. Nevertheless/none the less he gives generously to charity'. **None the less** is usually written as three words but **nevertheless** is spelt as one word. In modern usage **none the less** is sometimes written as one word, as **nonetheless**.

next and **this** can cause confusion. **Next** in one of its senses is used to mean the day of the week, month of the year, season of the year, etc, that will follow next, as in 'They are coming next Tuesday', 'We are going on holiday next June' and 'They are to be married next summer'. **This** can also be used in this sense and so ambiguity can occur. Some people use **this** to refer to the very next Tuesday, June, summer, etc, and use **next** for the one after that. Thus someone might say on Sunday, 'I'll see you next Friday', meaning the first Friday to come, but someone else might take that to mean a week on from that because they would refer to the first Friday to come as 'this Friday'. The only solution is to make sure exactly which day, week, season, etc, the other person is referring to.

nice

nice originally meant 'fine, subtle, requiring precision', as in 'There is rather a nice distinction between the two words', but it is widely used in the sense of 'pleasant, agreeable, etc', as in 'She is a nice person' and 'We had a nice time at the picnic'. It is overused and alternative adjectives should be found to avoid this, as in 'She is an amiable person' and 'We had an enjoyable time at the picnic'.

no one and **no-one** are interchangeable but the word is never written 'noone', unlike 'everyone'. **No one** and **no-one** are used with a singular verb, as in 'No one is allowed to leave' and 'No one is anxious to leave'. They are used by some people with a plural personal pronoun or possessive case when attempts are being made to avoid sexism, as in 'No one is expected to take their child away'. The singular form is grammatically correct, as in 'No one is expected to take his/her child away', but it is clumsy. 'No one is expected to take his child away' is sexist. Nobody is interchangeable with no one, as in 'You must tell no one/nobody about this'.

nobody *see* **no one**.

none can be used with either a singular verb or plural verb. Examples of sentences using a singular verb include 'There is none of the food left' and 'None of the work is good enough' and 'None of the coal is to be used today'. In sentences where none is used with a plural noun the verb was traditionally still singular, as in 'None of the books is suitable' and 'None of the parcels is undamaged'. This is still the case in formal contexts but, in the case of informal contexts, a plural verb is often used in modern usage, as in 'None of these things are any good'.

none the less *see* **nevertheless**.

not only is frequently used in a construction with 'but also', as in 'We have not only the best candidate but also the most efficient organization' and 'The organizers of the fête not only made a great deal of money for charity but also gave a great many people a great deal of pleasure'.

nought *see* **naught**.

noxious and **obnoxious** are liable to be confused. They both refer to unpleasantness or harmfulness but they are used in different contexts. **Noxious** is used of a substance, fumes, etc, and means 'harmful, poisonous', as in 'firemen overcome by noxious fumes' and 'delinquent children having a noxious influence on the rest of the class'. **Obnoxious** means 'unpleasant, nasty, offensive', as in 'He has the most obnoxious neighbours' and 'The child's parents let him off with the most obnoxious behaviour'. **Noxious** is used in formal and technical contexts rather than **obnoxious**.

nubile originally meant 'old enough to marry, marriageable' as in 'he has five nubile daughters'. In modern usage **nubile** is frequently used in the sense of 'sexually attractive', as in 'admiring the nubile girls sunbathing on the beach' and 'nubile models posing for magazine illustrations'.

numbers can be written in either figures or words. It is largely a matter of taste which method is adopted. As long as the method is consistent it does not really matter. Some establishments, such as a publishing house or a newspaper office, will have a house style. For example, some of them prefer to have numbers up to 10 written in words, as in 'They have two boys and three girls'. If this system is adopted, guidance should be sought as to whether a mixture of figures and words in the same sentence is acceptable, as in 'We have 12 cups but only six saucers', or whether the rule should be broken in such situations as 'We have twelve cups but only six saucers'.

nutritional and **nutritious** are liable to be confused. They both refer to 'nutrition, the process of giving and receiving nourishment' but mean different things. **Nutritional** means 'referring to nutrition', as in 'doubts about the nutritional value of some fast foods' and 'people who do not receive the minimum nutritional requirements'. **Nutritious** means 'nourishing, of high value as a food', as in 'nutritious homemade soups' and 'something slightly more nutritious than a plate of chips'.

O and **Oh** are both forms of an exclamation made at the beginning of a sentence. **Oh** is the usual spelling, as in 'Oh well. It's Friday tomorrow' and 'Oh dear, the baby's crying again'.

loan *see* **lend**.

objective and **subjective** are opposites. **Objective** means 'not influenced by personal feelings, attitudes, or prejudices', as in 'She is related to the person accused and so she cannot give an objective view of the situation' and 'It is important that all members of a jury are completely objective'. **Subjective** means 'influenced by personal feelings, attitudes and prejudices', as in 'It is only natural to be subjective in situations regarding one's children' and 'She wrote a very subjective report on the conference and did not stick to the facts'. **Objective** can also be a noun in the sense of 'aim, goal', as in 'Our objective was to make as much money as possible'. **Object** can also be used in this sense, as in 'Their main object is to have a good time'.

oblivious means 'unaware of, unconscious of, not noticing'. Traditionally it is followed by the preposition 'of', as in 'The lovers were oblivious of the rain' and 'When he is reading he is completely oblivious of his surroundings'. In modern usage its use with the preposition 'to' is also considered acceptable, as in 'They were oblivious to the fact that he was cheating them' and 'sleep soundly, oblivious to the noise'.

obnoxious *see* **noxious**.

obscene and **pornographic** are not interchangeable. **Obscene** means 'indecent, especially in a sexual way, offending against the accepted standards of decency', as in 'obscene drawings on the walls of the public toilet' and 'When his car was damaged he let out a stream of obscene language'. **Pornographic** means 'intended to arouse sexual excitement', as in 'pornographic videos' and 'magazines with women shown in pornographic poses'. **Obscene** is frequently misspelt. Note the *c* after the *s*.

oculist *see* **optician**.

of is sometimes wrongly used instead of the verb 'to have', as in 'He must of known she was lying' instead of 'He must have known she was lying'. The error arises because the two constructions sound alike when not emphasized.

Oh *see* **O**.

OK and **okay** are both acceptable spellings of an informal
word indicating agreement or approval, as in 'OK/okay,
I'll come with you', 'We've at last been given the OK/
okay to begin building'. When the word is used as a verb
it is more usually spelt **okay** because of the problem in
adding endings, as in 'They've okayed our plans at last'.
OK is sometimes written with full stops as **O.K.**

older *see* **elder**.

one is used in formal situations to indicate an indefinite
person where 'you' would be used in informal situations, as in 'One should not believe all one hears' and
'One should be kind to animals'. This construction can
sound rather affected. Examples of the informal 'you'
include 'You would've thought he would've had more
sense' and 'You wouldn't think anyone could be so stupid'. **One** when followed by 'of the' and a plural noun
takes a singular verb, as in 'One of the soldiers was
killed' and 'One of the three witnesses has died'. However, the constructions 'one of those . . . who' and 'one
of the . . . that' take a plural verb, as in 'He is one of
those people who will not take advice' and 'It is one of
those houses that are impossible to heat'.

only must be carefully positioned in written sentences to
avoid confusion. It should be placed before, or as close
as possible before, the word to which it refers. Compare 'She drinks only wine at the weekend', 'She drinks
wine only at the weekend' and 'Only she drinks wine at
the weekend'. In spoken English, where the intonation of
the voice will indicate which word **only** applies to it may
be placed in whichever position sounds most natural,

usually between the subject and the verb, as in 'She only drinks wine at the weekend'.

onto and **on to** are both acceptable forms in sentences such as 'The cat leapt onto/on to the table' and 'He jumped from the plane onto/on to the ground'. However, in sentences such as 'It is time to move on to another city' **onto** is not a possible alternative.

onward and **onwards** are not interchangeable. **Onward** is an adjective, as in 'onward motion' and 'onward progress'. **Onwards** is an adverb, as in 'march onwards' and 'proceed onwards'.

optician, ophthalmologist, optometrist and **oculist** all refer to 'a person who is concerned with disorders of the eyes' but they are not interchangeable. **Dispensing optician** refers to 'a person who makes and sells spectacles or contact lenses'. **Ophthalmic optician** refers to 'a person who tests eyesight and prescribes lenses'. **Optometrist** is another term for this. **Ophthalmologist** refers to 'a doctor who specializes in disorders of the eyes' and **oculist** is another name for this.

optimum means 'the most favourable or advantageous condition, situation, amount, degree, etc', as in 'A temperature of 20° is optimum for these plants'. It is mostly used as an adjective meaning 'most favourable or advantageous', as in 'the optimum speed to run the car at', 'the optimum time at which to pick the fruit' and 'the optimum amount of water to give the plants'. It should not be used simply as a synonym for 'best'.

optometrist *see* **optician**.

orientate and **orient** are both acceptable forms of the same word. **Orientate** is the more common in British

English but the shorter form, **orient**, is preferred by some people and is the standard form in American English. They are verbs meaning 'to get one's bearings', as in 'difficult to orientate/orient themselves in the mist on the mountain'; 'to adjust to new surroundings', as in 'It takes some time to orientate/orient oneself in a new job'; 'to direct at', as in 'The course is orientated/oriented at older students'; 'to direct the interest of to', as in 'try to orientate/orient students towards the sciences'.

orthopaedic and **paediatric** are liable to be confused. They both apply to medical specialties but they are different. **Orthopaedic** means 'referring to the treatment of disorders of the bones', as in 'attend the orthopaedic clinic with an injured back'. **Paediatric** means 'referring to the treatment of disorders associated with children', as in 'Her little boy is receiving treatment from a paediatric consultant'. In American English these are respectively spelt **orthopedic** and **pediatric**.

other than can be used when **other** is an adjective or pronoun, as in 'There was no means of entry other than through a trap door' and 'He disapproves of the actions of anyone other than himself'. Traditionally, it should not be used as an adverbial phrase, as in 'It was impossible to get there other than by private car'. In such constructions **otherwise than** should be used, as in 'It is impossible to get there otherwise than by private car'. However, **other than** used adverbially is common in modern usage.

otherwise traditionally should not be used as an adjective or pronoun, as in 'Pack your clothes, clean or otherwise' and 'We are not discussing the advantages, or otherwise, of the scheme at this meeting'. It is an adverb, as in 'We are in favour of the project but he obviously thinks otherwise' and 'The hours are rather long but otherwise the job is fine'. *See* **other than**.

owing to *see* **due to**.

p *see* **pence**.

paediatric *see* **orthopaedic**.

panacea and **placebo** are liable to be confused. **Panacea** means 'a universal remedy for all ills and troubles', as in 'The new government does not have a panacea for the country's problems'. It is often used loosely to mean any remedy for any problem, as in 'She thinks that a holiday will be a panacea for his unhappiness'. **Panacea** is pronounced pan-a-*see*-a. **Placebo** refers to 'a supposed medication that is just a harmless substance given to a patient as part of a drugs trial etc', as in 'She was convinced the pills were curing her headaches but the doctor has prescribed her a placebo'. It is pronounced pla-*see*-bo.

parameter is a mathematical term that is very loosely used in modern usage to mean 'limit, boundary, framework' or 'limiting feature or characteristic', as in 'work within the parameters of our budget and resources'. The word is over-used and should be avoided where possible. The emphasis is on the second syllable as par-*am*-it-er.

paranoid is an adjective meaning 'referring to a mental disorder, called **paranoia**, characterized by delusions of persecution and grandeur', as in 'a paranoid personality'. In modern usage it is used loosely to mean 'distrustful, suspicious of others, anxious etc', as in 'It is difficult to get to know him—he's so paranoid' and 'paranoid about people trying to get his job', when there is no question of actual mental disorder. **Paranoia** is pronounced par-a-*noy*-a.

paraphernalia means 'all the bits and pieces of equipment required for something', as in 'all the paraphernalia needed to take a baby on holiday', 'put his angling paraphernalia in the car'. Strictly speaking it is a plural noun but it is now frequently used with a singular verb, as in 'The artist's paraphernalia was lying all over the studio'. **Paraphernalia** is liable to be misspelt. Note the *er* before the *n*.

parlour *see* **sitting room**.

particular means 'special, exceptional', as in 'a matter of particular importance', or 'individual', as in 'Have you a particular person in mind?', and 'concerned over details, fastidious', as in 'very particular about personal hygiene'. **Particular** is often used almost meaninglessly, as in 'this particular dress' and 'this particular car', when **particular** does not add much to the meaning.

partner can be used to indicate one half of an established couple, whether the couple are married or living together, as in 'Her partner was present at the birth of the child'.

passed and **past** are liable to be confused. **Passed** is the past participle and past tense of the verb 'to pass', as in 'She has already passed the exam' and 'They passed an old man on the way'. **Past** is used as a noun, as in 'He was a difficult teenager but that is all in the past now' and 'He has a murky past'. It is also used as an adjective, as in 'I haven't seen him in the past few weeks'

and 'Her past experiences affected her opinion of men'.
Past can also be a preposition, as in 'We drove past
their new house', 'It's past three o'clock' and 'He's past
caring'. It can also be an adverb, as in 'He watched the
athletes running past' and 'The boat drifted past'.

patent, in British English, is usually pronounced *pay*-
tent, as in 'patent leather dancing shoes'. **Patent** in the
sense of 'obvious', as in 'his patent dislike of the situation' and 'It was quite patent that she loved him' is also
pronounced in that way. **Patent** in the sense of 'a legal
document giving the holder the sole right to make or sell
something and preventing others from imitating it', as in
'take out a patent for his new invention', can be pronounced either *pay*-tent or *pat*-ent. **Patent** in this last
sense can also be a verb, as in 'He should patent his invention as soon as possible'.

peddler and **pedlar** are not interchangeable in British
English. **Peddler** refers particularly to 'a person who
peddles drugs', as in 'drug-peddlers convicted and sent
to prison'. **Pedlar** refers to 'a person who sells small
articles from house to house or from place to place', as
in 'pedlars selling ribbons at the fair'.

pence, p and **pennies** are liable to be confused. **Pence**
is the plural form of 'penny', as in 'There are a hundred
pence in the pound'. It is commonly found in prices, as
in 'apples costing 10 pence each'. **Pence** has become
much more common than 'pennies', which tends to be
associated with pre-decimalization money (the British
currency was decimalized in 1972), as in 'There were
twelve pennies in one shilling'. **Pence** is sometimes
used as though it were singular, as in 'have no one-pence

pieces'. In informal contexts **p** is often used, as in 'Have you got a 10p (pronounced ten pee) piece' and 'Those chocolate bars are fifteen p'. **Pence** in compounds is not pronounced in the same way as pence was pronounced in compounds before decimalization. Such words as 'ten pence' are now pronounced *ten pens*, with equal emphasis on each word. In pre-decimalization days it was pronounced *ten*-pens, with the emphasis on the first word.

pennies *see* **pence**.

people is usually a plural noun and so takes a plural verb, as in 'The local people were annoyed at the stranger's behaviour' and 'People were being asked to leave'. In the sense of 'nation', 'race' or 'tribe' it is sometimes treated as a singular noun, as in 'the nomadic peoples of the world'. **People** acts as the plural of 'person', as in 'There's room for only one more person in that car but there's room for three people in this one'. In formal or legal contexts **persons** is sometimes used as the plural of 'person', as in 'The lift had a notice saying "Room for six persons only"'.

per capita is a formal expression meaning 'for each person', as in 'The cost of the trip will be £300 per capita'. It is a Latin phrase which has been adopted into English and literally means 'by heads'. It is pronounced per *ka*-pi-ta.

per cent is usually written as two words. It is used adverbially in combination with a number in the sense of 'in or for each hundred', as in 'thirty per cent of the people are living below the poverty line'. The number is sometimes written in figures, as in '50 per cent of the staff are married'. The symbol % is often used instead of the words 'per cent', especially in technical contexts, as in 'make savings of up to 30%'. **Per cent** in modern usage is sometimes used as a noun, as in 'They have agreed to lower the price by half a per cent'.

per means 'for each' and is used to express rates, prices, etc, as in 'driving at 60 miles per hour', 'cloth costing £5 per square metre', 'The cost of the trip is £20 per person' and 'The fees are £1000 a term per child'. It can also mean 'in each', as in 'The factory is inspected three times per year'.

per se is a Latin phrase that has been adapted into English and means 'in itself', as in 'The substance is not per se harmful but it might be so if it interacts with other substances' and 'Television is not per se bad for children'. It should be used only in formal contexts.

percentage refers to 'the rate, number or amount in each hundred', as in 'the number of unemployed people expressed as a percentage of the adult population' and 'What percentage of his salary is free?'. It is also used to mean proportion, as in 'Only a small percentage of last year's students have found jobs' and 'A large percentage of the workers are in favour of a strike'. In modern usage it is sometimes used to mean 'a small amount' or 'a small part', as in 'Only a percentage of the students will find work'.

perquisite *see* **prerequisite.**

person is now used in situations where 'man' was formerly used to avoid sexism in language. It is used when the sex of the person being referred to is either unknown or not specified, as in 'They are advertising for another person for the warehouse'. It often sounds more natural to use 'someone', as in 'They are looking for someone to help out in the warehouse'. **Person** is often used in compounds, as in **chairperson, spokesperson** and **salesperson**, although some people dislike this convention and some compounds, such as **craftsperson**, have not really caught on. **Person** has two possible plurals. *See* **people**. **Person with** and **people with** are phrases advocated in 'politically correct' language to avoid negative terms such as 'victim', 'sufferer', as in 'person with Aids'.

phenomenal means 'referring to a phenomenon'. It is often used to mean 'remarkable, extraordinary', as in 'a phenomenal atmospheric occurrence', and in modern usage it is also used loosely to mean 'very great', as in 'a phenomenal increase in the crime rate' and 'a phenomenal achievement'. This use is usually restricted to informal contexts.

phenomenon is a singular noun meaning 'a fact, object, occurrence, experience, etc, that can be perceived by the senses rather than by thought or intuition', as in 'She saw something coming out of the lake but it remained an unexplained phenomenon', and 'a strange, unusual or remarkable fact, event or person of some particular significance', as in 'Single parenthood is one of the phenomena of the 1990s'. The plural is **phenomena**, as in 'natural phenomena'. It is a common error to treat **phenomena** as a singular noun. Note the spelling of **phenomenon** as it is liable to be misspelt.

phone, which is a short form of 'telephone', is not regarded as being as informal as it once was. It is quite acceptable in sentences such as 'He is going to buy a mobile phone'. Note that **phone** is now spelt without an apostrophe.

phoney and **phony** are both acceptable spellings but **phoney** is the more common in British English. The word means 'pretending or claiming to be what one is not, fake', as in 'He has a phoney American accent' and 'There's something phoney about him'.

placebo *see* **panacea**.

plane and **aeroplane** mean the same thing, both referring to a 'a machine that can fly and is used to carry people and goods'. In modern usage **plane** is the usual term, as in 'The plane took off on time' and 'nearly miss the plane'. **Aeroplane** is slightly old-fashioned or unduly formal, as in 'Her elderly parents say that they refuse to travel by aeroplane'. The American English spelling is **airplane**. Note that **plane** is not spelt with an apostrophe although it is a shortened form.

pleaded and **pled** mean the same thing, both being the past tense and past participle of the verb 'to plead'. **Pleaded** is the usual form in British English, as in 'They pleaded with the tyrant to spare the child's life' and 'The accused pleaded guilty'. **Pled** is the usual American spelling.

plenty is used only informally in some contexts. It is acceptable in formal and informal contexts when it is followed by the preposition 'of ', as in 'We have plenty of food', or when it is used as a pronoun without the 'of' construction, as in 'You can borrow some food from us—we have plenty'. Some people think its use as an adjective, as in 'Don't hurry—we have plenty time' and 'There's plenty food for all in the fridge', should be restricted to informal contexts. As an adverb it is a acceptable in both formal and informal contexts in such sentences as 'Help yourself—we have plenty more'. However, such sentences as 'The house is plenty big enough for them' is suitable only for very informal or slang contexts.

political correctness is a modern movement aiming to remove all forms of prejudice in language, such as sexism, racism and discrimination against disabled people. Its aims are admirable but in practice many of the words and phrases suggested by advocates of political correctness are rather contrived or, indeed, ludicrous. The adjective is **politically correct**.

practicable and **practical** should not be used interchangeably. **Practicable** means 'able to be done or carried out, able to be put into practice', as in 'His schemes seem fine in theory but they are never practicable'. **Practical** has several meanings, such as 'concerned with action and practice rather than with theory', as in 'He has studied the theory but has no practical experience of the job'; 'suitable for the purpose for which it was made', as in 'practical shoes for walking'; 'useful', as in 'a practical device with a wide range of uses'; 'clever at doing and making things', as in 'She's very practical when it comes to dealing with an emergency'; 'virtual', as in 'He's not the owner but he's in practical control of the firm'.

practically can mean 'in a practical way', as in 'Practically, the scheme is not really possible', but in modern usage it is usually used to mean 'virtually', as in 'He practically runs the firm although he is not the manager', and 'almost', as in 'The driver of that car practically ran me over'.

prefer is followed by the preposition 'to' not 'than', as in
'She prefers dogs to cats', 'They prefer Paris to London'
and 'They prefer driving to walking'.

prerequisite and **perquisite** are liable to be confused
although they are completely different in meaning. **Perquisite** means 'money or goods given as a right in addition to one's pay', as in 'various perquisites such as a
company car'. It is frequently abbreviated to 'perks', as
in 'The pay's not very much but the perks are good'.
Prerequisite refers to 'something required as a condition for something to happen or exist', as in 'Passing the
exam is a prerequisite for his getting the job' and 'A
certain amount of studying is a prerequisite of passing
the exam'.

prevaricate and **procrastinate** are liable to be confused although they have completely different meanings. **Prevaricate** means 'to try to avoid telling the
truth by speaking in an evasive or misleading way', as in
'She prevaricated when the police asked her where she
had been the previous evening'. **Procrastinate** means
'to delay or postpone action', as in 'The student has
been procrastinating all term but now he has to get to
grips with his essay'.

preventative and **preventive** both mean 'preventing or
intended to prevent, precautionary', as in 'If you think
the staff are stealing from the factory you should take
preventative/preventive measures' and 'Preventative/
preventive medicine seeks to prevent disease and disorders rather than cure them'. **Preventive** is the more
frequently used of the two terms.

prima facie is a Latin phrase that has been adopted into

prognosis

English. It means 'at first sight, based on what seems to be so' and is mainly used in legal or very formal contexts, as in 'The police say they have prima facie evidence for arresting him but more investigation is required'. The phrase is pronounced *pri*-ma *fay*-shee.

prognosis *see* **diagnosis**.

programme and **program** are liable to cause confusion. In British English **programme** is the acceptable spelling in such senses as in 'a television programme', 'put on a varied programme of entertainment' 'buy a theatre programme' and 'launch an ambitious programme of expansion'. However, in the computing sense **program** is used. **Programme** can also be a verb meaning 'to plan, to schedule', as in 'programme the trip for tomorrow'; 'to cause something to conform to a particular set of instructions', as in 'programme the central heating system'; or 'to cause someone to behave in a particular way, especially to conform to particular instructions', as in 'Her parents have programmed her to obey them implicitly'. In the computing sense of 'to provide with a series of coded instructions', the verb is spelt **program** and the *m* is doubled to form the past participle, past tense and present participle, as **programmed** and **programming**. In American English **program** is the accepted spelling for all senses of both noun and verb.

protagonist was originally a term for 'the chief character in a drama', as in 'Hamlet is the protagonist in the play that bears his name'. It then came to mean also 'the leading person or participant in an event, dispute, etc', as in 'The protagonists on each side of the dispute had a meeting'. In modern usage it can now also mean 'a leading or notable supporter of a cause, movement, etc,' as in 'She was one of the protagonists of the feminist movement'.

provided and **providing** are used interchangeably, as in 'You may go, provided/providing that you have finished your work' and 'He can borrow the car provided/providing he pays for the petrol'. 'That' is optional. The phrases mean 'on the condition that'.

pudding *see* **dessert**.

pupil and **student** are not interchangeable. **Pupil** refers to 'a child or young person who is at school', as in 'primary school pupils and secondary school pupils'. **Student** refers to 'a person who is studying at a place of further education, at a university or college', as in 'students trying to find work during the vacations'. In modern usage senior **pupils** at secondary school are sometimes known as **students**. In American English student refers to people at school as well as to people in further education. **Pupil** can also refer to 'a person who is receiving instruction in something from an expert' as in 'The piano teacher has several adult pupils'. **Student** can also refer to 'a person who is studying a particular thing', as in 'In his leisure time he is a student of local history'.

quasi- is Latin in origin and means 'as if, as it were'. In English it is combined with adjectives in the sense of 'seemingly, apparently, but not really', as in 'He gave a quasi-scientific explanation of the occurrence which convinced many people but did not fool his colleagues', or 'partly, to a certain extent but not completely', as in 'It is a quasi-official body which does not have full powers'. **Quasi**- can also be combined with nouns to mean 'seeming, but not really', as in 'a quasi-socialist who is really a capitalist' and 'a quasi-Christian who will not give donations to charity'. **Quasi-** has several possible pronunciations. It can be pronounced *kway*-zi, *kway*-si or *kwah*-si

queer in the sense of 'homosexual' was formerly used only in a slang and derogatory or offensive way. However, it is now used in a non-offensive way by homosexual people to describe themselves, as an alternative to 'gay'.

question *see* **beg the question**; **leading question**.

quick is an adjective meaning 'fast, rapid', as in 'a quick method', 'a quick route' and 'a quick walker'. It should not be used as an adverb, as in 'Come quick', in formal contexts since this is grammatically wrong.

quite has two possible meanings when used with adjectives. It can mean 'fairly, rather, somewhat', as in 'She's quite good at tennis but not good enough to play in the team' and 'The house is quite nice but it's not what we're looking for'. Where the indefinite article is used, **quite** precedes it, as in 'quite a good player' and 'quite a nice house'. '**Quite** can also mean 'completely, totally', as in 'We were quite overwhelmed by their generosity' and 'It is quite impossible for him to attend the meeting'.

raison d'être is French in origin and is used in English to mean 'a reason, a justification for the existence of', as in 'Her children are her raison d'être' and 'His only raison d'être is his work'. The phrase is liable to be misspelt. Note the accent (^) on the first *e*. It is pronounced *ray*-zon detr.

rara avis is French in origin and means literally 'rare

bird'. In English it is used to refer to 'a rare or unusual person or thing', as in 'a person with such dedication to a company is a rara avis'. It is pronounced *ray*-ra *ayv*-is or *ra*-ra *ay*-vis.

ravage and **ravish** are liable to be confused. They sound rather similar although they have different meanings. **Ravage** means 'to cause great damage to, to devastate', as in 'low-lying areas ravaged by floods' and 'a population ravaged by disease', or 'to plunder, to rob', as in 'neighbouring tribes ravaging their territory'. **Ravish** means either 'to delight greatly, to enchant', as in 'The audience were ravished by the singer's performance'. It also means 'to rape', as in 'The girl was ravished by her kidnappers', but this meaning is rather old-fashioned and is found only in formal or literary contexts.

re- is a common prefix, meaning 'again', in verbs. In most cases it is not followed by a hyphen, as in 'retrace one's footsteps', 'a retrial ordered by the judge' and 'reconsider his decision'. However, it should be followed by a hyphen if its absence is likely to lead to confusion with another word, as in 're-cover a chair'/'recover from an illness', 're-count the votes'/'recount a tale of woe', 'the re-creation of a 17th-century village for a film set'/'play tennis for recreation' and 're-form the group'/'reform the prison system'. In cases where the second element of a word begins with *e*, **re-** is traditionally followed by a hyphen, as in 're-educate', re-entry' and 're-echo', but in modern usage the hyphen is frequently omitted.

re, meaning 'concerning, with reference to', as in 'Re your correspondence of 26 November', should be restricted to business or formal contexts.

readable *see* **legible**.

re-cover, **recover** *see* **re-**.

re-creation, **recreation** *see* **re-**.

referendum causes problems with regard to its plural form. It has two possible plural forms, **referendums** or **referenda**. In modern usage **referendums** is the more usual plural. **Referendum** means 'the referring of an issue of public importance to a general vote by all the people of a country', as in 'hold a referendum on whether to join the EC'.

re-form, **reform** *see* **re-**.

registry office and **register office** are interchangeable, although **registry office** is the more common term in general usage. The words refer to 'an office where civil marriage ceremonies are performed and where births, marriages and deaths are recorded', as in 'She wanted to be married in church but he preferred a registry office ceremony' and 'register the child's birth at the local registry office'.

rigour and **rigor** are liable to be confused. They look similar but they have completely different meanings. **Rigour** means 'severity, strictness', as in 'the rigour of the punishment', and 'harshness, unpleasantness', as in 'the rigour of the climate' (in this sense it is often in the plural, **rigours**), and 'strictness, detailedness', as in 'the rigour of the editing'. **Rigor** is a medical term meaning 'rigidity', as in 'muscles affected by rigor', or 'a feeling of chilliness often accompanied by feverishness', as in 'infectious diseases of which rigor is one of the symptoms'. **Rigor** is also short for **rigor mortis**, meaning 'the stiffening of the body that occurs after death'. The first syllable of **rigour** is pronounced to rhyme with 'big', but **rigor** can be pronounced either in this way or with the *i* pronounced as in 'ride'.

roof causes problems with regard to its plural form. The usual plural is **roofs**, which can be pronounced either as it is spelt, to rhyme with 'hoofs', or to rhyme with 'hooves'.

rout and **route** are liable to be confused. They look similar but are pronounced differently and have completely different meanings'. **Rout** as a noun means 'overwhelming defeat', as in 'the rout of the opposing army', and as a verb 'to defeat utterly', as in 'Their team routed ours last time'. **Route** refers to 'a way of getting somewhere', as in 'the quickest route' and 'the scenic route'. **Route** can also be a verb meaning 'to arrange a route for, to send by a certain route', as in 'route the visitors along the banks of the river'. **Rout** is pronounced to rhyme with 'shout'. **Route** is pronounced to rhyme with 'brute'.

scarfs and **scarves** are both acceptable spellings of the plural of 'scarf', meaning a piece of cloth worn around the neck or the head', as in 'a silk scarf at her neck' and 'wearing a head scarf'.

Scotch, Scots and **Scottish** are liable to be confused. **Scotch** is restricted to a few set phrases, such as 'Scotch whisky', 'Scotch broth' and 'Scotch mist'. As a noun **Scotch** refers to 'Scotch whisky', as in 'have a large Scotch with ice'. **Scots** as an adjective is used in such contexts as 'Scots accents', 'Scots people' and 'Scots attitudes'. As a noun **Scots** refers to the Scots language, as in 'He speaks standard English but he uses a few words of Scots.' The noun **Scot** is used to refer to 'a Scottish person', as in 'Scots living in London'. **Scot-**

tish is found in such contexts as 'Scottish literature', 'Scottish history' and 'Scottish culture'.

sculpt and **sculpture** are interchangeable as verbs meaning 'to make sculptures, to practise sculpting', as in 'commissioned to sculpt/sculpture a bust of the chairman of the firm' and 'She both paints and sculpts/sculptures.

seize Note the *ei* combination, which is an exception to the '*i* before *e* except after *c*' rule.

sentiment and **sentimentality** are liable to be confused. They are related but have different shades of meaning. **Sentiment** means 'feeling, emotion', as in 'His actions were the result of sentiment not rationality'. It also means 'attitude, opinion', as in 'a speech full of anti-Christian sentiments'. **Sentimentality** is the noun from the adjective **sentimental** and means 'over-indulgence in tender feelings', as in 'dislike the sentimentality of the love songs' and 'She disliked her home town but now speaks about it with great sentimentality'.

sexism in language has been an issue for some time, and various attempts have been made to avoid it. For example, 'person' is often used where 'man' was traditionally used and 'he/she' substituted for 'he' in situations where the sex of the relevant person is unknown or unspecified.

ship *see* **boat**.

sine qua non is a Latin phrase that has been adopted into English and means 'essential condition, something that is absolutely necessary', as in 'It is a sine qua non of the agreement that the rent is paid on time'. It is used only in formal or legal contexts.

sitting room, **living room**, **lounge** and **drawing**

room all refer to 'a room in a house used for relaxation and the receiving of guests'. Which word is used is largely a matter of choice. Some people object to the use of **lounge** as being pretentious but it is becoming increasingly common. **Drawing room** is a more formal word and applies to a room in rather a grand residence.

skilful, as in 'admire his skilful handling of the situation' is frequently misspelt. Note the single *l* before the *f*. In American English the word is spelt **skillful**.

slander *see* **libel**.

sometime and **some time** are liable to be confused. **Sometime** means 'at an unknown or unspecified time', as in 'We must get together sometime' and 'I saw her sometime last year'. There is a growing tendency in modern usage to spell this as **some time**. Originally **some time** was restricted to meaning 'a period of time', as in 'We need some time to think'.

spelled and **spelt** are both acceptable forms of the past tense and past participle of the verb 'to spell', as in 'They spelled/spelt the word wrongly' and 'He realized that he had spelled/spelt the word wrongly'.

stadium causes problems with regard to its plural form. **Stadiums** and **stadia** are both acceptable. **Stadium** is derived from Latin and the original plural form followed the Latin and was **stadia.** However, anglicized plural forms are becoming more and more common in foreign words adopted into English, and **stadiums** is now becoming the more usual form.

stanch and **staunch** are both acceptable spellings of the word meaning 'to stop the flow of', as in 'stanch/staunch the blood from the wound in his head' and 'try to stanch/staunch the tide of violence'. **Staunch** also means 'loyal, firm', as in 'the team's staunch supporters'.

start *see* **commence**.

stationary and **stationery** are liable to be confused. They sound alike but have completely different meanings. **Stationary** means 'not moving, standing still', as in 'stationary vehicles'. **Stationery** refers to 'writing materials', as in 'office stationery'. An easy way to differentiate between them is to remember that **stationery** is bought from a 'stationer', which, like 'baker' and 'butcher', ends in -*er*.

staunch *see* **stanch**.

stimulant and **stimulus** are liable to be confused. Formerly the distinction between them was quite clear but now the distinction is becoming blurred. Traditionally **stimulant** refers to 'a substance, such as a drug, that makes a person more alert or more active', as in 'Caffeine is a stimulant'. **Stimulus** traditionally refers to 'something that rouses or encourages a person to action or greater effort', as in 'The promise of more money acted as a stimulus to the work force and they finished the job in record time'. In modern usage the words are beginning to be used interchangeably. In particular, **stimulus** is used in the sense of **stimulant** as well as being used in its own original sense.

straight away and **straightaway** are both acceptable ways of spelling the expression for 'without delay, at once', as in 'attend to the matter straight away/straightaway'.

strata *see* **stratum**.

stratagem and **strategy** are liable to be confused. They look and sound similar but they have different meanings. **Stratagem** means 'a scheme or trick', as in 'think of a stratagem to mislead the enemy' and 'devise a stratagem to gain entry to the building'. **Strategy** refers to 'the art of planning a campaign', as in 'generals meeting to put together a battle strategy', and 'a plan or policy, particularly a clever one, designed for a particular purpose', as in 'admire the strategy which he used to win the game'.

stratum and **strata** are liable to be confused. **Stratum** is the singular form and **strata** is the plural form of a word meaning 'a layer or level', as in 'a stratum of rock' and 'different strata of society'. It is a common error to use **strata** as a singular noun.

student *see* **pupil**.

subconscious and unconscious are used in different contexts. **Subconscious** means 'concerning those areas or activities of the mind of which one is not fully aware', as in 'a subconscious hatred of her parents' and 'a subconscious desire to hurt her sister'. **Unconscious** means 'unaware', as in 'She was unconscious of his presence' and 'unconscious of the damage which he had caused', and 'unintentional', as in 'unconscious humour' and 'an unconscious slight'. **Unconscious** also means 'having lost consciousness, insensible', as in 'knocked unconscious by the blow to his head'.

subjective *see* **objective.**

such and **like** are liable to be confused. **Such** is used to introduce examples, as in 'herbs, such as chervil and parsley' and 'citrus fruits, such as oranges and lemons'. **Like** introduces comparisons. 'She hates horror films supper

like *Silence of the Lambs*', and 'Very young children, like very old people, have to be kept warm.'

supper *see* **dinner**.

syndrome in its original meaning refers to 'a set of symptoms and signs that together indicate the presence of a physical or mental disorder', as in 'Down's syndrome'. In modern usage it is used loosely to indicate 'any set of events, actions, characteristics, attitudes that together make up, or are typical of, a situation', as in 'He suffers from the "I'm all right Jack" syndrome and doesn't care what happens to anyone else' and 'They seem to be caring people but they are opposing the building of an Aids hospice in their street—a definite case of "the not in my back yard" syndrome'.

tea *see* **dinner**.

teach *see* **learn**.

telephone *see* **phone**.

terminal and **terminus** in some contexts are interchangeable. They both refer to 'the end of a bus route, the last stop on a bus route, the building at the end of a bus route', as in 'The bus doesn't go any further—this is the terminus/terminal', but **terminus** is the more common term in this sense. They can also both mean 'the end of a railway line, the station at the end of a railway line', but **terminal** is the more common term in this sense. **Terminal** can refer to 'a building containing the arrival and departure areas for passengers at an airport' and 'a building in the centre of a town for the arrival and departure of air passengers'. **Terminal** also refers to 'a point of connection in an electric circuit', as in 'the positive and negative terminals', and 'apparatus, usually consisting of a keyboard and screen, for communicating with the central processor in a computing system', as in 'He has a dumb terminal so he can read information but not input it'. As an adjective **terminal** means 'of, or relating to, the last stage in a fatal illness', as in 'a terminal disease' and 'terminal patients'.

than is used to link two halves of comparisons or contrasts, as in 'Peter is considerably taller than John is', 'He is older than I am' and 'I am more informed about the situation than I was yesterday'. Problems arise when the relevant verb is omitted. In order to be grammatically correct, the word after 'than' should take the subject form if there is an implied verb, as in 'He is older than I (am)'. However this can sound stilted, as in 'She works harder than he (does)', and in informal contexts this usually becomes 'She works harder than him'. If there is no implied verb, the word after **than** is in the object form, as in 'rather you than me!'

the the definite article, which usually refers back to something already identified or to something specific, as in 'Where is the key?, 'What have you done with the book that I gave you?' and 'We have found the book that had we lost'. It is also used to denote someone or something as being the only one, as in 'the House of Lords', 'the King of Spain' and 'the President of Russia' and to indicate a class or group, as in 'the aristocracy', 'the cat family' and 'the teaching profession'. The is sometimes pronounced 'thee' when it is used to identify someone or something unique or important, as in 'Is that the John Frame over there?' and 'She is the fashion designer of the moment'.

their and **there** are liable to be confused because they sound similar. **There** means 'in, to or at that place', as in 'place it there' and 'send it there'. **Their** is the possessive of 'they', meaning 'of them, belonging to them', as in 'their books' and 'their mistakes'.

their and **they're** are liable to be confused because they sound similar. **Their** is the possessive of 'they', meaning 'of them, belonging to them', as in 'their cars' and 'their attitudes'. **They're** is a shortened form of 'they are', as in 'They're not very happy' and 'They're bound to lose'.

their used in conjunction with 'anyone', everyone', 'no one' and 'someone', is becoming increasingly common, even in textbooks, although this use is ungrammatical. The reason for this is to avoid the sexism of using 'his' when the sex of the person being referred to is either unknown or unspecified, and to avoid the clumsiness of 'his/her' or 'his or her'. Examples of **they** being so used include 'Everyone must do their best' and 'No one is to take their work home'.

this *see* **next**.

till and **until** are more or less interchangeable except that **until** is slightly more formal, as in 'They'll work till they drop' and 'Until we assess the damage we will not know how much the repairs will cost'.

toilet, **lavatory**, **loo** and **bathroom** all have the same meaning but the context in which they are used sometimes varies. **Toilet** is the most widely used of the words and is used on signs in public places. The informal **loo** is also very widely used. **Lavatory** is less common nowadays although it was formerly regarded by all but the working class and lower-middle class as the most acceptable term. **Bathroom** in British English usually refers to 'a room containing a bath', but in American English it is the usual word for **toilet**. **Ladies** and **gents** are terms for **toilet**, particularly in public places. **Powder room** also means this, as does the American English **rest room**.

town *see* **city**.

trade names should be written with a capital letter, as in 'Filofax' and 'Jacuzzi'. When trade names are used as verbs they are written with a lower case letter, as in 'hoover the carpet'.

try to and **try and** are interchangeable in modern usage. Formerly **try and** was considered suitable only in spoken and very informal contexts, but it is now considered acceptable in all but the most formal contexts, as in 'Try to/and do better' and 'They must try to/and put the past behind them'.

ultra is used as a prefix meaning 'going beyond', as in 'ultraviolet' and 'ultrasound', or 'extreme, very', as in 'ultra-sophisticated', 'ultra-modern', and 'ultra-conservative'. Compounds using it may be spelt with or without a hyphen. Words such as 'ultrasound' and 'ultraviolet' are usually spelt as one word, but words with the second sense of **ultra**, such as 'ultra-sophisticated', are often hyphenated.

unconscious *see* **subconscious**.

under way, meaning 'in progress', is traditionally spelt as two words, as in 'Preparations for the conference are under way'. In modern usage it is frequently spelt as one word, as in 'The expansion project is now underway'. It is a common error to write 'under weigh'.

underhand and **underhanded** are interchangeable in the sense of 'sly, deceitful', as in 'He used underhand/ underhanded methods to get the job' and 'It was underhand/underhanded of him to not to tell her that he was leaving'. **Underhand** is the more common of the two terms.

uninterested *see* **disinterested**.

unique traditionally means 'being the only one of its kind', as in 'a unique work of art' and 'everyone's fingerprints are unique' and so cannot be modified by such words as 'very', 'rather', 'more', etc, although it can be modified by 'almost' and 'nearly'. In modern usage **unique** is often used to mean 'unrivalled, unparalleled, outstanding', as in 'a unique opportunity' and 'a unique performance'.

unreadable *see* **illegible**.

until *see* **till**.

up and **upon** mean the same and are virtually interchangeable, except that **upon** is slightly more formal. Examples include 'sitting on a bench', 'the carpet on the floor', 'the stamp on the letter', caught with the stolen goods on him' and 'something on his mind'; and 'She threw herself upon her dying mother's bed', 'a carpet of snow upon the ground' and 'Upon his arrival he went straight upstairs'.

upward and **upwards** are not interchangeable. **Upward** is used as an adjective, as in 'on an upward slope' and 'an upward trend in prices'. **Upwards** is an adverb, as in 'look upwards to see the plane'.

vacation, meaning 'holiday', in British English is mostly restricted to a university or college situation, as in 'students seeking paid employment during their vacation'. In American English it is the usual word for 'holiday'.

verbal and **oral** are liable to be confused. **Oral** means 'expressed in speech', as in 'an oral, rather than a written examination'. **Verbal** means 'expressed in words', as in 'He asked for an instruction diagram but he was given verbal instructions' and 'They were going to stage a protest match but they settled for a verbal protest'. It is also used to mean 'referring to the spoken word, expressed in speech', as in 'a verbal agreement'. Because of these two possible meanings, the use of **verbal** can lead to ambiguity. In order to clarify the situation, **oral** should be used when 'expressed in speech' is meant. **Verbal** can also mean referring to verbs, as in 'verbal endings'.

vice versa means 'the other way round, with the order reversed', as in 'He will do his friend's shift and vice versa' and 'Mary dislikes John and vice versa'. It is pronounced vis-e ver-sa, vi-si ver-sa or vis ver-sa and is derived from Latin.

vis-à-vis means 'in relation to', as in 'their performance vis-à-vis their ability' and 'the company's policy vis-à-vis early retirement'. It is pronounced vee-za-vee and is derived from French. Note the accent on the *a*.

-ways *see* **-wise**.

what ever and **whatever** are not interchangeable. **What ever** is used when 'ever' is used for emphasis, as in 'What ever does he think he's doing?' and 'What ever is she wearing'. **Whatever** means 'anything, regardless of what, no matter what', as in 'Help yourself to whatever you want' and 'Whatever he says I don't believe him'.

which and **what** can cause problems. In questions **which**

whisky

is used when a limited range of alternatives is suggested, as in 'Which book did you buy in the end?' and **what** is used in general situations, as in 'What book did you buy?'

whisky and **whiskey** both refer to a strong alcoholic drink distilled from grain. **Whisky** is made in Scotland and **whiskey** in Ireland and America. **Whisky** is the usual British English spelling.

who and **whom** cause problems. **Who** is the subject of a verb, as in 'Who told you?', 'It was you who told her' and 'the girls who took part in the play'. **Whom** is the object of a verb or preposition, as in 'Whom did he tell?', 'To whom did you speak?' and 'the people from whom he stole'. In modern usage **whom** is falling into disuse, especially in questions, except in formal contexts. **Who** is used instead even although it is ungrammatical, as in 'Who did you speak to?' **Whom** should be retained when it is a relative pronoun, as in 'the man whom you saw', 'the person to whom he spoke' and 'the girl to whom she gave the book'.

whose and **who's** are liable to be confused. They sound alike but have different meanings. **Whose** means 'of whom' or 'of which', as in 'the woman whose child won', 'the boy whose leg was broken', 'Whose bicycle is that?' and 'the firm whose staff went on strike'. **Who's** is a shortened form of 'who is', as in 'Who's that?', 'Who's first in the queue?' and 'Who's coming to the cinema?'

-wise and **-ways** cause problems. Added to nouns, **-wise** can form adverbs of manner indicating either 'in such a position or direction', as in 'lengthwise' and 'clockwise', and 'in the manner of', as in 'crabwise'. In modern usage **-wise** is frequently used to mean 'with reference to', as in 'Weatherwise it was fine', 'Workwise all is well' and 'Moneywise they're not doing too well'. The suffix **-ways** has a more limited use. It means 'in such a way, direction or manner of', as in 'lengthways' and 'sideways'.

woman *see* **lady**.

Xmas is sometimes used as an alternative and shorter form of 'Christmas'. It is common only in a written informal context and is used mainly in commercial situations, as in 'Xmas cards on sale here' and 'Get your Xmas tree here'. When pronounced it is the same as 'Christmas'. The X derives from the Greek *chi*, the first letter of *Christos*, the Greek word for Christ.

X-ray is usually written with an initial capital letter when it is a noun meaning 'a photograph made by means of X-rays showing the bones or organs of the body', as in 'take an X-ray of the patient's chest'. Another term for the noun **X-ray** is 'radiograph'. As a verb it is also usually spelt with an initial capital, as 'After the accident he had his leg X-rayed', but it is sometimes spelt with an initial lower-case letter, as in 'have his chest x-rayed'.

you is used in informal or less formal situations to indicate an indefinite person referred to as 'one' in formal situations. Examples include 'You learn a foreign language more quickly if you spend some time in the country where it is spoken', 'You would think that they would make sure that their staff are polite', 'You can get used to anything in time' and 'You have to experience the situation to believe it'. **You** in this sense must be distinguished from **you** meaning the second person singular', as in 'You have missed your bus', 'You must know where

your

you left your bag' and 'You have to leave now'. *See*
one.

your and **you're** are liable to be confused. **Your** is a possessive adjective meaning 'belonging to you, of you', as
in 'That is your book and this is mine', 'Your attitude is
surprising' and 'It is your own fault'. **You're** is a shortened form of 'you are', as in 'You're foolish to believe
him', 'You're going to be sorry' and 'You're sure to do
well'. Note the spelling of the pronoun **yours**, as in
'This book is yours' and 'Which car is yours?' It should
not be spelt with an apostrophe as it is not a shortened
form of anything.

Spelling

-able and -ible are both used to form adjectives. It is easy to confuse the spelling of words ending in these. *See* **Adjectives liable to be misspelt**.

accent refers to certain symbols used on some foreign words adopted into English. In modern usage, which has a tendency to punctuate less than was formerly the case, accents are frequently omitted. For example, an actor's part in a play is now usually spelt 'role' but originally it was spelt 'rôle', the accent on *o* being called a circumflex.

The accent is most likely to be retained if it affects the pronunciation. Thus 'cliché' and 'divorcé' usually retain the acute accent, as it is called, on the *e*. On the other hand, the accent known as the cedilla is frequently omitted from beneath the *c* in words such as 'façade/facade', although it is there to indicate that the *c* is soft, pronounced like an *s*, rather than a hard sound pronounced like a *k*.

apostrophe *see* **Punctuation** section.

book titles these can cause problems as to spelling and style. How they are treated in publications, business reports, etc, depends largely on the house style of the firm concerned. However, they are generally written in documents, letters, etc, as they appear on their title pages, that is with the first letter of the first word and of the following main words of the title in capital letters, and those of words of lesser importance, such as the articles, prepositions and coordinate conjunctions, in lowercase letters, as in The Guide to Yoga, Hope for the Best and In the Middle of Life.

Some people, and some house-style manuals, prefer to put the titles in italic, as in *A Room with a View* and *A Guide to Dental Health*. Others prefer to put book titles in quotation marks, as in 'Gardening for Beginners'. Such a convention can make use of either single or double quotation marks. Thus either 'Desserts for the Summer' or "Desserts for the Summer" is possible provided that the writer is consistent throughout any one piece of writing.

If the title of a book is mentioned in a piece of direct speech in quotation marks it goes within the opposite style of quotation marks from the piece in direct speech. Thus if the direct speech is within single quotation marks, the book title goes within double quotation marks, as in 'Have you read "Wuthering Heights" or are you not a Bronte fan?' If the direct speech is within double quotation marks, the book title goes between single quotation marks, as in "Would you say that 'Animal Farm' was your favourite Orwell novel?"

It is even quite common for book titles to appear in documents both in italic type and with quotation marks. To some extent the punctuation of book titles is a matter of choice as long as they are consistent, but there is a growing tendency to have as little punctuation as possible and to have as uncluttered a page as possible.

buildings can cause problems with regard to capital letters. The proper noun attached to the name of the building should have an initial capital letter, as should have the common noun that may be part of the name, as in The White House and The National Portrait Gallery.

businesses and **organizations** often cause problems with regard to their names or titles. In general the initial letters of the main words of the title should be in capital letters and the words of lesser importance, such as the articles, coordinating conjunctions and prepositions, should be in lower case, except when they are the first word of the title, as in 'The Indian Carpet Company', 'Kitchens for All' and 'Capital Industrial Cleaners'. Obviously, when the names of people are involved these should have initial capital letters, as in 'Jones and Brown'.

capital letters are used in a number of different situations.

The first word of a sentence or a direct quotation begins with a **capital letter**, as in 'They left early', 'Why have they gone?' and 'He said weakly, "I don't feel very well"'.

The first letter of a name or proper noun is always a **capital letter**, as in 'Mary Brown', 'John Smith', 'South America', 'Rome', 'speak Italian', 'Buddhism', 'Marxism'.

Capital letters are also used in the titles of people, places or works of art, as in 'Uncle Fred', 'Professor Jones', 'Ely Cathedral', Edinburgh University', 'reading *Wuthering Heights*', 'watching *Guys and Dolls*', 'listen to Beethoven's Third Symphony' and 'a copy of *The Potato Eaters* by van Gogh'. They are also used in the titles of wars and historical, cultural and geological periods, doubling of consonants

as in 'the Wars of the Roses', 'the Renaissance', 'the Ice Age'.

Note that only the major words of titles, etc, are in capital letters, words, such as 'the', 'on', 'of', etc, being in lower-case letters.

A capital letter is used as the first letter of days of the week, months of the year, and religious festivals, as in 'Monday', 'October', 'Easter', 'Yom Kippur'. It is a matter of choice whether the seasons of the year are given capital letters or not, as in 'spring/Spring', 'autumn/Autumn'.

Apart from 'I', pronouns are lower-case except when they refer to God or Christ, when some people capitalize them, as in 'God asks us to trust in Him'.

Trade names should be spelt with an initial capital letter, as in 'Filofax', 'Jacuzzi', 'Xerox', 'Biro', 'Hoover'. When verbs are formed from these, they are spelt with an initial lower-case letter, as 'xerox the letter', 'hoover the carpet'.

doubling of consonants There are a few rules that can help you decide whether or not to double a consonant.

In words of one syllable ending in a single consonant preceded by a single vowel, the consonant is doubled when an ending starting with a vowel is added, as in 'drop' and 'dropped', 'pat' and 'patting' and 'rub' and 'rubbing'.

In words of more than one syllable that end in a single consonant preceded by a single vowel, the consonant is doubled if the stress is on the last syllable, as in 'begin' and 'beginning', 'occur' and 'occurring', 'prefer' and 'preferred', 'refer' and 'referring' and 'commit' and 'committed'. In similar words where the stress is not on the last syllable, the consonant does not double, as in 'bigot' and 'bigoted' and 'develop' and 'developed'

Exceptions to this rule include words ending in 'l'. The 'l' doubles even in cases where the last syllable containing it is unstressed, as in 'travel' and 'travelled' and 'appal' and 'appalling'. 'Worship', in which the stress is on the first syllable, is also an exception, as in 'worshipped'.

geographical features these should be written with initial capital letters. They include the common nouns that are part of the name of the feature, as in Niagara Falls, Atlantic Ocean, River Thames, Mount Everest and Devil's Island.

hyphen *see* **Punctuation** section.

indefinite article a and an are the forms of the indefinite article.

The form a is used before words that begin with a consonant sound, as in *a* box, *a* garden, *a* road, *a* wall.

The form an is used before words that begin with a vowel sound, as in *an* apple, *an* easel, *an* ostrich, *an* uncle.

Note that it is the *sound* of the initial letter that matters and not the *spelling*. Thus a is used before words beginning with a *u* when they are pronounced with a *y* sound as though it were a consonant, as *a* unit, *a* usual occurrence. Similarly an is used, for example, before words beginning with the letter *h* where this is not pronounced, as in *an* heir, *an* hour, *an* honest man.

Formerly it was quite common to use an before words that begin with an *h* sound and also begin with an unstressed syllable, as *an* hotel, *an* historic occasion, but nowadays it is more usual to use *a* in such cases.

months of the year these are spelt with initial capital letters, as in January, February, March, April, May, June, July, August, September, October, November and December.

plural nouns singular nouns in English form plural forms in different ways.

Most in add *s* to form the plural, as in 'cats', 'machines' and 'boots'.

Words ending in -*s*, -*x*, -*z*, -*ch* and -*sh* add *es*, as in 'buses', 'masses', 'foxes', 'fezzes or fezes', 'churches' and 'sashes'.

Nouns ending in a consonant followed by *y* have -*ies* in the plural, as 'fairies' and 'ladies', but note 'monkey', where the *y* is preceded by a vowel and becomes 'monkeys'. Proper nouns ending in *y* add *s*, as in 'the two Germanys'.

Some words ending in *f* have *ves* in the plural, as 'wives' and 'halves', but some simply add *s* to the singular form, as 'beliefs'. Some words ending in *f* can either add *s* or change to *ves*, as 'hoofs or hooves'.

Words ending in *o* cause problems as some end in *oes* in the plural, as 'potatoes' and 'tomatoes', and some end in *s*, as in 'pianos', while some can be spelt either way and have to be learned or looked up in a dictionary etc. Shortened forms, such as 'photo' and 'video', add simply *s*, as 'photos', 'videos'.

Some words have the same form in the plural as they do in the singular, such as 'sheep' and 'deer'. Some are plural in form already and so do not change. These include 'trousers' and 'scissors'.

Several words in English have irregular plural forms

which just have to be learned or looked up in a dictionary, etc. These include 'men', 'mice' and 'feet'.

Some foreign words adopted into English used to retain the foreign plural form in English but this is becoming less common and, at the very least there is now often an English-formed alternative, as 'gateaux/gateaus', 'index/indices', 'formulae/formulas', 'appendixes/appendices'. However, several nouns of foreign extraction retain the foreign-style plural in English, such as 'criteria' and 'crises'.

Commonly misspelt words

All of us have problem words that cause spelling difficulties but there are some words that are generally misspelt. These include:

A

abbreviation
abscess
absence
abysmal
accelerator
accessible
accessories
accommodate
accompaniment
accumulate
accurate
accustomed
achieve

aching
acknowledge
acknowledge-
    ment/
acknowledgment
acquaint
acquaintance
acquiesce
acquiescence
acquire
acquit
acquittal
acreage
across

actual
additional
address
adequate
adieu
adjacent
admissible
admittance
adolescence
adolescent
advantageous
advertisement
advice
advise

aerate

aerate	already	apparently
aerial	although	appearance
aesthetic	aluminium	appendicitis
affect	ambiguous	appreciate
affiliation	amethyst	approval
afforestation	ammunition	aquarium
aggravate	anachronism	aquiline
aggravation	anaesthetic	arbiter
aggregate	analyse	arbitrary
aggression	analysis	arbitration
aggressive	anarchist	archaeology
aghast	ancestor	architectural
agnosticism	ancestry	Arctic
agoraphobia	anemone	arguably
agreeable	angrily	arrangement
agreed	anguish	arrival
aisle	annihilate	artichoke
alcohol	annihilation	ascend
alfresco	anniversary	ascent
alibis	announcement	asphalt
align	annulled	asphyxiate
alignment	annulment	asphyxiation
allege	anonymous	assassin
allergic	anorak	assassinate
alleys	answered	assessment
alligator	Antarctic	assistance
allocate	antibiotic	associate
allotment	antithesis	asthma
allotted	anxiety	asthmatic
almond	apartheid	astrakhan
alms	apologize	atheist
alphabetically	appalling	atrocious

attach
attendant
attitude
aubergine
auburn
auctioneer
audible
aural
automatic
autumn
awful
awkward

B

bachelor
bagatelle
baggage
bailiff
ballast
ballerina
banana
banister
bankruptcy
banquet
barbecue
barometer
barrister
basically
basis
bassoon
battalion
bazaar

beautiful
befriend
beguile
behaviour
beleaguer
belief
believe
belligerent
benefited
bequeath
berserk
besiege
bettered
bevelled
bewitch
bias
bicycle
biennial
bigamous
bigoted
bilingual
biscuit
bivouacked
blancmange
blasphemous
blasphemy
bleary
blitz
bodily
bonfire
bootee
borough

bouquet
bourgeois
boutique
bracketed
braille
brassiere
breadth
breathalyser
brief
broccoli
brochure
bronchitis
bruise
brusque
buccaneer
Buddhist
budding
budgerigar
budgeted
buffeted
bulletin
bumptious
bungalow
buoyancy
buoyant
bureau
bureaucracy
business
buttoned

C

cabbage

cafeteria	ceiling	clientele
caffeine	cellophane	clique
camouflage	cemetery	coalesce
campaign	centenary	cocoa
campaigned	centilitre	coconut
cancelled	centimetre	coffee
cancerous	certainty	cognac
candour	champagne	coincidence
cannabis	championed	colander
cannibal	chancellor	collaborate
canvassing	changeable	collapsible
capability	channelled	colleague
capillary	characteristic	colonel
capitalist	chasm	colossal
caravan	chauffeur	comically
carbohydrate	cheetah	commandeer
carburettor	cherish	commemorate
career	chief	commentator
caress	chilblain	commercial
caries	chintz	commiserate
carriage	chiropody	commission
cartoonist	chisel	commissionaire
cashier	choreographer	commitment
cassette	choreography	committal
castanets	chronically	committed
casualty	chrysanthemum	committee
catalogue	cigarette	communicate
catarrh	cinnamon	commuter
catechism	circuitous	companion
catering	cistern	comparative
cauliflower	civilian	comparison
cautious	claustrophobia	compatibility

compelled
competitive
computer
conceal
concealment
conceit
conceive
concession
concurrent
concussion
condemned
condescend
confectionery
conference
confetti
congeal
congratulations
conjunctivitis
conned
connoisseur
conscience
conscientious
conscious
consequently
consignment
consolation
conspicuous
constitute
consumer
contemptible
continent
continuous

contraception
contradictory
controlled
controller
controversial
convalesce
convenient
convertible
conveyed
convolvulus
coolly
cooperate
cooperative
coordinate
copying
coquette
corduroy
co-respondent
coronary
correspondence
correspondent
corridor
corroborate
corrugated
cosmopolitan
cosseted
councillor
counselling
counterfeit
courageous
courteous
crèche

credible
credited
crematorium
creosote
crescent
crisis
criterion
crocheted
crocodile
croupier
crucial
crucifixion
cruelly
cruise
cryptic
cubicle
cupful
curable
curiosity
curious
currency
curriculum vitae
customary
cynic
cynicism
cynosure

D
dachshund
daffodil
dahlia
dais

damage
dandruff
darkened
debatable
debauched
debility
deceased
deceit
deceive
deciduous
decipher
decoyed
decrease
decreed
defamatory
defeat
defendant
defied
definite
definitely
dehydrate
deign
deliberate
delicatessen
delicious
delinquent
delirious
demeanour
demonstrate
denouement
denunciation
dependence

depth
derailment
dermatitis
derogatory
descend
descendant
desiccate
desperate
detach
detachable
detergent
deterred
deterrent
deuce
develop
developed
development
diabetes
diagnosis
dialogue
diametrically
diaphragm
diarrhoea
difference
different
dilapidated
dilemma
dilettante
diminish
diminution
dinosaur
diphtheria

diphthong
disadvantageous
disagreeable
disagreed
disagreement
disappearance
disappeared
disappoint
disapproval
disastrous
disbelief
disbelieve
discipline
discotheque
discouraging
discourteous
discrepancy
discrimination
discussion
disease
disguise
dishevelled
dishonourable
disillusion
disinfectant
disinherited
dismissal
disobeyed
disparage
dispelled
disposal
dispossess

dissatisfaction
dissatisfy
dissect
disseminate
dissent
dissimilar
dissipated
dissipation
dissociate
dissolute
dissuade
distilled
distillery
distinguish
distraught
disuse
divisible
documentary
doggerel
domineering
donate
doubt
dragooned
drastically
draughty
drooled
drooped
drunkenness
dubious
dumbfounded
dungarees
duress

dutiful
dynamite
dysentery
dyspepsia

E
eccentric
ecclesiastic
ecologically
economically
ecstasy
eczema
effective
effervescence
efficacious
efficient
effrontery
eightieth
elaborate
electrician
elevenses
eligible
emancipate
embarrass
embarrassment
emergence
emergent
emolument
emotional
emphasize
employee
emptied

enable
encourage
encyclopedia
endeavour
endurance
energetically
enervate
engineer
enough
ensuing
entailed
enthusiasm
enumerate
epilepsy
equalize
equalled
equipped
erroneous
erudite
escalator
escapism
espionage
essence
essential
estranged
etiquette
euthanasia
eventually
evidently
exaggerate
exaggeration
exalt

exasperate

exasperate
exceed
exceedingly
excellent
excessive
exchequer
excommunicate
exercise
exhaust
exhibit
exhilarate
exorcise
explanation
exquisite
extinguish
extraneous
extravagant

F

fabulous
facetious
faeces
Fahrenheit
fallacious
fanatic
farcical
fascinate
fatigue
fatuous
February
feeler
feign

ferocious
festooned
feud
feudal
fevered
fiasco
fibre
fictitious
fiend
fierce
fiery
filial
finesse
flabbergasted
flaccid
flammable
flannelette
fluent
fluoridate
fluoride
fluoridize
foliage
forcible
foreigner
forfeit
forthwith
fortieth
fortuitous
fortunately
frailty
frankincense
fraudulent

freedom
freight
frequency
friend
frolicked
fuchsia
fugitive
fulfil
fulfilled
fulfilment
fullness
fulsome
furious
furniture
furthered

G

gaiety
galloped
garrison
garrotted
gases
gateau
gauge
gazetteer
geisha
generator
genuine
gerbil
gesticulate
ghastly
ghetto

gigantic
gingham
giraffe
glamorous
glamour
glimpse
global
gluttonous
glycerine
gnarled
gnash
goitre
gossiped
government
graffiti
grammar
grandeur
gratefully
gratitude
gratuitous
greetings
gregarious
grief
grieve
grovelled
gruesome
guarantee
guarantor
guard
guardian
guest
guillotine

guinea
guise
guitar
gymkhana
gypsy/gipsy

H
haemoglobin
haemorrhage
halcyon
hallucination
hammered
handfuls
handicapped
handkerchief
happened
harangue
harass
harlequin
haughty
hazard
hearse
height
heightened
heinous
heir
herbaceous
hereditary
heroism
hesitate
hiccup, hiccough
hideous

hierarchy
hieroglyphics
hijack
hilarious
hindrance
hippopotamus
holiday
holocaust
homonym
honorary
honour
hooligan
horoscope
horrible
horticulture
hullabaloo
humorous
humour
hurricane
hurried
hygiene
hyphen
hypnosis
hypochondria
hypocrisy
hypotenuse
hypothesis
hypothetical
hysterical

I
icicle

ideological	incommunicado	ingratiate
idiosyncrasy	inconceivable	ingredient
ignorance	incongruous	inhabitant
illegible	incontrovertible	inheritance
illegitimate	incorrigible	inhibition
illiberal	incredulous	iniquitous
illiterate	incriminate	initiate
imaginative	incubator	initiative
imitation	incurred	innate
immaculate	indefatigable	innocuous
immediate	indefinable	innumerable
immemorial	indefinite	innumerate
immoral	independence	inoculate
immovable	independent	insecticide
impasse	indescribable	inseparable
impeccable	indict	insincere
imperative	indictment	insistence
imperceptible	indigenous	instalment
imperious	indigestible	instantaneous
impetuous	indomitable	intercept
implacable	indubitable	interference
impresario	ineligible	interior
imprisoned	inescapable	intermediate
imprisonment	inexcusable	intermittent
inaccessible	inexhaustible	interpret
inadmissible	infallible	interpretation
inappropriate	infatuated	interrogate
inaugural	inferred	interrupt
incandescent	infinitive	interview
incessant	inflamed	intrigue
incipient	inflammable	intrinsically
incognito	inflationary	intuition

intuitive
invariably
inveigle
inveterate
involuntary
involvement
irascible
irrelevant
irreparable
irreplaceable
irresistible
irresponsible
irrevocable
irritable
italicize
itinerant
itinerary

J
jackal
Jacuzzi
jeopardize
jettisoned
jewellery
jodhpurs
juggernaut
jugular

K
kaleidoscopic
karate
keenness

khaki
kidnapped
kilometre
kiosk
kitchenette
kleptomania
knick-knack
knowledgeable
kowtow

L
labelled
laboratory
labyrinth
lackadaisical
laddered
lager
language
languor
languorous
laryngitis
larynx
lassitude
latitude
laundered
launderette
layette
league
leanness
ledger
legendary
legible

legitimate
length
lengthened
leukaemia
levelled
liaise
liaison
lieu
lieutenant
lilac
limousine
lineage
linen
lingerie
linguist
liqueur
literature
litre
livelihood
loneliness
loosened
loquacious
lorgnette
lucrative
lucre
luggage
lugubrious
luminous
luscious
lustre
luxurious
lyric

macabre

M
macabre
maelstrom
magician
magnanimous
mahogany
maintenance
malaise
malaria
malignant
manageable
management
mannequin
manoeuvre
mantelpiece
manually
margarine
marijuana
marquee
martyr
marvellous
marzipan
masochist
massacre
matinee
mayonnaise
meagre
measurement
medallion
medieval
mediocre
melancholy

meningitis
meringue
messenger
meteorological
metropolitan
microphone
midday
migraine
mileage
milieu
millionaire
mimicked
mimicry
miniature
miraculous
mirrored
miscellaneous
mischief
mischievous
misogynist
misshapen
misspell
misspent
modelled
modelling
morgue
mortgage
mosquito
mountaineer
moustache
multitudinous
muscle

museum
mysterious
mythical

N
naive
narrative
naughty
nausea
nautical
necessary
necessity
negligence
negligible
negotiate
neighbourhood
neither
neurotic
neutral
niche
niece
ninetieth
ninth
nocturnal
nonentity
notably
noticeably
notoriety
nuance
numbered
numerate
numerous

nutrient
nutritious

O
obedient
obese
obituary
oblige
oblique
oblivious
obnoxious
obscene
obscenity
obsessive
obstetrician
occasion
occupancy
occupier
occupying
occurred
occurrence
octogenarian
odorous
odour
offence
offered
official
officious
ominous
omission
omitted
oneself

opaque
ophthalmic
opinion
opponent
opportunity
opposite
orchestra
ordinary
original
orthodox
orthopaedic
oscillate
ostracize
outlying
outrageous
overdraft
overrate
overreach
overwrought
oxygen

P
pacifist
pageant
pamphlet
panacea
panegyric
panicked
papered
parachute
paraffin
paragraph

paralyse
paralysis
paraphernalia
parcelled
parliament
paroxysm
parquet
partially
participant
particle
partner
passenger
passers-by
pastime
patterned
pavilion
peaceable
peculiar
pejorative
pencilled
penicillin
peppered
perceive
perennial
perilous
permissible
permitted
pernicious
perpetrate
persistence
personnel
persuasion

perusal

perusal	positive	promiscuous
pessimism	possession	pronunciation
pessimistically	possibility	propeller
pesticide	posthumous	proposal
phantom	potatoes	proprietor
pharmacy	precede	prosecute
pharyngitis	precedent	protagonist
pharynx	precinct	protein
phenomenon	precipice	provocation
phial	precocious	prowess
phlegm	preference	psalm
physician	preferred	psyche
physiotherapist	prejudice	psychiatric
picketed	preliminary	psychic
picnic	prepossessing	publicly
picnicked	prerequisite	pursuit
picturesque	prerogative	putative
pioneered	prescription	pyjamas
pious	presence	
piteous	preservative	**Q**
pitiful	prestige	quarrelsome
plaintiff	prestigious	questionnaire
plausible	pretentious	queue
pleurisy	prevalent	quintet
pneumonia	priest	
poignant	primitive	**R**
politician	procedure	rabies
pollution	proceed	radioed
polythene	procession	radios
porridge	professional	railing
portrait	profiteering	rancour
portray	prohibit	ransack

rapturous
reassurance
rebelled
rebellious
recalcitrant
receipt
receive
recommend
reconnaissance
reconnoitre
recruitment
recurrence
redundant
referee
reference
referred
regatta
regrettable
regretted
rehabilitation
reign
relevant
relief
relieve
reminisce
reminiscence
remuneration
rendezvous
repertoire
repetitive
reprieve
reprisal

requisite
rescind
resemblance
reservoir
resistance
resourceful
responsibility
restaurant
restaurateur
resurrection
resuscitate
retrieve
reunion
reveille
revelry
revenue
reversible
rhapsody
rheumatism
rhododendron
rhomboid
rhubarb
rhyme
rhythm
ricochet
righteous
rigorous
rigour
risotto
riveted
rogue
roughage

roulette
royalty
rucksack
ruinous
rummage
rumour

S
sabotage
sacrilege
saddened
salmon
salvage
sanctuary
sandwich
sanitary
sapphire
satellite
scaffolding
scandalous
scenic
sceptre
schedule
scheme
schizophrenic
schooner
sciatica
science
scissors
scruple
scrupulous
scurrilous

scythe	sluice	strait-laced
secretarial	smattering	straitjacket
secretary	smithereens	strategic
sedative	snivelled	strength
sedentary	soccer	strenuous
sensitive	solemn	stupor
separate	solicitor	suave
sergeant	soliloquy	subpoena
serrated	soloist	subtle
serviceable	sombre	succeed
serviette	somersault	successful
settee	sophisticated	successor
shampooed	sovereign	succinct
shattered	spaghetti	succulent
sheikh	spectre	succumb
sheriff	spherical	suddenness
shield	sphinx	suede
shovelled	sponsor	sufficient
shuddered	spontaneity	suffocate
siege	spontaneous	suicide
significant	squabble	sullenness
silhouette	squandered	summoned
simply	squawk	supercilious
simultaneous	staccato	superfluous
sincerely	staggered	supersede
sixtieth	stammered	supervise
skeleton	statistics	supervisor
skilful	statutory	supplementary
slanderous	stealth	surgeon
slaughter	stereophonic	surveillance
sleigh	stirrup	surveyor
sleight of hand	storage	susceptible

suspicious
sweetener
sycamore
symmetry
sympathize
symphony
synagogue
syndicate
synonym
syringe

T

tableau
taciturn
taffeta
tangerine
tangible
tattoo
technique
teenager
televise
temperature
tenuous
terrifically
terrifying
territory
terrorist
therapeutic
therefore
thief
thinness
thirtieth

thorough
thoroughfare
threshold
thrombosis
throughout
thwart
thyme
tightened
titivate
tobacconist
toboggan
toffee
tomatoes
tomorrow
tonsillitis
topsy turvy
tornadoes
torpedoes
torpor
tortoiseshell
tortuous
totalled
tourniquet
towelling
trafficked
tragedy
traitorous
tranquillity
tranquillizer
transcend
transferable
transferred

transparent
travelled
traveller
tremor
troublesome
trousseau
truism
trustee
tsetse
tuberculosis
tumour
tunnelled
tureen
turquoise
twelfth
typhoon
tyranny

U

unanimous
unconscious
undoubted
unduly
unequalled
unique
unnecessary
unremitting
unrequited
unrivalled
upheaval
uproarious

vaccinate

V

vaccinate
vacuum
vague
vanilla
variegate
vehement
vendetta
veneer
ventilator
verandah
vermilion
veterinary
vetoes
vice versa
vicissitude
vigorous
vigour
viscount
visibility
vivacious
vociferous

voluminous
volunteered
vulnerable

W

walkie-talkie
walloped
warrior
wastage
watered
weakened
wearisome
Wednesday
weight
weird
whereabouts
wherewithal
widened
width
wield
wintry
witticism

wizened
woebegone
wooden
woollen
worsened
worship
worshipped
wrapper
wrath
wreak
writhe

X

xylophone

Y

yield
yoghurt

Z

zealous
zigzagged

Adjectives liable to be misspelt

-able and -ible are both used to form adjectives. It is easy to confuse the spelling of words ending in these. The following adjectives are likely to be misspelt.

-able:

abominable	adaptable	advisable
acceptable	adorable	agreeable

amiable
approachable
available
bearable
beatable
believable
calculable
capable
changeable
comfortable
commendable
conceivable
definable
delectable
demonstrable
dependable
desirable
discreditable
disreputable
durable
enviable
excitable
excusable
expendable
foreseeable
forgettable
forgivable
healable
hearable
immovable
impassable
impeccable

implacable
impracticable
impressionable
indescribable
indispensable
inimitable
insufferable
lamentable
manageable
measurable
memorable
nameable
non-flammable
objectionable
operable
palpable
pleasurable
preferable
readable
recognizable
regrettable
renewable
reputable
sizeable
stoppable
tenable
tolerable
transferable
understandable
undoable
unmistakable
usable

variable
viable
washable
wearable
winnable
workable

ible:
accessible
admissible
audible
collapsible
combustible
compatible
comprehensible
contemptible
credible
defensible
destructible
digestible
discernible
divisible
edible
exhaustible
expressible
fallible
feasible
flexible
forcible
gullible
indelible
intelligible

irascible

irascible	repressible	risible
negligible	reproducible	sensible
perceptible	resistible	susceptible
permissible	responsible	tangible
possible	reversible	visible

Punctuation

Punctuation is the use of punctuation marks within a written text to enhance its meaning or fluency or to indicate aspects of pronunciation.

accent *see* **Spelling** section.

apostrophe a form of punctuation that is mainly used to indicate possession. Many spelling errors centre on the position of the apostrophe in relation to *s*.

Possessive nouns are usually formed by adding *'s* to the singular noun, as in 'the girl's mother', and 'Peter's car'; by adding an apostrophe to plural nouns that end in *s*, as in 'all the teachers' cars'; by adding *'s* to irregular plural nouns that do not end in *s*, as in 'women's shoes'.

In the possessive form of a name or singular noun that ends in *s*, *x* or *z*, the apostrophe may or may not be followed by *s*. In words of one syllable the final *s* is usually added, as in 'James's house', 'the fox's lair', 'Roz's dress'. The final *s* most frequently omitted in names, particularly in names of three or more syllables, as in 'Euripides' plays'. In many cases the presence or absence of final *s* is a matter of convention.

The apostrophe is also used to indicate omitted letters in contracted forms of words, as in 'can't' and 'you've'. They are sometimes used to indicate missing century numbers in dates, as in 'the '60s and '70s', but are not used at the end of decades, etc, as in '1960s', not '1960's'

Generally apostrophes are no longer used to indicate omitted letters in shortened forms that are in common use, as in 'phone' and 'flu'.

brackets

Apostrophes are often omitted wrongly in modern usage, particularly in the media and by advertisers, as in 'womens hairdressers', 'childrens helpings'. In addition, apostrophes are frequently added erroneously (as in 'potato's for sale' and 'Beware of the dog's'). This is partly because people are unsure about when and when not to use them and partly because of a modern tendency to punctuate as little as possible.

brackets are used to enclose information that is in some way additional to a main statement. The information so enclosed is called **parenthesis** and the pair of brackets enclosing it can be known as **parentheses**. The information that is enclosed in the brackets is purely supplementary or explanatory in nature and could be removed without changing the overall basic meaning or grammatical completeness of the statement. Brackets, like commas and dashes, interrupt the flow of the main statement but brackets indicate a more definite or clearcut interruption. The fact that they are more visually obvious emphasizes this.

Material within brackets can be one word, as in 'In a local wine bar we had some delicious crepes (pancakes)' and 'They didn't have the chutzpah (nerve) to challenge her'. It can also take the form of dates, as in 'Robert Louis Stevenson (1850–94) wrote *Treasure Island*' and '*Animal Farm* was written by George Orwell (1903–50)'.

The material within brackets can also take the form of a phrase, as in 'They served lasagne (a kind of pasta) and some delicious veal' and 'They were drinking Calvados (a kind of brandy made from apples)' or in the form of a clause, as in 'We were to have supper (or so they called it) later in the evening' and 'They went for a walk round the loch (as a lake is called in Scotland) before taking their departure'.

It can also take the form of a complete sentence, as in 'He was determined (we don't know why) to tackle the problem alone' and 'She made it clear (nothing could be more clear) that she was not interested in the offer'. Sentences that appear in brackets in the middle of a sentence are not usually given an initial capital letter or a full stop, as in 'They very much desired (she had no idea why) to purchase her house'. If the material within brackets comes at the end of a sentence the full stop comes outside the second bracket, as in 'For some reason we agreed to visit her at home (we had no idea where she lived).'

If the material in the brackets is a sentence which comes between two other sentences it is treated like a normal sentence with an initial capital letter and a closing full stop, as in 'He never seems to do any studying. (He is always either asleep or watching television.) Yet he does brilliantly in his exams.' Punctuation of the main statement is unaffected by the presence of the brackets and their enclosed material except that any punctuation that would have followed the word before the first bracket follows the second bracket, as in 'He lives in a place (I am not sure exactly where), that is miles from anywhere.'

There are various shapes of brackets. Round brackets are the most common type. Square brackets are sometimes used to enclose information that is contained inside other information already in brackets, as in '(Christopher Marlowe [1564–93] was a contemporary of Shakespeare)' or in a piece of writing where round brackets have already been used for some other purpose. Thus in a dictionary if round brackets are used to separate off the pronunciation, square brackets are sometimes used to separate off the etymologies.

Square brackets are also used for editorial comments in a scholarly work where the material within brackets is more of an intrusion to the flow of the main statement than is normally the case with bracketed material. Angle brackets and brace brackets tend to be used in more scholarly or technical contexts.

capital letters *see* **Spelling** section.

colon a punctuation mark (:) that is used within a sentence to explain, interpret, clarify or amplify what has gone before it. 'The standard of school work here is extremely high: it is almost university standard', 'The fuel bills are giving cause for concern: they are almost double last year's'. 'We have some new information: the allies have landed'. A capital letter is not usually used after the colon in this context.

The colon is also used to introduce lists or long quotations, as in 'The recipe says we need: tomatoes, peppers, courgettes, garlic, oregano and basil', 'The boy has a huge list of things he needs for school: blazer, trousers, shirts, sweater, ties, shoes, tennis shoes, rugby boots, sports clothes and leisure wear' and 'One of his favourite quotations was: "If music be the food of love play on"'.

The colon is sometimes used in numerals, as in '7:30 a.m.', '22:11:72' and 'a ratio of 7:3'. It is used in the titles of some books, for example where there is a subtitle or explanatory title, as in 'The Dark Years: the Economy in the 1930s'.

In informal writing, the dash is sometimes used instead of the colon, indeed the dash tends to be overused for this purpose.

comma a very common punctuation mark (,). In modern usage there is a tendency to adopt a system of minimal punctuation and the comma is one of the casualties of this new attitude. Most people use the comma considerably less frequently than was formerly the case.

However there are certain situations in which the comma is still commonly used. One of these concerns lists. The individual items in a series of three or more items are separated by commas. Whether a comma is put before the 'and' which follows the second-last item is now a matter of choice. Some people dislike the use of a comma before 'and' in this situation, and it was formerly considered wrong. Examples of lists include—'at the sports club we can play tennis, squash, badminton and table tennis', 'We need to buy bread, milk, fruit and sugar', and 'They are studying French, German, Spanish and Russian'. The individual items in a list can be quite long, as in 'We opened the door, let ourselves in, fed the cat and started to cook a meal' and 'They consulted the map, planned the trip, got some foreign currency and were gone before we realized it'. Confusion may arise if the last item in the list contains 'and' in its own right, as in 'In the pub they served ham salad, shepherd's pie, pie and chips and omelette'. In such cases it as well to put a comma before the final 'and'.

In cases where there is a list of adjectives before a noun, the use of commas is now optional although it was formerly standard practice. Thus both 'She wore a long, red, sequinned dress' and 'She wore a long red sequinned dress' are used. When the adjective immediately before the noun has a closer relationship with it than the other adjectives no comma should be used, as in 'a beautiful old Spanish village'.

The comma is used to separate clauses or phrases that are parenthetical or naturally cut off from the rest of a sentence, as in 'My mother, who was of Irish extraction, was very superstitious'. In such a sentence the clause within the commas can be removed without altering the basic meaning. Care should be taken to include both commas. Commas are not normally used to separate main clauses and relative clauses, as in 'The woman whom I met was my friend's sister'. Nor are they usually used to separate main clauses and subordinate clauses, as in 'He left when we arrived' and 'They came to the party although we didn't expect them to'. If the subordinate clause precedes the main clause, it is sometimes followed by a comma, especially if it is a reasonably long clause, as in 'Although we stopped and thought about it, we still made the wrong decision'. If the clause is quite short, or if it is a short phrase, a comma is not usually inserted, as in 'Although it rained we had a good holiday' and 'Although poor they were happy'. The use of commas to separate such words and expression from the rest of the sentence to which they are related is optional. Thus one can write 'However, he could be right' or 'However he could be right'. The longer the expression is, the more likely it is to have a comma after it, as in 'On the other hand, we may decide not to go'.

Commas are always used to separate terms of address, interjections or question tags from the rest of the sentence, as in 'Please come this way, Ms Brown, and make yourself at home', 'Now, ladies, what can I get you?' and 'It's cold today, isn't it?'

Commas may be used to separate main clauses joined by a coordinating conjunction, but this is not usual if the clauses have the same subject or object, as in 'She swept the floor and dusted the table'. In cases where the subjects are different and the clauses are fairly long, it is best to insert a comma, as in 'They took all the furniture with them, and she was left with nothing'.

A comma can be inserted to avoid repeating a verb in the second of two clause, as in 'he plays golf and tennis, his brother rugby'.

dash a punctuation mark in the form of a short line that indicates a short break in the continuity of a sentence, as in 'He has never been any trouble at school—quite the reverse', 'I was amazed when he turned up—I thought he was still abroad'. In such situations it serves the same purpose as brackets, except that it is frequently considered more informal. The dash should be used sparingly. Depending on it too much can lead to careless writing with ideas set down at random rather than turned into a piece of coherent prose. The dash can be used to emphasize a word or phrase, as in 'They said goodbye then—forever'. It can also be used to add a remark to the end of a sentence, as in 'They had absolutely no money—a regular state of affairs towards the end of the month.'

The dash can also be used to introduce a statement that amplifies or explains what has been said, as in 'The burglars took everything of value—her jewellery, the silver, the TV set, her hi-fi and several hundred pounds.' It can be used to summarize what has gone before, as in direct speech

'Disease, poverty, ignorance—these are the problems facing us.

The dash is also used to introduce an afterthought, as in 'You can come with me—but you might not want to'. It can also introduce a sharp change of subject, as in 'I'm just making tea—what was that noise?' It can also be used to introduce some kind of balance in a sentence, as in 'It's going to take two of us to get this table out of here—one to move it and one to hold the door open.'

The dash is sometimes found in pairs. A pair of dashes acts in much the same way as a set of round brackets. A pair of dashes can be used to indicate a break in a sentence, as in 'We prayed—prayed as we had never prayed before—that the children would be safe', 'It was—on reflection—his best performance yet', and 'He introduced me to his wife—an attractive pleasant woman—before he left'.

Dashes are used to indicate hesitant speech, as in 'I don't—well—maybe—you could be right'. They can be used to indicate the omission of part of a word or name, as in 'It's none of your b—business', 'He's having an affair with Mrs D—'.

They can also be used between points in time or space, as in 'Edinburgh–London' and '1750–1790.'

direct speech *see* **quotation marks**.

exclamation mark a punctuation mark **(!)** which occurs at the end of an exclamation, which is a word, phrase or sentence called out with strong feeling of some kind as in 'Get lost!', 'What a nerve!', 'Help!', 'Ouch!', 'Well I never!', 'What a disaster!', 'I'm tired of all this!' and 'Let me out of here!'

full stop a punctuation mark consisting of a small dot (.).

Its principal use is to end a sentence that is not a question or an exclamation, as in 'They spent the money.', 'She is studying hard.', 'He has been declared redundant and is very upset.' and 'Because she is shy, she rarely goes to parties.'

The full stop is also used in decimal fractions, as in '4.5 metres', '6.3 miles' and '12.2 litres'. It can also be used in dates, as in '22.2.94', and in times, as in '3.15 tomorrow afternoon'.

In modern usage the tendency is to omit full stops from abbreviations. This is most true of abbreviations involving initial capital letters as in TUC, BBC, EEC and USA. In such cases full stops should definitely not be used if one or some of the initial letters do not belong to a full word. Thus, television is abbreviated to TV and educationally subnormal to ESN.

There are usually no full stops in abbreviations involving the first and last letters of a word (contractions) Dr, Mr, Rd, St, but this is a matter of taste.

Abbreviations involving the first few letters of a word, as in 'Prof' (Professor) are the most likely to have full stops, as in 'Feb.' (February), but again this is now a matter of taste.

For the use of the full stop in direct speech *see* **direct speech**. The full stop can also be called **point** or **period**.

hyphen a small stroke (-) that is used to join two words together or to indicate that a word has been broken at the end of a line because of lack of space. It is used in a variety of situations.

The hyphen is used as the prefixed element in a proper noun, as in 'pre-Christian', 'post-Renaissance',

hyphen

'anti-British', 'anti-Semitic', 'pro-French' and 'pro-Marxism'. It is also used before dates or numbers, as in 'pre-1914', 'pre-1066', 'post-1920', 'post-1745'. It is also used before abbreviations, as in 'pro-BBC', 'anti-EEC' and 'anti-TUC'.

The hyphen is used for clarification. Some words are ambiguous without the presence of a hyphen. For example, 're-cover', as in 're-cover a chair', is spelt with a hyphen to differentiate it from 'recover', as in 'The accident victim is likely to recover'. Similarly, it is used in 're-form', meaning 'to form again', as in 'They have decided to re-form the society which closed last year', to differentiate the word from 'reform', meaning 'to improve, to become better behaved', as in 'He was wild as a young man but he has reformed now'. Similarly 're-count' in the sense of 'count again', as in 're-count the number of votes cast', is spelt with a hyphen to differentiate it from 'recount' in the sense of 'tell', as in 'recount what happened on the night of the accident'.

The hyphen was formerly used to separate a prefix from the main element of a word if the main element begins with a vowel, as in 'pre-eminent', but there is a growing tendency in modern usage to omit the hyphen in such cases. At the moment both 'pre-eminent' and 'pre-eminent' are found. However, if the omission of the hyphen results in double *i*, the hyphen is usually retained, as in 'anti-inflationary' and 'semi-insulated'.

The hyphen was formerly used in words formed with the prefix *non-*, as in 'non-functional', 'non-political', 'non-flammable' and 'non-pollutant'. However there is a growing tendency to omit the hyphen in such cases, as in 'nonfunctional' and 'nonpollutant'. At the moment both forms of such words are common.

The hyphen is usually used with 'ex-' in the sense of 'former', as in 'ex-wife' and 'ex-president'.

The hyphen is usually used when 'self-' is prefixed to words, as in 'self-styled', 'a self-starter' and 'self-evident'.

Use or non-use of the hyphen is often a matter of choice, house style or frequency of usage, as in 'drawing-room' or 'drawing room', and 'dining-room' or 'dining room'. There is a modern tendency to punctuate less frequently than was formerly the case and so in modern usage use of the hyphen in such expressions is less frequent. The length of compounds often affects the inclusion or omission of the hyphen. Compounds of two short elements that are well-established words tend not to be hyphenated, as in 'bedroom' and 'toothbrush'. Compound words with longer elements are more likely to be hyphenated, as in 'engine-driver' and 'carpet-layer'.

Some fixed compounds of two or three or more words are always hyphenated, as in 'son-in-law', 'good-for-nothing' and 'devil-may-care'.

Some compounds formed from phrasal verbs are sometimes hyphenated and sometimes not. Thus both 'take-over' and 'takeover' are common, and 'run-down' and 'rundown' are both common. Again the use of the hyphen is a matter of choice. However some words formed from phrasal verbs are usually spelt without a hyphen, as in 'breakthrough'.

Compound adjectives consisting of two elements, the second of which ends in -ed, are usually hyphenated, as

hyphen

in 'heavy-hearted', 'fair-haired', 'fair-minded' and 'long-legged'.

Compound adjectives when they are used before nouns are usually hyphenated, as in 'gas-fired central heating', 'oil-based paints', 'solar-heated buildings' and 'chocolate-coated biscuits'.

Compounds containing some adverbs are usually hyphenated, sometimes to avoid ambiguity, as in 'his best-known opera', a 'well-known singer', 'an ill-considered venture' and 'a half-planned scheme'.

Generally adjectives and participles preceded by an adverb are not hyphenated if the adverb ends in -ly, as in 'a highly talented singer', 'neatly pressed clothes' and 'beautifully dressed young women'.

In the case of two or more compound hyphenated adjectives with the same second element qualifying the same noun, the common element need not be repeated but the hyphen should be, as in 'two- and three-bedroom houses' and 'long- and short-haired dogs'.

The hyphen is used in compound numerals from 21 to 99 when they are written in full, as in 'thirty-five gallons', 'forty-four years', 'sixty-seven miles' and 'two hundred and forty-five miles'. Compound numbers such as 'three hundred' and 'two thousand' are not hyphenated.

Hyphens are used in fractions, as in 'three-quarters', 'two-thirds', and 'seven-eighths'.

Hyphens are also used in such number phrases as 'a seventeenth-century play', 'a sixteenth-century church', 'a five-gallon pail', 'a five-year contract' and a 'third-year student'.

The other use of hyphens is to break words at the ends

of lines. Formerly people were more careful about where they broke words. Previously, words were broken up according to etymological principles, but there is a growing tendency to break words according to how they are pronounced. Some dictionaries or spelling dictionaries give help with the division and hyphenation of individual words. General points are that one-syllable words should not be divided and words should not be broken after the first letter of a word or before the last letter. Care should be taken not to break up words, for example by forming elements that are words in their own right, in such a way as to mislead the reader. Thus divisions such as 'therapist' and 'mans-laughter' should be avoided.

inverted comma *see* **quotation marks.**

italic type a sloping typeface that is used for a variety of purposes. It is used to differentiate a piece of text from the main text, which is usually in Roman type. For example, it is used sometimes for the titles of books, newspapers, magazines, plays, films, musical works and works of art, as in 'he is a regular reader of *The Times*', 'She reads *Private Eye*', 'Have you read *Animal Farm* by George Orwell', 'He has never seen a production of Shakespeare's *Othello*', 'We went to hear Handel's *Messiah*', '*Mona Lisa* is a famous painting'. Sometimes such titles are put in quotation marks rather than in italics.

Italic type is also sometimes used for the names of ships, trains, etc, as in 'the launch of *The Queen Elizabeth II*', 'She once sailed in *The Queen Mary*' and 'Their train was called *The Flying Scotsman*'.

Italic type is also used for the Latin names of plants and animals, as in 'of the genus *Lilium*', 'trees of the genus *Pyrus*', '*Panthera pardus*' and '*Canis lupus*'.

Italic type is sometimes used for foreign words that have been adopted into the English language but have never been fully integrated. Examples include *bête noire*, *raison d'être*, *inter alia* and *Weltschmerz*.

Italic type can also sometimes be used to draw attention to a particular word, phrase or passage, as in 'How do you pronounce *formidable*?', or to emphasize a word or phrase, as in 'Is he *still* in the same job?'

ligature a printed character combining two letters in one, as in æa and œ. It is sometimes called a digraph.

line-break the division of a word at the end of a line for space purposes. This is marked by a hyphen.

lower-case letter the opposite of capital letter. It is also known informally as 'small letter'. Lower-case letters are used for most words in the language. It is capital letters that are exceptional in their use.

oblique a diagonal mark (/) that has various uses. Its principal use is to show alternatives, as in 'he/she', 'Dear Sir/Madam', 'two/three-room flat' and 'the budget for 1993/4'. The oblique is used in some abbreviations, as in 'c/o Smith' (meaning 'care of Smith'). The word 'per' is usually shown by means of an oblique, as in 60km/h (60 kilometres per hour).

paragraph a subdivision of a piece of prose. Many people find it difficult to divide their work into paragraphs. Learning to do so can be difficult but it is an area of style that improves with practice.

A paragraph should deal with one particular theme or point of the writer's writing or argument. When that has been dealt with, a new paragraph should be started.

However, there are other considerations to be taken into account. If the paragraph is very long it can appear off-putting visually to the would-be reader and can be difficult to make one's way through. In such cases it is best to subdivide themes and shorten paragraphs. On the other hand, it is best not to make all one's paragraphs too short as this can create a disjointed effect. It is best to try to aim for a mixture of lengths to create some variety.

Traditionally it was frowned upon to have a one-sentence paragraph but there are no hard and fast rules about this. Usually it takes more than one sentence to develop the theme of the paragraph, unless one is a tabloid journalist or copywriter for an advertising firm, and it is best to avoid long, complex sentences.

The opening paragraph of a piece of writing should introduce the topic about which one is writing. The closing paragraph should sum up what one has been writing about. New paragraphs begin on new lines and they are usually indented from the margin. In the case of dialogue in a work of fiction, each speaker's utterance usually begins on a new line for the clarification of the reader.

parentheses *see* **brackets**.

period *see* **full stop**.

point *see* **full stop**.

punctuation mark one of the standardized symbols used in punctuation, as the **full stop**, **comma, question mark**, etc.

question mark the punctuation mark (?) that is placed at the end of a question or interrogative sentence, as in 'Who is he?', 'Where are they?', 'Why have they gone?', 'Whereabouts are they?', 'When are you going?' and 'What did he say?'. The question mark is sometimes known as the **query**.

quotation marks or **inverted commas** are used to enclose material that is part of **direct speech**, which is the reporting of speech by repeating exactly the actual words used by the speaker. In the sentence:

Peter said, 'I am tired of this.'

'I am tired of this' is a piece of direct speech because it represents exactly what Peter said. Similarly, in the sentence:

Jane asked, 'Where are you going?'

'Where are you going?' is a piece of direct speech since it represents what Jane said.

Quotation marks are used at the beginning and end of pieces of direct speech. Only the words actually spoken are placed within the quotation marks, as in:

'If I were you,' he said, 'I would refuse to go.'

The quotation marks involved can be either single or double, according to preference or house style.

If there is a statement such as 'he said' following the piece of direct speech, a comma is placed before the second inverted comma, as in:

'Come along,' he said.

If the piece of direct speech is a question or exclamation, a question mark or exclamation mark is put instead of the comma, as in:

'What are you doing?' asked John.

'Get away from me!' she screamed.

If a statement such as 'he said' is placed within a sentence in direct speech, a comma is placed after 'he said' and the second part of the piece of direct speech does not begin with a capital letter, as in:

'I know very well,' he said, 'that you do not like me.'

If the piece of direct speech includes a complete sentence, the sentence begins with a capital letter, as in:

'I am going away,' she said, 'and I am not coming back. I don't feel that I belong here anymore.'

Note that the full stop at the end of a piece of direct speech that is a sentence should go before the closing inverted comma.

If the piece of direct speech quoted takes up more than one paragraph, quotation marks are placed at the beginning of each new paragraph. However, quotation marks are not placed at the end of each paragraph, just at the end of the final one.

When writing a story, etc, that includes dialogue or conversation, each new piece of direct speech should begin on a new line or sometimes in a new paragraph.

Quotation marks are not used only to indicate direct speech. For example, they are sometimes used to indicate the title of a book or newspaper.

The quotation marks used in this way can be either single or double, according to preference or house style. If a piece of direct speech contains the title of a poem, song, etc, it should be put in the opposite type of quotation marks to those used to enclose the piece of direct speech. Thus, if single quotation marks have been used

Roman type

in the direct speech, then double quotation marks should be used for the title within the direct speech, as in:

'Have you read "Ode to a Nightingale" by Keats?' the teacher asked.

If double quotation marks have been used for the direct speech, single quotation marks should be used for the title, as in:

"Have you read 'Ode to a Nightingale' by Keats?" the teacher asked.

Roman type the normal upright type used in printing, not bold or italic type.

semicolon (;) a rather formal form of punctuation. It is mainly used between clauses that are not joined by any form of conjunction, as in 'We had a wonderful holiday; sadly they did not', 'She was my sister; she was also my best friend' and 'He was a marvellous friend; he is much missed'. A dash is sometimes used instead of a semicolon but this more informal.

The semicolon is also used to form subsets in a long list or series of names so that the said list seems less complex, as in 'The young man who wants to be a journalist has applied everywhere. He has applied to *The Times* in London; *The Globe and Mail* in Toronto; *The Age* in Melbourne; *The Tribune* in Chicago'.

The semicolon is also sometimes used before 'however', 'nevertheless' 'hence', etc, as in 'We have extra seats for the concert; however you must not feel obliged to come'.

Style

abbreviation a shortened form of words, usually used as a space-saving technique and becoming increasingly common in modern usage. Abbreviations cause problems with regard to punctuation. The common question asked is whether the letters of an abbreviation should be separated by full stops. In modern usage the tendency is to omit full stops from abbreviations. This is most true of abbreviations involving initial capital letters, as in TUC, BBC, EC and USA. In such cases full stops should definitely not be used if one or some of the initial letters do not belong to a full word. Thus 'television' is abbreviated to TV and 'educationally subnormal' to ESN.

There are usually no full stops in abbreviations involving the first and last letters of a word (contractions)—Dr, Mr, Rd, St—but this is a matter of taste.

An abbreviation involving the first few letters of a word, as in 'Prof' (Professor), is the most likely to a have full stop, as in 'Feb.' (February), but again this is now a matter of taste.

Plurals of abbreviations are mostly formed by adding lower-case *s*, as in Drs, JPs, TVs. Note the absence of apostrophes. *See also* **acronym**.

acronym a word that, like some abbreviations, is formed from the initial letters of several words. Unlike abbreviations, however, acronyms are pronounced as words rather than as just a series of letters. For example, OPEC (Organization of Petroleum Producing Countries) is pronounced *o-pek* and is thus an acronym, unlike USA

(United States of America) which is pronounced as a series of letters and not as a word (*yoo-ess-ay,* not *yoo-say* or *oo-sa*) and is thus an abbreviation.

Acronyms are written without full stops, as in UNESCO (United Nations Educational, Scientific and Cultural Organization). Mostly acronyms are written in capital letters, as in NASA (National Aeronautics and Space Administration). However, very common acronyms, such as Aids (Acquired Immune Deficiency Syndrome), can be written with just an initial capital, the rest of the letters being lower case.

Acronyms that refer to a piece of scientific or technical equipment are written like ordinary words in lower-case letters, as laser (light amplification by simulated emission of radiation.

affix refers to an element that is added to the root or stem of a word to form another word. Affixes can be in the form of **prefixes** or **suffixes**. A prefix is added to the beginning of a word, as audio in audiovisual, an affix to the end, as -aholic in workaholic.

back formation the process of forming a new word by removing an element from an existing word. This is the reversal of the usual process since many words are formed by adding an element to a base or root word. Examples of back formation include 'burgle' from 'burglary'; 'caretake' from 'caretaker'; 'donate' from 'donation; 'eavesdrop' from 'eavesdropper'; 'enthuse' from 'enthusiasm'; 'intuit' from 'intuition'; 'liaise' from 'liaison'; 'reminisce' from 'reminiscence'; 'televise' from 'television'.

base the basic element in word formation, also known as **root** or **stem**, e.g. in the word 'infectious' 'infect' is the base.

blend a word that is formed by the merging of two other words or elements, as in 'brunch' from 'breakfast' and 'lunch'; 'camcorder' from 'camera' and 'recorder'; 'chocoholic' from 'chocolate' and 'alcoholic'; 'motel' from 'motor' and 'hotel'; 'smog' from 'smoke' and 'fog'; 'televangelist' from 'television' and 'evangelist'.

book titles *see* **Spelling** section and **italic type** in **Punctuation** section.

borrowing the taking over into English of a word from a foreign language and also to the word so borrowed. Many words borrowed into English are totally assimilated as to spelling and pronunciation. Others remain obviously different and retain their own identity as to spelling or pronunciation, as *raison d'être*, borrowed from French. Many of them have been so long part of the English language, such as since the Norman Conquest, that they are no longer thought of as being foreign words. However the process goes on, and recent borrowings include *glasnost* and *perestroika* from Russian.

From French, Latin and Greek have been the main sources of our borrowings over the centuries. However, we have borrowed extensively from other languages as well. These include Italian, from which we have borrowed many terms relating to music, art and architecture. These include *piano*, *libretto*, *opera*, *soprano*, *tempo*, *corridor*, *fresco*, *niche*, *parapet* and *grotto*, as well as many food terms, such as *macaroni*, *pasta*, *semolina* and *spaghetti*.

From the Dutch we have acquired many words relating to the sea and ships since they were a great seafaring nation. These include *cruise*, *deck*, *skipper* and *yacht*. Through the Dutch/Afrikaans connection we have borrowed *apartheid*, *boss* and *trek*.

From German we have borrowed *dachshund*, *hamster*, *frankfurter*, *kindergarten* and *waltz*, as well as some words relating to World War II, for example, *blitz*, *flak* and *strafe*.

From Norse and the Scandinavian languages have come a wide variety of common words, such as *egg*, *dirt*, *glitter*, *kick*, *law*, *odd*, *skill*, *take*, *they*, *though*, as well as some more modern sporting terms such as *ski* and *slalom*.

From the Celtic languages have come *bannock*, *bog*, *brogue*, *cairn*, *clan*, *crag*, *slogan* and *whisky*, and from Arabic have come *algebra*, *alkali*, *almanac*, *apricot*, *assassin*, *cypher*, *ghoul*, *hazard*, *mohair*, *safari*, *scarlet* and *talisman*.

The Indian languages have provided us with many words, originally from the significant British presence there in the days of the British Empire. They include *bungalow*, *chutney*, *dinghy*, *dungarees*, *gymkhana*, *jungle*, *pundit* and *shampoo*. In modern times there has been an increasing interest in Indian food and cookery, and words such as *pakora*, *poppadom*, *samosa*, etc, have come into the language.

From the South American languages have come *avocado*, *chocolate*, *chilli*, *potato*, *tobacco* and *tomato*. From Hebrew have come *alphabet*, *camel*, *cinnamon* and *maudlin*, as well as more modern borrowings from Yiddish such as *bagel*, *chutzpah*, *schmaltz* and *schmuck*.

From the native North American languages have come *anorak*, *kayak*, *raccoon* and *toboggan*, and from the Aboriginal language of Australia have come *boo-merang* and *kangaroo*.

Judo, *bonsai* and *tycoon* have come from Japanese, *rattan* from Malay and *kung-fu*, *sampan* and *ginseng* from Chinese.

The borrowing process continues. With Britain becoming more of a cosmopolitan and multi-cultural nation the borrowing is increasing.

cliché a word or expression that has lost a lot of its impact through over use and overexposure. For example, 'accidents will happen' and 'across the board'.

coinage the invention of a new word or expression.

colloquialism a term used to describe an expression of the kind used in informal conversation.

derivative a word that has been formed from a simpler word or word element. For example, 'sweetly' is a derivative of 'sweet', 'peaceful' is a derivative from 'peace', 'clinging' is derived from 'cling' and 'shortest' is derived from 'short'.

dialect the language of a region or community with regard to vocabulary, structure, grammar and pronunciation.

doubles words that habitually go together, as in 'out and out', 'neck and neck', 'over and over', 'hale and hearty', 'rant and rave', 'fast and furious', 'hue and cry', 'stuff and nonsense', 'rough and ready', 'might and main', 'give and take', 'ups and downs', 'fair and square', 'high and dry' and 'wear and tear'. Doubles are also sometimes called **dyads**.

doublets pairs of words that have developed from the same original word but now differ somewhat in form and usually in meaning. Examples include 'human' and 'humane', 'shade' and 'shadow', 'hostel' and 'hotel', 'frail' and 'fragile', and 'fashion' and 'faction'.

dyads see **doubles**.

EFL English as a foreign language.

etymology the origin and history of a word; the study of the history of words.

euphemism *see* **Euphemism** section.

figurative a term that refers to words that are not used literally. For example, 'mine' in the sense of 'excavation in the earth from which coal, tin, etc, is taken' is a literal use of the word. 'Mine' in the sense of 'He is a mine of information' is a figurative use of the word.

first language *same as* **mother tongue**.

formal the term used to refer to speech and writing that is characterized by more complicated and more difficult language and by more complicated grammatical structures. Short forms and contractions are avoided in formal speech and writing.

gobbledygook a noun that is used informally to refer to pretentious and convoluted language of the type that is found in official documents and reports. It is extremely difficult to understand and should be avoided and 'plain English' used instead.

hybrid a word that is formed from words or elements derived from different languages, such as 'television'.

idiolect a person's own style of language with regard to vocabulary, structure, etc, is known as idiolect, as in 'He is the son of academic parents and has rather a formal idiolect'.

homograph *see* **Homograph** section.

homonym *see* **Homonym** section.

homophone *see* **Homophone** section.

jargon refers to the technical or specialized language used by a particular group, e.g. doctors, computer engineers, sociologists, etc, to communicate with each other within their specialty. It should be avoided in the general language as it will not be clear to the ordinary person exactly what is meant.

journalese a derogatory name for the style of writing and choice of vocabulary supposedly found in newspapers. It is usually the style of writing in tabloid newspapers, such as widespread use of clichés, sensational language and short sentences, that is meant by the term.

language the means by which human beings communicate using words. Language can refer either to spoken or written communication. It can also refer to the variety of communication used by a particular nation or state, as in 'the French language'.

    The term can also be used to refer to the style and vocabulary of a piece of writing, as in 'The language of his novels is very poetic'. It can also be used to denote the particular style and variety of language that is used in a particular profession or among a particular group of people with some common interest, as in 'legal language', 'technical language', etc. Such specialist language is sometimes referred to rather pejoratively as legalese, 'computerese', etc. *See* **jargon**.

lexicography the art and practice of defining words, selecting them and arranging them In dictionaries or glossaries.

lingua franca a language adopted as a common language by speakers whose mother tongues are different from each other. This enables people to have a common medium of communication for various purposes, such as trading. Examples include Swahili in East Africa, Hausa in West Africa and Tok Pisin in Papua New Guinea. The term historically referred to a language that was a mixture of Italian, French, Greek, Spanish and Arabic, used for trading and military purposes.

linguistics the systematic, scientific study of language. It describes language and seeks to establish general principles rather than to prescribe rules of correctness.

loanword a word that has been taken into one language from another. From the point of view of the language taking the word in, the word is known as a borrowing. Some loanwords become naturalized or fully integrated into the language and have a pronunciation and spelling reflecting the conventions of the language which has borrowed them. Other loanwords retain the spelling and pronunciation of the language from which they have been borrowed. These include 'Gastarbeiter', borrowed from German and meaning 'a foreign worker'.

localism a word or expression the use of which is restricted to a particular place or area. The area in question can be quite small, unlike dialect words or 'regionalism'.

malapropism the incorrect use of a word, often through confusion with a similar-sounding word. It often arises from someone's attempt to impress someone else with a knowledge of long words or of technical language.

mother tongue the language that one first learns, the language of which one is a native speaker.

native speaker *see* **mother tongue**.

neologism a word that has been newly coined or newly introduced into the language, as 'camcorder', 'Jacuzzi' and 'karaoke'.

palindrome a word which reads the same backwards a forwards, such as 'level' or 'madam'. It can also apply to a phrase, as 'Able was I ere I saw Elba'.

pangram a phrase or sentence which contains all the letters of the alphabet. The ideal pangram contains each letter only once, but this is quite difficult to do, if the result is to be meaningful.

officialese a derogatory term for the vocabulary and style of writing often found in official reports and documents and thought of as being pretentious and difficult to understand. It is usually considered to be the prime example of gobbledegook.

orthography the study or science of how words are spelt.

philology the science, especially comparative, of languages and their history and structure.

prefix *see* **affix**.

redundancy *same as* **tautology**.

retronym a word or phrase that has had to be renamed slightly in the light of another invention, etc. For example, an ordinary guitar has become 'acoustic guitar' because of the existence of 'electric guitar'. Leather has sometimes become 'real leather' because of the existence of 'imitation leather'.

root *same as* **base**.

semantics the study of the historical development and change of word meaning

slang the name given to a set of highly colloquial words and phrases, often rapidly changing and ephemeral, which are regarded as being below the level of educated standard speech. The term is also used to refer to the language used by a particular group of people e.g. surfer's slang.

stem *same as* **base**.

stress emphasis placed on a particular sound or syllable of a word by pronouncing it with more force than those surrounding it.

suffix *see* **affix**.

synonym a word which has the same, or a similar, meaning to another word.

tautology unnecessary repetition, as in 'new innovations', 'a see-through transparent material' and 'one after the other in succession'. In these examples 'new', 'see-through' and 'in succession' are all unnecessary or **redundant** because the idea which they convey is conveyed by 'innovations', 'transparent' and 'one after the others respectively.

Pronunciation

accent commonly refers to a regional or individual way of speaking or pronouncing words, as in 'a Glasgow accent'.

cedilla the **diacritic** used in French to indicative a soft pronunciation, as 'façade'. *See also* **umlaut**.

consonant a speech sound which is produced by a closing movement, either partial or total, involving the vocal organs, such as the lips, teeth, tongue or the throat, which forms such a narrow constriction that the sound of air can be heard passing through. The term also applies to a letter of the alphabet sounded in this way. *See* **vowel**.

dental produced by the tip of the tongue positioned near the front teeth, as in the pronunciation of the letter 'd'.

diacritic a mark placed a either above or below a letter to indicate a certain emphasis or pronunciation.

diaeresis a mark that is placed over a vowel to indicate that it is sounded separately from a neighbouring vowel, as in 'naïve', 'Chloë'.

digraph a group of two letters representing one sound, as in 'ay' in 'hay', 'ey' in 'key', 'oy' in 'boy', 'ph' in 'phone' and 'th' in 'thin'. When the digraph consists of two letters physically joined together, as 'æa', it is called a 'ligature'.

diphthong a speech sound that changes its quality within the same single syllable. The sound begins as for one vowel and moves on as for another. Since the sound glides from one vowel into another, a diphthong is sometimes called a **gliding vowel**. Examples include the vowels

231

disyllabic

sounds in 'rain', 'weigh', 'either', 'voice', 'height', 'aisle', 'road', 'soul', 'know', 'house', 'care', 'pure', 'during', 'here' and 'weird'.

disyllabic a term that describes a word with two syllables. For example, 'window' is disyllabic, since it consists of the syllable 'win' and the syllable 'dow'. Similarly 'curtain' is disyllabic since it consists of the syllable 'cur' and 'tain'.

elision the omission of a speech sound or syllable, as in the omission of 'd' in one of the possible pronunciations of 'Wednesday' and in the omission of 'ce' from the pronunciation of 'Gloucester'.

fricative a sound produced by forcing air through a partly closed passage, as in the pronunciation of 'th'.

gliding vowel same as **diphthong**.

hiatus a break in pronunciation between two vowels that come together in different syllables, as in 'Goyaesque' and 'cooperate'.

inflection a varying of tone or pitch.

International Phonetic Alphabet a system of written symbols designed to enable the speech sounds of any language to be consistently represented. Some of the symbols are the ordinary letters of the Roman alphabet but some have been specially invented. The alphabet was first published in 1889 and is commonly known as **IPA**.

intrusive r the pronunciation of the *r* sound between two words or syllables where the first of these ends in a vowel sound and the second begins with a vowel sound and where there is no 'r' in the spelling. It appears in such phrases as 'law and order', which is frequently pronounced as 'lawr and order'.

IPA *see* **International Phonetic Alphabet**.

labial formed by closing, or partially closing, the lips, as in the pronunciation of the letter 'm'.

labiodental produced by the lips and teeth together, as in the pronunciation of the letter 'v'.

length mark a mark used in phonetics in relation to a vowel to indicate that it is long. This can take the form of a 'macron', a small horizontal stroke placed above a letter, or a symbol resembling a colon placed after a vowel in the IPA pronunciation system.

macron *see* **length mark**.

phoneme the smallest unit of speech.

phonetics the science connected with pronunciation and the representation of speech sounds.

plosive denoting a burst of air, such as is produced when pronouncing the letter 'p'.

sibilant suggesting a hissing sound, as that produced when pronouncing the letter 's'.

umlaut the **diacritic** which indicates a change of vowel sound in German, as in *mädchen*.

spoonerism the accidental or deliberate transposition of the initial letters of two or more words when speaking, as in 'the queer old dean' instead of 'the dear old queen', 'a blushing crow' instead of a 'crushing blow' and 'a well-boiled icicle' instead of a 'well-oiled bicycle'. Spoonerisms are called after the Reverend William Archibald Spooner (1844–1930) of Oxford University.

velar produced by the back of the tongue on the soft palate, as in the pronunciation of the letter 'g' in the word 'grand', etc.

voiceless spoken without using the vocal cords, as in the pronunciation of the letter 'p'.

vowel a sound produced by the passage of air through the larynx, virtually unobstructed, no part of the mouth being closed and none of the vocal organs being so close together that the sound of air can be heard passing between them. The term is also applied to a letter of the alphabet sounded in this way. The vowels in the alphabet are a, e, i, o and u.

Words liable to be mispronounced

abdomen is now usually pronounced with the emphasis on the first syllable (*ab*-do-men).

acumen is now usually pronounced *ak*-yoo-men, with the emphasis on the first syllable, although formerly the stress was usually on the second syllable (yoo).

adult may be pronounced with the emphasis on either of the two syllables. Thus *a*-dult and a-*dult* are both acceptable although the pronunciation with the emphasis on the first syllable (*a*-dult) is the more common.

adversary is commonly pronounced with the emphasis on the first syllable (*ad*-ver-sar-i) although in modern usage it is also found with the emphasis on the second syllable (ad-*ver*-sar-i).

aged has two possible pronunciations depending on the sense. When it means 'very old', as in 'aged men with white beards', it is pronounced *ay*-jid. When it means 'years of age', as in 'a girl aged nine', it is pronounced with one syllable, *ayjd*.

banal should rhyme with 'canal', with the emphasis on the second syllable (ba-*nal*).

blackguard, meaning 'a scoundrel', has an unusual pronunciation. It is pronounced *blagg*-ard.

brochure is usually pronounced *bro*-sher, despite the *ch* spelling, rather than bro-*shoor*, which is French-sounding.

Celtic is usually pronounced kel-tik.

cervical has two possible pronunciations. Both *ser*-vik-al, with the emphasis on the first syllable, and ser-*vik*-al, with the emphasis on the second syllable which has the same sound as in *Vik*ing in 'cervical cancer'.

chamois in the sense of 'a kind of cloth (made from the skin of the chamois antelope) used for polishing or cleaning' is pronounced *sham*-mi. In the sense of 'a kind of antelope', it is pronounced *sham*-wa.

chiropodist is usually pronounced kir-*op*-od-ist with an initial *k* sound, but the pronunciation shir-*op*-od-ist with an initial *sh* sound is also possible.

clandestine usually has the emphasis on the second syllable, as klan-*des*-tin', but it is acceptable to pronounce it with the emphasis on the first syllable, as *klan*-des-tin.

comparable is liable to be mispronounced. The emphasis should be on the first syllable, as in *kom*-par-able. It is often mispronounced with the emphasis on the second syllable.

contrary has two possible pronunciations. When it means 'opposite', as in 'On the contrary, I would like to go very much', it is pronounced with the emphasis on the first syllable (*kon*-trar-i). When it means 'perverse, stubborn', as in 'contrary children' it is pronounced with the emphasis on the second syllable, which is pronounced to rhyme with 'Mary'.

controversy is usually pronounced with the emphasis on the first syllable (*kon*-tro-ver-si). In modern usage there is a growing tendency to place the emphasis on the second syllable (kon-*tro*-ver-si).

dais meaning 'platform' or 'stage', is now usually pronounced as two syllables, as day-is. Formerly it was pronounced as one syllable, as days.

decade is pronounced with the emphasis on the first syllable as *dek*-ayd. An alternative but rare pronunciation is dek-*ayd*.

demonstrable is most commonly pronounced di-*mon*-strabl, with the emphasis on the second syllable, in modern usage. Previously the emphasis was on the first syllable as *dem*-on-strabl.

explicable is now usually pronounced with the emphasis on the second syllable (ex-*plik*-ibl). Formerly it was commonly pronounced with the emphasis on the first syllable (*ex*-plikibl).

exquisite has two possible pronunciations. It is most usually pronounced with the emphasis on the first syllable (*ex*-kwis-it) but some prefer to put the emphasis on the second syllable (iks-*kwis*-it).

finance can be pronounced in two ways. The commoner pronunciation has the emphasis on the second syllable and the first syllable pronounced like the fin of a fish (fin-*ans*). The alternative pronunciation has emphasis on the first syllable, which then is pronounced as fine (*fin*-ans).

formidable may be pronounced with the emphasis on the first syllable as *for*-mid-ibl or with the emphasis on the second syllable as for-*mid*-ibl.

forte the usual pronunciation is *for*-tay but it can also be pronounced as single syllable fort. The word means 'someone's strong point', as in 'Putting people at their ease is not her forte' and 'The chef's forte is desserts'. There is also a musical word **forte** meaning 'loud' or 'loudly'. It is of Italian origin and is pronounced either *for*-ti or *for*-tay.

foyer the most widely used pronunciation is foi-ay but it can also be pronounced fwah-yay following the original French pronunciation.

harass traditionally is pronounced with the stress on the first syllable, as *har*-as. However, in modern usage there is an increasing tendency to put the emphasis on the second syllable, as har-*as*, which is how the word is pronounced in America.

heinous is most commonly pronounced *hay*-nis, although *hee*-nis also exists.

hospitable can be pronounced in two ways. The more traditional pronunciation has the emphasis on the first syllable, as *hos*-pit-ibl. In modern usage it is sometimes pronounced with the emphasis on the second syllable, as hos-*pit*-ibl.

impious the emphasis should be on the first syllable as *im*-pi-us. This is unlike 'impiety' where the stress is on the second syllable.

incomparable the emphasis should be on the second syllable and not the third. It should be pronounced in-*kom*-pir-ibl.

inventory unlike the word 'invention', the emphasis is on the first syllable as *in*-ven-tri or *in*-ven-tor-i.

kilometre has two possible pronunciations in modern usage. It can be pronounced with the emphasis on the first syllable, as *kil*-o-meet-er, or with the emphasis on the second syllable, as kil-*om*-it-er. The first of these is the more traditional pronunciation but the second is becoming common.

laboratory should be pronounced with the emphasis on the second syllable, as lab-*or*-a-tor-i or lab-*or*-a-tri. In American English the emphasis is on the first syllable.

lamentable should be pronounced with the emphasis on the first syllable, as *lam*-en-tabl. However it is becoming common to place the emphasis on the second syllable in the same way that 'lament' does.

longevity should be pronounced lon-*jev*-iti. Some people pronounce it lon-*gev*-iti, but this is rarer.

machinations should be pronounced mak-in-*ay*-shunz but mash-in *ay*-shunz is becoming increasingly common in modern usage.

mandatory the emphasis should be on the first syllable, as *man*-da-tor-i.

margarine formerly the usual pronunciation was mar-ga-reen but now the most common pronunciation is mar-ja-reen.

migraine is pronounced *mee*-grayn in British English but the American pronunciation of *mi*-grayn, in which the first syllable rhymes with 'eye', is sometimes used in Britain.

motif is pronounced with the emphasis on the second syllable, as mo-*teef*.

naïve is pronounced ni-*eev*, with the emphasis on the second syllable, and the first syllable rhyming with 'my'. The accent on the *ï* (called a diaeresis) indicates that the two vowels *a* and *i* are to be pronounced separately.

necessarily is traditionally pronounced with the emphasis on the first syllable, but this is often very difficult to say except when one is speaking exceptionally carefully. Because of this difficulty it is often pronounced with the emphasis on the third syllable although this is considered by many people to be incorrect.

niche the most common pronunciation is *nitch*, but *neech*, following the French pronunciation, is also a possibility.

pejorative in modern usage it is pronounced with the emphasis on the second syllable, as in pi-*jor*-at-iv.

phlegm is pronounced *flem*.

prestige is pronounced prez-*teezh*.

primarily is traditionally pronounced with the emphasis on the first syllable, as *prim*-ar-el-i. Since this is difficult to say unless one is speaking very slowly and carefully, it is becoming increasingly common to pronounce it with the emphasis on the second syllable, as prim-*err*-el-i.

quay the spelling of the word does not suggest the pronunciation, which is *kee*.

questionnaire formerly the acceptable pronunciation was kes-tyon-*air*, but in modern usage kwes-chon-*air* is more common.

schedule is usually pronounced *shed*-yool in British English. However, the American English pronunciation *sked*-yool is now sometimes found in British usage.

subsidence has two acceptable pronunciations. It can be pronounced either sub-*sid*-ens, with the emphasis on the middle syllable which rhymes with 'hide', or *sub*-sid-ens, with the emphasis on the first syllable and with the middle syllable rhyming with 'hid'.

suit is pronounced *soot* or *syoot*.

suite is pronounced *sweet*.

swingeing is pronounced *swin*-jing, not like swinging.
trait is traditionally pronounced *tray* but *trayt* is also an
 acceptable pronunciation in modern usage
victuals is pronounced *vitlz*.
vitamin is pronounced vit-a-min, with the first syllable
 rhyming with 'lit' in British English. In American English the first syllable rhymes with 'light'.

Words Liable to be Confused

Some words with totally different meanings are liable to be confused, often, but not always, because they are pronounced in a similar way or have similar spellings. Below is a list of words which are often confused, together with short examples of usage to help you to differentiate them.

accept	accept a gift
except	everyone except Mary
access	access to the building; access to computer data
excess	an excess of food at the picnic
adapter	the adapter of the novel for TV
adaptor	an electrical adaptor
addition	an addition to the family
edition	a new edition of the book
adverse	an adverse reaction to the drug
averse	not averse to the idea
advice	seek legal advice
advise	We advise you to go
affect	badly affected by the news
effect	the effects of the drug
alley	a bowling alley
allay	allay the child's fears

allusion, delusion

allusion	make no allusion to recent events
delusion	under the delusion that he is immortal
illusion	an optical illusion
altar	praying at the altar
alter	alter the dress
alternately	feeling alternately hot and cold
alternatively	we could drive there – alternatively we could walk
amend	amend the law
emend	emend the text before printing
angel	heavenly angels
angle	a triangle has three angles; a new angle to the story
annex	annex a neighbouring country
annexe	build an annexe to the house
antiquated	antiquated attitudes
antique	valuable antique furniture
arisen	a problem has arisen
arose	a problem arose today
ascent	the ascent of Everest
assent	he gave his assent to the proposal
astrology	believers in astrology read horoscopes
astronomy	astronomy involves the scientific study of the stars and the planets
ate	we ate bread and cheese
eaten	we have eaten too much

aural	an aural impairment requiring a hearing aid; an aural comprehension test
oral	both oral and written language exams; oral hygiene recommended by the dentist
bad	bad men arrested by the police
bade	we bade him farewell
bail	the accused was granted bail
bale	a bale of cotton; bale out; bale out water; bale out of an aircraft
ballet	practising ballet steps
ballot	voting by means of a secret ballot
bare	bare feet
bear	bear the pain; bear children; bears looking for food
base	at the base of the pillar; base the argument on facts
bass	sing bass; fishermen catching bass
bath	lie soaking in the bath; bath the baby
bathe	bathe in the sea; bathe a wound
baton	the conductor's baton; a relay baton
batten	secure the broken door with wooden battens; batten down the hatches
beach	building sand castles on the beach
beech	beech and oak trees
been	having been famous
being	being poor scared her

beat, beet

beat	beat them at tennis; beat the dog with a stick
beet	sugar beet; soup made with beet
beat	we should beat them
beaten	we should have beaten them
became	she became famous
become	he wants to become a doctor
beer	a pint of beer
bier	a funeral bier
began	the child began to cry
begun	it had begun to rain
belief	have belief in his son's abilities
believe	believe that his son could succeed
beside	the bride stood beside the groom
besides	besides, he has no money; who, besides your mother, was there
bit	the dog bit the postman
bitten	he was bitten by a rat
blew	the wind blew; the hat blew away
blown	the wind had blown fiercely; the papers have been blown away
bloc	the African bloc of countries
block	a block of flats; a block of wood; block a pipe
boar	shooting wild boar
bore	the speaker is a bore
boast	boast about his achievements
boost	give a boost to the economy

bonny	a bonny little girl with beautiful hair
bony	the man's bony knees
born	babies born in hospital
borne	I could not have borne the pain; water-borne diseases
bouquet	a bouquet of roses
bookie	place a bet with a bookie
bow	take a bow after the performance; bow to the queen
bough	the bow of a tree
boy	boys and girls
buoy	a mooring buoy in the bay
breach	a breach of the peace; breach the enemy's defences
breech	the breech of a gun; a breech delivery of a baby
bread	bread and butter
bred	born and bred
break	break an arm
brake	failure of the car's brakes; brake suddenly on seeing the dog in the road
breath	take a deep breath
breathe	breathe deeply
bridal	the bridal party going to the church
bridle	the horse's bridle
broke	the watch fell and broke
broken	the watch was broken

brooch, broach

brooch	wear a silver brooch
broach	afraid to broach the subject
buffet	[buffit] heavy waves regularly buffet the cliffs
buffet	[boofay] serve a cold buffet at the party; the station buffet
but	he was dead, but his family did not know
butt	butt in rudely to the conversation; the goat will butt you; a cigarette butt
calf	a cow and her calf; the calf of the leg
calve	hoping the cow would calve soon
callous	a cruel, callous tyrant
callus	the callus on her finger
came	they came late
come	they promised to come
cannon	soldiers firing cannons
canon	the canons of the cathedral; the canons and principles of the Christian church
canvas	a bag made of canvas; the canvas painted by a local artist
canvass	canvass for votes
carton	a carton of milk
cartoon	children laughing at TV cartoons
cast	the whole cast came on stage; cast a quick glance; a cast in the eye
caste	the caste system in India
censor	appoint a film censor; censor letters
censure	censure the child's unruly behaviour

cereal	cereal crops; breakfast cereal
serial	a magazine serial
chafe	tight shoes will chafe your heels; chafe at the delay
chaff	separate the wheat from the chaff
chartered	a chartered surveyor; a chartered boat
charted	the charted areas of the region
cheap	buy cheap clothes at the market
cheep	birds beginning to cheep
check	check the addition; check the tyre pressure; act as a check on her extravagance
cheque	pay by cheque
checked	a checked tablecloth
chequered	a chequered career
choose	you may choose a cake
chose	she chose a peach from the fruit dish
chosen	you have chosen well; the chosen few
chord	a musical chord; strike a chord
cord	the cord of a dressing gown; spinal cord; vocal cord
coarse	made of some coarse material; a coarse sense of humour
course	taking a French course; a golf course; in due course
coma	the patient is still in a coma
comma	put a comma instead of the full stop

commissionaire, commissioner

commissionaire	the hotel commissionaire
commissioner	a police commissioner
compliment	embarrassed at being paid a compliment
complement	a full complement of staff; the complement of a verb
complimentary	complimentary remarks; complimentary tickets
complementary	complementary medicine; a complementary amount; complementary angles
compulsive	a compulsive gambler
compulsory	compulsory to wear school uniform
concert	an orchestral concert
consort	the queen's consort
confident	confident of success
confidant	he was the king's trusted confidant
confidante	she was the queen's closest confidante
conscience	suffering from a guilty conscience
conscious	he was knocked out but is conscious now; conscious that she was all alone; a conscious decision
conservative	wear conservative clothes; a conservative, rather than radical, approach
Conservative	the Conservative Party in British politics

consul	he was British consul in Rome then
council	she was elected to the town council
counsel	counsel for the defence; seeking professional counsel
contemptible	a contemptible act of cowardice; a contemptible fellow
contemptuous	contemptuous of the achievements of others; contemptuous of the law
continual	disturbed by continual interruptions; in continual pain
continuous	a continuous line of cars; a continuous roll of paper
coop	a hencoop
coup	a military coup
corps	an army corps; the corps de ballet
corpse	a corpse found in a shallow grave
councillor	a town councillor
counsellor	a bereavement counsellor
courtesy	treat the visitors with courtesy
curtsy	curtsy to the queen
credible	a credible story
creditable	a creditable performance
credulous	credulous enough to believe anything
crevasse	a crevasse in the glacier
crevice	a crevice in the rock
cue	a billiards cue; an actor famous for missing his cue
queue	the bus queue

curb	curb their extravagance
kerb	cars parked by the kerb
currant	a currant bun
current	unable to swim against the strong current
cygnet	a swan and her cygnets
signet	a signet ring
cymbal	banging the cymbals
symbol	a symbol of purity; a mathematical symbol
dairy	milk from the dairy
diary	writing in her diary every night
dear	dear friends; clothes which are too dear
deer	hunting deer
dependant	trying to provide for his wife and other dependants
dependent	dependent on her family for personal care
deprecate	strongly deprecate the behaviour of the gang of youths
depreciate	depreciate in value
desert	camels in the desert; He deserted his wife and family
dessert	have chocolate cake for dessert
detract	detract from his reputation as an actor
distract	try not to distract the driver
device	a device designed to save water
devise	devise a rescue plan

devolution	the population voted for the de-volution of power from the government to the assembly
evolution	the theory of evolution was first proposed by Charles Darwin
dew	the morning dew
due	payment is due now; in due course
did	you did enough; He did steal the money
done	you have done enough
die	very ill and likely to die
dye	about to dye her fair hair black
died	the poet died young
dyed	he dyed his white shirt blue
dinghy	a dinghy capsizing in the storm
dingy	a dingy basement flat
disadvantageous	disadvantageous to one of the teams; disadvantageous, rather than favourable, circumstances
disadvantaged	disadvantaged people in society
discomfit	the question seemed to discomfit her
discomfort	living in great discomfort
discriminating	discriminating in their choice of wines
discriminatory	discriminatory against women

discus	throwing the discus
discuss	discuss the matter
distinct	see a distinct improvement; a style quite distinct from others
distinctive	the distinctive markings of the zebra
draft	a first draft of a report
draught	there was a draught in the room from the open window; a draught of cold beer
dragon	a dragon breathing fire
dragoon	the dragoon guards; We dragooned her into helping us
drank	we drank some white wine
drunk	to have drunk too much; a drunk woman staggering down the street
drunken	a drunken, violent man; a drunken brawl
drew	the child drew a picture
drawn	he has drawn a picture of a house
driven	we were driven home by my father
drove	we drove home after midnight
dual	serve a dual purpose
duel	fight a duel
economic	a country facing economic disaster; charging an economic rent for the flat
economical	the economical use of resources; an economical car to run; economical with the truth
eerie	in the eerie atmosphere of a thick mist
eyrie	the eagle's eyrie

elder	Mary has two brothers and James is the elder
eldest	John has three sisters and Jill is the eldest
elicit	elicit information
illicit	an illicit love affair
eligible	eligible for promotion; an eligible bachelor
legible	scarcely legible handwriting
elude	elude capture by the police
allude	allude to facts which he had concealed
emigrant	emigrants weeping for their native land
immigrant	illegal immigrants to the country
emigration	the poor standard of living led to mass emigration from the country
immigration	anxious to reduce the extent of immigration into the country
emission	the emission of poisonous gases
omission	the omission of her name from the invitation list
emotional	an emotional person; an emotional reaction
emotive	an emotive subject
employee	hiring several new employees
employer	asking their employer for an increase in salary
enormity	the enormity of the crime
enormousness	the enormousness of the elephant

envelop, envelope

envelop	she wanted to envelop the child in her arms; Mist began to envelop the mountains
envelope	a brown envelope
enviable	an enviable affluent lifestyle
envious	envious of other people's wealth
epitaph	carve an epitaph on a gravestone
epithet	King Alfred was given the epithet 'great'
equable	an equable climate; an equable temperament
equitable	an equitable system
erotic	erotic picture of naked women
erratic	an erratic driver; impulsive, erratic behaviour
ewe	a ewe and her lambs
yew	the yew tree in the graveyard
exceedingly	exceedingly beautiful
excessively	excessively fond of alcohol
exceptional	a singer of exceptional talent; an exceptional amount of rain
exceptionable	find their behaviour exceptionable
executioner	bring the condemned man to the executioner
executor	an executor of a will
exercise	physical exercise; an English exercise
exorcise	exorcise evil spirits

exhausting	an exhausting climb
exhaustive	an exhaustive search
expand	expand the business; metals expanding in the heat
expend	expend a great deal of energy
expansive	his knowledge of literature was expansive
expensive	spending a lot of money on expensive meals
expedient	politically expedient
expeditious	a parcel sent by the most expeditious method
extant	old customs which are still extant in some areas
extinct	an endangered species that is likely to be extinct soon; a volcano that has been extinct for centuries
faint	feel faint; a faint noise
feint	a feint in fencing
fair	a fair result; fair hair; sideshows at a fair
fare	bus fare; How did you fare in the exam?
fate	suffer a terrible fate; by a strange twist of fate
fête	a fête in aid of charity
fearful	fearful of being left behind; what a fearful smell
fearsome	see a fearsome sight

feat, feet

feat	perform a brave feat
feet	sore feet
fiancé	Jill and her fiancé
fiancée	Jim and his fiancée
final	a final warning
finale	all the cast took part in the final
flair	have a flair for languages
flare	send up a flare as a signal for help; make the fire flare up; a skirt with a slight flare
flammable	clothes made of flammable material
inflammable	highly inflammable substances such as petrol
flea	bitten by a flea
flee	people beginning to flee from the burning houses
fleshy	fleshy upper arms; a fleshy fruit
fleshly	fleshly pleasures
flu	suffering from flu
flue	cleaning the flue
flew	the bird flew away
flown	the bird has flown away
floe	an ice floe
flow	the flow of water
flour	flour to make bread
flower	pick a flower from the garden

flout	flout the new school rule
flaunt	flaunt her long legs
font	babies christened at the font
fount	printed in a small size of fount
forbade	she forbade them to leave
forbidden	she was forbidden to leave
foresaw	we foresaw trouble
foreseen	the problem could not have been foreseen
forgave	we forgave them
forgiven	we have forgiven them
forgot	we forgot about the party
forgotten	I had forgotten the event
formally	formally dressed
formerly	formerly the president of the club
fort	soldiers defending the fort
forte	tact is not his forte
foul	commit a foul on the football pitch; a foul smell
fowl	a chicken is a type of fowl
found	they found the missing child
founded	their grandfather founded the firm
freeze	freeze the vegetables; freeze to death
frieze	a decorative frieze
froze	we froze the meat immediately
frozen	frozen vegetables; have frozen to death

funeral, funereal

funeral	mourners at the funeral
funereal	solemn funereal music
gaff	blow the gaff
gaffe	a social gaffe
gamble	decide to gamble on a horse in the next race
gambol	lambs beginning to gambol about
gate	shut the gate
gait	a shuffling gait
gave	he gave money to the poor
given	we had been given some money
gentle	a gentle touch; a gentle breeze
genteel	a genteel tea party
glacier	a glacier beginning to melt
glazier	a glazier mending the window
goal	score a goal
gaol	escape from gaol
gone	he has gone
went	she went yesterday
gorilla	a gorilla in the zoo
guerrilla	guerrillas fighting in the mountains
grate	a fire burning in the grate
great	a great improvement; a great man
grew	the plants grew well
grown	the plant had grown tall
grief	weeping from grief
grieve	time to grieve for her dead husband

grill	put the meat under the grill
grille	a metal grille on the window
grisly	the grisly sight of a decaying body
grizzly	a grizzly bear
hail	a hail storm; a hail of bullets; hail a taxi
hale	hale and hearty
hair	cut off her hair
hare	a running hare
half	a half of the apple
halve	halve the apple
hangar	an aeroplane hangar
hanger	a clothes hanger
hanged	they hanged the murderer
hung	they hung the pictures
heal	the wound began to heal
heel	a blister on the heel
hear	hear the news
here	here and there
hereditary	a hereditary title
heredity	part of his genetic heredity
heron	a heron catching fish
herring	fishermen catching herring
hid	we hid the treasure
hidden	they have hidden the treasure
hoard	a hoard of treasure
horde	a horde of invaders

honorable	an honorable gentleman; honorable deeds
honorary	the honorary post of secretary
hoop	jump through a hoop
whoop	a whoop of delight
human	a human being
humane	the humane killing of the injured animal
idle	too idle to work
idol	the pop star as teenage idol; worshipping an idol
imaginary	the child's imaginary friend
imaginative	an imaginative story; an imaginative person
immoral	wicked and immoral
immortal	no one is immortal
inapt	an inapt remark
inept	an inept attempt
incredible	find the story incredible
incredulous	incredulous enough to believe anything
industrial	an industrial estate
industrious	studious and industrious
ingenious	an ingenious plan
ingenuous	an ingenuous young person
its	a dog wagging its tail
it's	it's raining
jam	strawberry jam; a traffic jam; the machine seemed to jam
jamb	a door jamb

jib	jib at the high price
jibe	ignore the nasty jibe
judicial	a judicial enquiry into the accident
judicious	a judicious choice of words
junction	a road junction
juncture	at this juncture we went home
key	a door key
quay	the boat tied to the quay
knead	knead the bread dough
kneed	he kneed his attacker in the stomach
knew	we knew him slightly
know	we did not know him
known	if I had known
knight	a knight in shining armour
night	a stormy night
laid	we laid the patient on the bed; they laid a new carpet
lain	he had lain injured for days
lair	the animal's lair
layer	a layer of dust
laterally	moving laterally; thinking laterally
latterly	latterly she was very ill
lath	a lath of wood
lathe	using a lathe in the factory
lead	pipes made of lead
led	he led the group

leak, leek

leak	a leak in the pipe
leek	a leek to make soup
licence	have a driving licence
license	to license the sale of alcohol
lifelong	a lifelong ambition
livelong	the livelong day
lighted	a lighted match
lit	we lit the fire; we have lit the fire
lightening	lightening the load
lightning	struck by lightning; a lightning decision
liqueur	an after-dinner liqueur
liquor	strong liquor such as whisky
liquidate	liquidate a debt; liquidate an asset; liquidate an enemy
liquidize	liquidize the soup
literal	a literal translation
literary	literary and artistic tastes
literate	people who are scarcely literate
loath/loth	loath/loth to join in
loathe	I loathe him
local	the local shops; drinking at his local
locale	a perfect locale for a rock concert
loose	loose clothing
lose	lose your luggage; lose weight
loot	the thieves' loot
lute	playing the lute

lumbar	lumbar pain
lumber	to lumber along awkwardly
luxuriant	luxuriant vegetation
luxurious	a luxurious lifestyle
magnate	a shipping magnate
magnet	a fridge magnet
mail	deliver the mail
male	male and female
main	the main reason
mane	the lion's mane
maize	grow maize
maze	get lost in the maze
manner	a friendly manner
manor	a manor surrounded by beautiful gardens
masterful	she prefers masterful men
masterly	a masterly performance
mat	a door mat
matt, matte	matt/matte paint
meat	meat such as beef
meet	meet a friend
medal	a gold medal
meddle	meddle in the affairs of others
mediate	mediate between the rival groups
meditate	meditate to relax

melted, molten

melted	the ice cream melted; melted chocolate
molten	molten lava
metal	chairs made of metal
mettle	a test of the football team's mettle
meter	read the gas meter
metre	a metre of silk
miner	a coal miner
minor	a minor incident; legally still a minor
missal	members of the congregation carrying missals
missile	hit by a missile
mistaken	a case of mistaken identity; we were mistaken
mistook	I mistook him for you in the dark
model	a model of a ship; a fashion module
module	a space module; a software module; a study module
momentary	a momentary lapse of memory
momentous	a momentous decision
moral	the moral of the story; a person with no morals
morale	morale was low in the firm
motif	decorated with a motif of roses
motive	a motive for murder
muscle	strain a muscle
mussel	eat fresh mussels

naturalist	a naturalist interested in local flowers
naturist	naked people on a naturist beach
naval	a naval cadet
navel	your navel is in the middle of your abdomen
negligent	negligent parents
negligible	a negligible amount of money
net	caught in a net
net, nett	net, nett profit
niceness	appreciate the old lady's niceness
nicety	the nicety of the distinction
notable	a notable figure in the town
noticeable	a noticeable improvement
nougat	nougat is a sweet
nugget	a nugget of gold; a nugget of information
oar	the boat's oars
ore	iron oar
observance	the observance of school rules
observation	keep the patient under observation
of	made of gold; tired of working; a glass of wine
off	run off; switch off; badly off
official	an official report; official duties; council official
officious	upset at the officious manner of the hotel receptionist

organism, orgasm

organism	an organism found in the water supply
orgasm	to reach orgasm
outdoor	an outdoor sport
outdoors	playing outdoors
overcame	we overcame the enemy
overcome	an enemy difficult to overcome
overtaken	he had overtaken the other runners
overtook	they overtook the car in front
pail	a pail of water
pale	looking pale; a pale colour
pain	suffering from pain
pane	a pane of glass
pair	a pair of gloves
pare	he began to pare his toenails
pear	an apple and a pear
palate	the soft palate
palette	an artist's palette
pallet	a straw pallet
passed	she passed the exam; we passed the other car; the feeling passed
past	past times; in the past; walking past the church; a mile past the village
pastel	pastel colours
pastille	sucking a throat pastille
pâté	chicken liver pâté on toast
patty	a small meat patty

peace	warring nations now at peace
piece	a piece of cake
peak	a mountain peak; talent at its peak
peek	peek through the window
peal	the bells began to peal
peel	peel an orange
pearl	a pearl necklace
purl	knit two, purl two
pedal	pedal the bike
peddle	peddle their wares
pendant	wearing a silver pendant
pendent	pendent lights lighting up the room
perceptible	a perceptible improvement
perceptive	a perceptive remark
perpetrate	perpetrate a crime
perpetuate	perpetuate the myth
persecute	persecute members of other religions
prosecute	prosecute thieves
personal	a personal letter; a personal assistant
personnel	the person in charge of office personnel
phase	the next phase of the development; phase in the changes
faze	nothing seems to faze her
pigeon	a pigeon looking for food
pidgin	pidgin English
place	a sunny place; get a place at university
plaice	plaice and chips

plain, plane

plain	a plain carpet; rather a plain girl; corn growing on the plain
plane	a plane taking off; the plane used by the joiner; writing on a different plane from other crime writers
plaintiff	evidence on behalf of the plaintiff
plaintive	a plaintive cry
plate	the food on the plate
plait	wearing her hair in a plait
plum	eating a plum
plumb	plumb straight; plumb in the middle; plumb the depths; plumb-in the bath
politic	not politic to ask any questions
political	political parties
pour	pour water
pore	pore over the book; a clogged pore
practice	go to football practice
practise	to practise dance steps
pray	pray to God
prey	the fox's prey; prey on one's mind
precede	the leader who preceded the present one; precede them into the room
proceed	You may proceed; proceed to cause trouble
precipitate	rash, precipitate action; precipitate economic panic
precipitous	a precipitous slope

premier	a meeting of European premiers; one of the country's premier actors
première	the premiere of the film
premises	seek new office premises
premise	based on a mistaken premise
prescribe	prescribe antibiotics for the disease
proscribe	proscribe the carrying of dangerous weapons
principal	the college principal
principle	a person of principle; the principle of the steam engine
prise	prise open the lid of the tin
prize	win a prize
program	a computer program
programme	a theatre programme
proof	no proof of his guilt
prove	able to prove her innocence
prophecy	the gift of prophesy; her prophecy came true
prophesy	prophesy that there would be a war
prostate	the prostate gland
prostrate	lying prostrate on the ground
purposely	leave the book behind purposely
purposefully	walk purposefully into the room
quash	quash a rebellion; quash a conviction
squash	squash the tomatoes; squash the insect with his foot

quiet, quite

quiet	a quiet child; a quiet time of day
quite	quite good; quite right
racket	the noisy children made quite a racket; a drugs racket; tennis racket
racquet	tennis racquet (variant spelling)
rain	get wet in the rain
reign	in the reign of the last king
rein	a horse's reins
raise	raise one's arm; raise a family
raze	raze the whole street to the ground
ran	they ran away
run	he started to run; She had run away
rang	they rang the bell
rung	they had rung the bell
rap	rap at the window
wrap	wrap the presents
rapt	with rapt attention
wrapped	we wrapped the presents
read	I read the book last week
red	a red dress
real	made of real leather; a real friend
reel	a reel of thread; dance a reel
refuge	seek refuge from the storm
refugee	a political refugee
regal	a regal wave of the hand
regale	regale them with his adventures

relief	bring relief from pain
relieve	relieve the pain
rest	rest after work
wrest	wrest the knife from his hand
retch	feel sick and begin to retch
wretch	the poor wretch
review	the review of the play; the annual salary review
revue	a musical revue
rhyme	children reciting a rhyme; cook rhymes with book
rime	rime on the grass on a cold morning
ridden	she had ridden the horse home
rode	he rode a fine stallion
right	the right person for the job; the right to be free; the right hand
rite	a religious rite
write	write in pencil
risen	the sun had risen
rose	the sun rose
road	the road through the town
rode	the child rode her bicycle
roe	cod roe
row	a row of green beans; row a boat
role	play the role of Hamlet; the parental role
roll	a roll of carpet; a ham roll; roll a ball

rote	learn the answers by rote
wrote	he wrote a letter
rough	a rough material; rough weather
ruff	a lace ruff at the neck
rout	rout the enemy
route	the shortest route to the town
rung	the bottom rung of the ladder; we had rung the bell
wrung	she wrung her hands in grief
rye	grow rye and barley
wry	a wry smile; a wry sense of humour
sail	the sail of a boat; go for a sail
sale	an end-of-season sale
salon	a hair-dressing salon
saloon	a saloon car; a saloon bar
sang	they sang a song
sung	we had sung a song earlier
sank	the ship sank
sunk	the ship has sunk
sunken	a sunken wreck
saviour	the saviour of the organization; Christ the saviour
savour	savour the delicious food
saw	we saw him go
seen	I have seen the film before
sawed	we sawed the wood
sawn	all the wood has been sawn

scared	scared of the dark
scarred	scarred for life in the accident
scene	a scene in the play; the scene of the accident
seen	have seen the play
scent	the scent of roses
sent	she sent a letter
sceptic	a sceptic arguing with the believers
septic	a septic wound; a septic tank
scraped	he scraped the car on the gate
scrapped	they scrapped their original plans
sculptor	a statue by a famous sculptor
sculpture	carve a piece of sculpture
seam	sew the seam of a dress; a seam of coal
seem	they seem familiar
seasonal	seasonal hotel work
seasonable	seasonable weather for spring
seasoned	a seasoned dish of stew; seasoned travellers
secret	a secret hideout; their engagement was a secret
secrete	secrete the money under the floorboards
see	I see a light
sea	boats sailing on the sea
sensual	a sensual mouth
sensuous	the sensuous feel of the silk sheets

series, serious

series	a series of disasters; a TV series
serious	a serious matter; looking serious
sew	sew new curtains
sow	sow seeds
sewed	she sewed tiny stitches
sewn	the dress which she had sewn
shaken	she was shaken by the accident
shook	he shook the child angrily
shear	to shear sheep
sheer	a sheer slope; sheer impertinence; sheer silk
shelf	put the book on the shelf
shelve	shelve the plan
shoe	a high-heeled shoe
shoo	shoo the dog away
showed	we showed them the house
shown	he has shown me the book
shrank	the child shrank back in fear; the dress shrank in the wash
shrunk	the child had shrunk from the angry man; the dress had shrunk
sight	the sight of the woman crying
site	the battle site; a building site
singeing	singeing a blouse with an iron
singing	singing a song
slay	slay an enemy in battle
sleigh	a sleigh ride in the snow

slow	at a slow pace
sloe	a ripe sloe
soar	soar up high
sore	a sore finger
solder	to solder metal
soldier	a soldier in the British army
sole	the sole reason; the sole of the foot; a dish of sole
soul	body and soul; a poor old soul
some	some people
sum	the sum total
son	a son and two daughters
sun	lie in the sun on the beach
soot	soot falling down the chimney
suit	an evening suit
sped	the car sped away into the night
speeded	we speeded up to pass the car in front
spoke	she spoke with feeling
spoken	he has spoken to the parents
sprang	he sprang to his feet
sprung	the lion had sprung over the fence
stair	a stone stair
stare	stare into space
stake	a stake missing from the fence; stake a claim
steak	eat a large steak

stalk	the stalk of the flower
stock	a large stock of goods; stocks and shares
stank	he stank of beer
stunk	the room had stunk for days
stationary	the car was stationary
stationery	a shop stocking stationery
statue	stone statues in the grounds of the house
statute	pass a new statute
steal	steal the money from the till
steel	tools made of steel
stile	climb over the stile
style	dress with style; a style of writing
stimulant	athletes taking illegal stimulants
stimulus	the stimulus of a valuable prize
storey	the top storey of the house
story	tell a story
straight	a straight road; a straight answer
strait	the Bering Strait
straightened	she had her teeth straightened
straitened	in straitened circumstances
strategy	the team's winning strategy; devise a strategy to counteract bullying
stratagem	devise a stratagem to mislead the enemy
strewed	they strewed flowers
strewn	flowers were strewn

tail, tale

strife	quarrelling and strife
strive	strive to overcome the difficulty
striven	we haven striven to succeed
strove	they strove to win
suede	a jacket made of real suede
swede	cutting up a swede for dinner
suit	wearing a smart suit; a law suit; a suit of cards
suite	a three-piece suite; a suite of rooms; a ballet suite
summary	a summary of the report; his summary dismissal
summery	sunny, summery weather
sundae	an ice cream sundae
Sunday	have a rest on Sunday
surplice	the priest's surplice
surplus	a surplus of food at the party
swam	we swam in the river
swum	he has swum across the river
swingeing	a swingeing blow; swingeing cuts
swinging	a swinging gate; the swinging sixties
swollen	her eye has swollen up; swollen glands
swelled	her injured ankle swelled
swore	they swore they would find the killer
sworn	he has sworn to get revenge
tail	the dog's tail
tale	tell a tale

taken, took

taken	she has taken the book
took	she took the book
taper	a lighted taper; The road seems to taper there
tapir	a tapir is a pig-like animal
taught	he taught us maths
taut	a taut rope; a face taut with concentration
tea	a cup of tea
tee	a golf tee
team	a football team
teem	the town will teem with tourists
tear	wipe away a tear
tier	one tier of the wedding cake
teeth	have two teeth extracted
teethe	the child has begun to teethe
temporal	temporal, not spiritual
temporary	a temporary post
their	their home
there	stay there
they're	they're quarrelling again
thorough	a thorough cleaning
through	pass through
thrash	thrash the youth with a belt
thresh	thresh the corn
threw	he threw the ball
through	go through the door

threw	he threw the ball
thrown	he had thrown the ball
throes	in the throes of studying for exams
throws	he throws the ball
thyme	flavour the sauce with thyme
time	what time is it?; not enough time
tic	a nervous tic
tick	the tick of the clock; the dog bitten by the tick; in a tick; a tick at a correct answer
timber	a house made of timber
timbre	the timbre of his voice
tire	runners beginning to tire
tyre	change a car tyre
to	go to town
too	she wants to go too
two	two or three times
toe	injure a toe
tow	tow the broken-down car
tomb	the tomb of the Egyptian king
tome	struggling to read a legal tome
topi	wear a topi in the hot sun
toupee	a bald man wearing a toupee
tore	she tore her dress
torn	she has torn her dress; a torn dress

trait	dishonesty is an unpleasant trait
tray	tea served on a tray
treaties	signing treaties to end the war
treatise	write a treatise on company law
trod	she trod on the cat's tail
trodden	she had trodden on some mud
troop	a troop of soldiers; troop out of school
troupe	a troupe of actors
turban	hair hidden by a turban
turbine	a turbine engine
tycoon	a business tycoon
typhoon	a ship damaged in a typhoon
unaware	unaware of what had happened
unawares	taken unawares by the attack
unconscionable	an unconscionable delay
unconscious	knocked unconscious by the blow; unconscious of the recent event
undid	they undid all the damage
undone	the damage could not be undone
unexceptional	a disappointing, unexceptional performance
unexceptionable	unnecessary complaints about unexceptionable behaviour
unwanted	unwanted guests
unwonted	speak with unwonted enthusiasm

urban	prefer urban to rural life
urbane	an urbane young man
vacation	go on vacation to America
vocation	have a vocation to be a priest
vain	a vain young woman; a vain attempt
vane	a weather vane
vein	inject the drug into a vein; a vein of pessimism in the novel
vale	the Vale of Evesham
veil	a hat with a veil; draw a veil over the incident
veracity	doubt the veracity of the account
voracity	the voracity of the youth's appetite
vertex	the vertex of a cone
vortex	the swimmer was caught in a vortex of water and drowned
vigilant	be vigilant because of pickpockets
vigilante	the thief was caught by a vigilante
wafer	an ice cream wafer; a Communion wafer
waver	begin to waver about the decision
waif	a starving waif
waive	waive the extra charges
wave	wave to their departing guests
waist	a leather belt round the waist
waste	liquid waste from the factory; a waste of food

want, wont

want	want more money; for want of enough money
wont	she was wont to arrive late
warden	the warden of the hostel
warder	a prison warder
ware	kitchen ware; stallholders selling their wares
wear	wear a skirt; show signs of wear
way	the quickest way home; the correct way to do it
weigh	weigh the apples
weak	invalids too weak to get out of bed
week	go to the supermarket every week
weakly	weakly children who did not survive
weekly	look forward to their weekly visit
went	they went quite suddenly; She went pale
gone	he has gone home; She had gone deaf
wet	a wet day; wet the floor
whet	whet the appetite
whit	not care a whit
wit	find his wit amusing; a person of wit and intelligence
whole	the whole group
hole	dig a hole

withdrawn	he has withdrawn from the election; a shy, withdrawn child
withdrew	he withdrew from the election
wittily	he spoke wittily after dinner
wittingly	she wittingly told a lie
woe	sadness and woe
woo	woo her and marry her
woke	she woke early
woken	she had woken early
wore	he wore the shoes
worn	he had worn the shoes; an old, worn carpet
would	we knew she would go
wood	a pine wood
wove	he wove the material
woven	he has woven the material
weaved	the cyclist weaved in and out of the line of traffic
wreak	wreak vengeance; wreak havoc
wreck	wreck the car; wreck their plans
wreath	a holly wreath
wreathe	mist had begun to wreathe the mountain peaks
wrote	she wrote the letter
written	she has written the letter

yoke, yolk

yoke	the yoke of a dress; the yoke of a plough
yolk	egg yolk
yore	in days of yore
your	your house
you're	you're wrong

Affixes

Affix refers to an element that is added to the root or stem of a word to form another word. Affixes can be in the form of **prefixes or suffixes**. A prefix is added to the beginning of a word, as audio in audiovisual, an affix to the end, as -aholic in workaholic. Some common affixes are listed below.

a-, an- a prefix meaning without or not, as amoral, anonymous and atypical.

-able, -ible a suffix meaning 'that can be', as laughable, washable, horrible and edible.

aero- a prefix meaning **1** air, as aerobics and aeroplane, **2** aeroplane, as aerodrome.

agro-, agri- a prefix meaning field, as agriculture and agrochemicals.

-aholic a suffix indicating an addiction, formed on analogy with alcoholic, as workaholic and shopaholic. It sometimes becomes **-oholic**, as chocoholic.

ambi- a prefix meaning two or both as ambivalent, having mixed or uncertain feelings about something and ambidextrous, able to use both the right and left hand with equal skill.

-ana a suffix meaning 'things associated with', as Americana.

ante- a prefix meaning before, as antenatal, before birth.

anti- a prefix meaning against. It is used in many words that have been established In English for a long time, as antipathy, a feeling of hostility or dislike, but it has also been used to form many modern words, as anti-freeze, anti-nuclear and anti-warfare.

arch- a prefix meaning chief, as archbishop, archduke and arch-enemy.

-arch a suffix meaning ruler or leader, as monarch and patriarch.

astro- a prefix meaning star, as in astrology, astronomy, astronaut, astrophysics.

-athon, -thon a suffix meaning large-scale or long-lasting contest or event, such as swimathon. Such words are formed on analogy with the word marathon.

audio- a prefix referring to hearing. It is found in several words that have been established in the language for some time, as audition, but it is also used to form many modern words, as audiotape and audiovisual.

auto- a prefix meaning of or by itself, as autobiography, autograph and automatic, meaning working by itself.

bi- a prefix meaning two, as in bicycle, bifocal, bilingual and bisect. Bi- forms words in English in which it means half, and other words in which it means twice. This can give rise to confusion in such words as biweekly and bimonthly, where there are two possible sets of meanings. Biweekly can mean either every two weeks or twice a week so that one would not be able to be certain about the frequency of a biweekly publication. Similarly, a bimonthly publication might appear either twice a month or once every two months.

biblio- a prefix meaning book, as bibliophile, a person who is fond of or collects books, and bibliography.

bio- a prefix meaning life or living material, as biography and biology.

-bound a suffix meaning **1** confined or restricted, as housebound and snowbound, **2** It can also mean obligated, as duty-bound.

by- a prefix **1** meaning subordinate, secondary, as by-product, **2** around, as in by-pass.

cardi- a prefix meaning heart, as cardiology and cardiac.

cent-, centi- a prefix meaning hundred, as centenary and centigrade.

chrono- a prefix meaning time, as chronology and chronicle.

-cide a suffix meaning killing, as infanticide, patricide and pesticide.

circum- a prefix meaning around, as circumnavigate and circumvent.

con-, com- a prefix meaning together with, as connect, compare and compound.

contra- a prefix meaning opposite or against, as contrary, contradict and contraflow.

deca- a prefix meaning ten, as decade and decathlon.

deci- a prefix meaning tenth, as decibel and decimal

demi- a prefix meaning half, as demigod.

di- a prefix meaning two or double, as in dioxide, dilemma, diphthong and disyllabic.

dia- a prefix meaning **1** through, as in diaphanous, **2** apart, as in diacritical, diaphragm and dialysis, **3** and across, as in diameter.

dis- a prefix indicating opposite or meaning not, as disappear, disapprove, dislike, disobey, dispossess, distrust and disunite.

-dom a suffix meaning state or condition, as in boredom, freedom, officialdom, martyrdom, **2** rank or status, as in earldom, dukedom, **3** domain or territory as in kingdom.

dys- a prefix meaning, bad, impaired or abnormal, as dys-
functional and dyslexia, dyspepsia

eco- a prefix indicating ecology. Following the increased
awareness of the importance of the environment, there
has been a growing interest in ecology and many words
beginning with eco- have been added to the English
language. Some of these are scientific terms such as
ecotype, ecosystem or ecospecies. Others are more
general terms, such as ecocatastrophe and ecopolitics,
and some are even slang terms, such as ecofreak and
econut.

-ectomy a suffix that indicates surgical removal, as hyster-
ectomy (the surgical removal of the womb), mastectomy
(the surgical removal of a breast) and appendicectomy
(the surgical removal of the appendix).

-ed a suffix that forms the past tense and past participles
of regular verbs, as in asked, caused, dropped and es-
caped.

-ee a suffix that is used as part of nouns that are the re-
cipients of an action, as in deportee (a person who has
been deported); employee, and interviewee. The prefix
can also be used as part of a noun indicating a person
who acts or behaves in a particular way, as absentee (a
person who absents himself/herself) and escapee (a person who escapes).

electro- a prefix meaning electric, electrical as electro-
magnetic.

-en a suffix with several functions. In one sense it indicates causing to be, as broaden, darken, gladden, lighten
and sweeten. It also indicates a diminutive or small version of something, as chicken and maiden. It also indi-

cates what something is made of, as in silken and wooden. It is also used to form the past participle of many irregular verbs, such as broken and fallen.

en- a prefix indicating causing to be, as in enrich and enlarge, and putting into, as endanger and enrage. enslave.

equi- a prefix meaning equal, as equidistant and equivalent.

-er a suffix with several functions. It can indicate a person who does something, as in bearer, cleaner, employer, farmer, manager. Some words in this category can also end in '-or', as in adviser/advisor. It can also indicate a person who is engaged in something, as in lawyer. It also indicates a thing that does something, as in blender, cooker, mower, printer and strainer. It can also indicate the comparative form of an adjective, as in darker, fairer, older, shorter and younger. It can also indicate someone who comes from somewhere, as in Londoner.

-ese a suffix that indicates belonging to, coming from and is used of people and languages, as Chinese, Japanese and Portuguese. By extension it refers to words indicating some kind of jargon, as computerese, journalese and legalese.

-esque a suffix of French origin that means in the style or fashion of, as in Junoesque, statuesque, Picassoesque, Ramboesque.

-ess a suffix that was formerly widely used to indicate the feminine form of a word, as authoress from author, poetess from poet, editress from editor, and sculptress from sculptor. In many cases the supposed male form, such as author, is now considered a neutral form and so

-est

is used of both a woman and a man. Thus a woman as well as a man may be an author, a poet, an editor and a sculptor, etc. Some words ending in -ess remain, as princess, duchess, heiress and hostess. Actress and waitress are still also fairly widespread.

-est a suffix that indicates the superlative forms of adjectives, as biggest, smallest and ugliest.

-ette a suffix indicating **1** a diminutive or smaller version, as cigarette and kitchenette, **2** imitation, as in flannelette and leatherette, **3** a female version, as usherette, a female usher in a cinema. In this last sense it is sometimes used disparagingly, as in jockette (a derogatory word for a female jockey) and hackette a derogatory word for a female journalist.

Euro- a prefix meaning **1** referring to Europe, as in Eurovision, **2** (more commonly now) referring to the European Community, as in Euro-MP, Eurocrat and Eurocurrency.

ex- a prefix meaning former, as ex-chairman, ex-president, ex-wife.

extra- a prefix meaning beyond, outside as in extramarital, meaning outside marriage and extra-curricular, meaning outside the curriculum.

-fold a suffix meaning 'times', multiplied by, as in fourfold, a hundredfold.

for- a prefix with several meanings. These include prohibition, as forbid; abstention as in forbear, forgo and forswear; neglect, as forsake; excess, intensity, as forlorn; and away, off, apart, as forgive.

fore- a prefix meaning **1** before, as forecast, foregoing and forefathers, **2** front as forehead, foreground.

-form a suffix meaning **1** having the form of, as cruci-
form, meaning in the form of a cross, **2** having such a
number of, as uniform, multiform.

-ful a suffix indicating **1** the amount that fills something,
as handful, spoonful and bagful, **2** full of, as beautiful,
truthful and scornful, **3** having the qualities of, as mas-
terful, **4** apt to, able to, as forgetful and useful.

-free a suffix used to form adjectives indicating absence
of, freedom from as carefree, trouble-free, anxiety-free,
tax-free, lead-free.

-friendly a modern suffix formed on analogy with user-
friendly to mean helpful to, supporting, as child-friendly
and environment-friendly.

-gate a modern suffix that is added to a noun to indicate
something scandalous. Most of the words so formed are
short-lived and forgotten about almost as soon as they
are invented. In modern usage they are frequently used
to apply to sexual scandals, but originally -gate was restricted to some form of political scandal. The suffix is
derived from Watergate, and refers to a political scandal
in the United States during President Richard Nixon's
re-election campaign in 1972, when Republican agents
were caught breaking into the headquarters of the Demo-
cratic Party in Washington, which were in a building
called the Watergate Building. The uncovering of the
attempts to cover up the break-in led to Richard Nixon's
resignation.

geo- a prefix meaning earth, as geography and geology.

-gram a suffix meaning **1** writing or drawing, as telegram,
electrocardiogram and diagram, **2** used in modern usage
to indicate a greeting or message, as in kissogram.

-graph a suffix meaning **1** written or recorded, as autograph, monograph, photograph, **2** an instrument that records, as seismograph, tachograph and cardiograph.

gynaec-, gynaeco- a prefix meaning female, woman, as gynaecology.

-hand a suffix meaning **1** worker, as deckhand, farmhand and cowhand, **2** position, as right-hand and left-hand.

haem-, haemo- a prefix meaning blood, as haemorrhage and haematology.

hemi- a prefix meaning half, as hemisphere.

hetero- a prefix meaning other, another, different, as heterosexual.

holo- a prefix meaning complete, whole, as holistic

homo- a prefix meaning same, as in homogenous, homonym and homosexual.

-hood a suffix meaning state or condition, as babyhood, childhood, manhood, priesthood, womanhood and widowhood.

hydro- a prefix meaning water, as hydro-electric and hydrophobia. It also means 'hydrogen', as in hydrochloride.

hyper- a prefix meaning over, above, as hyperactive, hypercritical and hypersensitive.

hypo- a prefix meaning under, as hypothermia and hypodermic.

-ian a suffix indicating **1** a profession, job or pastime, as comedian, musician, optician, physician, **2** proper names, as Dickensian, Orwellian and Shakespearian.

-iana a suffix which is a form of form of **-ana** and indicates memorabilia or collections relating to people or places of note, as Churchilliana.

-ible *see* **-able.**

-ics a suffix indicating science or study, as electronics, genetics, and politics.

-ify a suffix indicating 'making or becoming', as clarify, purify, satisfy and simplify.

infra- a prefix meaning below or beneath, as infrared and infrastructure.

-in a suffix meaning **1** in or into, as income, inside and invade, **2** not, as incurable, incapable and inconvenient

-ine a suffix indicating 'belonging to', as canine, divine and feline.

-ing a suffix used to form the present participle of verbs, as living, going and running.

inter- a prefix meaning between, as in intercity, intercontinental and interstate.

intra- a prefix meaning within, as intravenous.

-ise and **-ize** are both verb endings. In British English there are many verbs that can be spelt ending in either **-ise** or **-ize**, as 'computerise/ize', 'economise/ize', 'finalise/ize', 'hospitalise/ize', 'modernise/ize', 'organise/ize', 'realise/ize', 'theorise/ize'. There are a few verbs that cannot be spelt **-ize**. These include 'advertise', 'advise', 'comprise', 'despise', 'exercise', 'revise', 'supervise' and 'televise'.

-ish a suffix meaning **1** somewhat, as baldish, smallish and youngish, **2** nationality, as Spanish, Turkish and Polish.

-ism a suffix indicating **1** a state or condition, as conservatism, egotism and heroism, sometimes an abnormal state, as alcoholism. **2** doctrine, theory or system of beliefs, as Catholicism and Marxism. **3** discrimination or prejudice, as ageism, discrimination on the grounds of age, often against old or older people, classicism, discrimination on the grounds of social class, racism, discrimination on the grounds of race and sexism, discrimination on the grounds of sex or gender, often against women.

iso- a prefix meaning equal, as in isobar, isotherm and isosceles.

-ist a suffix indicating believer, supporter, practitioner, as in atheist, fascist, feminist and Methodist.

-ite a suffix indicating a believer, supporter, practitioner, as in Thatcherite and Trotskyite.

-itis a suffix indicating an illness or disease, as bronchitis, a disease of the chest and hepatitis, a disease of the liver.

-ize see **-ise.**

kilo- a prefix meaning a thousand, as in kilogram, kilohertz, kilolitre, kilometre and kilowatt.

-kin a suffix that indicates a diminutive or smaller version, as in lambkin and mannikin.

-kind a suffix indicating a group of people, as in humankind, mankind, womankind.

-less a suffix meaning **1** without or lacking added to nouns to form adjectives, as expressionless, fearless, harmless, homeless and hopeless, **2** without being able to be measured, as ageless, countless, priceless and timeless.

-let a suffix indicating a diminutive or smaller form of something, as in booklet, coverlet, droplet, islet, piglet, starlet and streamlet.

-like a suffix indicating similarity, as in childlike, dreamlike, lifelike and warlike.

-ling a suffix indicating a diminutive or smaller version of something, as duckling, gosling and nestling.

-logue a suffix meaning conversation or discussion, as dialogue, monologue, prologue and travelogue.

-ly a common adverbial ending, as hurriedly, sharply and tightly.

macro- a prefix meaning large in size or scope, as in macrobiotic, macrocosm and macrostructure.

-mania a suffix indicating abnormal or obsessive behaviour, as kleptomania and pyromania.

mal- a prefix meaning **1** bad, unpleasant, as malodorous, having an unpleasant smell, **2** imperfect, faulty, as malformation and malfunctioning.

-man a suffix used with nouns to form nouns indicating someone's job, as barman, chairman, clergyman, policeman and salesman. In modern usage, when attempts are being made to remove sexism from the language, alternatives have been sought for any words ending in -man. Formerly, words ending in -man were often used whether or not the person referred to was definitely known to be a man. Different ways have been found to avoid the sexism of -man. Salesman has been changed in many cases to salesperson, chairman often becomes chairperson or chair. Similarly, fireman has become fire-fighter and policeman frequently becomes police officer.

-mate a suffix referring to someone who shares something with someone, as classmate, roommate, schoolmate, team-mate and workmate.

mega- a prefix meaning very large, as megabucks and megastar. Many words using mega- in this way are modern and many are also informal or slang. In technical language mega- means a million times bigger than the unit to which it is attached, as in megabyte, megacycle, megahertz and megawatt.

meta- a prefix meaning alteration or transformation, as metamorphosis.

-meter a suffix meaning a measuring instrument, as altimeter, barometer, speedometer and thermometer.

-metre a suffix indicating meter, the unit of length, as centimetre, kilometre and millimetre.

micro- a prefix meaning very small, as microscope and microsurgery.

milli- a prefix meaning a thousand, as millisecond and millennium.

mini- a prefix meaning very small or least, as minimum, minimal, and miniature. Mini- is frequently used to form modern words, as minibus, minicab, mini-computer, mini-cruise and miniskirt. Modern words beginning with mini- can often be spelt either with a hyphen or without.

mis- a prefix meaning badly, wrongly, as in misbehave, miscalculate, mistreat and misunderstanding.

-monger a suffix meaning dealer, trader, as fishmonger and ironmonger. As well as being used for occupations in which people sell things, it is used for people who 'trade' in less tangible things, as in gossipmonger, rumourmonger, scaremonger and warmonger.

mono- a prefix meaning one or single, as monochrome, monologue, monoplane and monosyllabic.

multi- a prefix indicating many, as in multiply and multitude. Multi- is frequently used to form new modern words, as in multi-media, multi-purpose, multi-storey and multi-talented.

-naut a suffix meaning navigator, as in astronaut and cosmonaut.

neo- a prefix meaning new or recent, as neologism and neo-natal.

neuro- a prefix meaning nerve, as neurology, neuron and neurosurgery.

non- a prefix meaning not, as nonsense and nonconformist.

-ock a suffix indicating a diminutive form, as hillock and bullock.

-ocracy a suffix meaning a form of government, as democracy, bureaucracy and meritocracy.

-ology a suffix meaning study of, as biology and geology.

-oholic *see* **-aholic**.

-ology a suffix meaning study of, as in biology, geology and technology.

omni- a prefix meaning all, as in omnipotent and omnivorous.

-osis a suffix meaning **1** a disease as tuberculosis. **2** a development or process, as metamorphosis, a complete or major change.

para- a prefix meaning **1** beside, as paramilitary, paramedic and paranormal. **2** (defence) against, as parasol and parapet.

pen- a prefix meaning almost, as peninsula and penultimate.

per- a prefix meaning through, as permit.

peri- a prefix meaning round, as perimeter and periphery.

-phile a suffix meaning someone who loves or likes someone or something very much, as Francophile, someone

who loves France, bibliophile, someone who loves
books.

-phobe a suffix meaning someone who hates or fears
someone or something very much, as Europhobe and
Francophobe. The condition has the suffix **-phobia**,
as Europhobia, and there is a whole range of conditions of this kind, as claustrophobia, hatred or fear of
enclosed spaces. *See* section in the **Wordfinder** on
Phobias.

-phone a suffix meaning sound or voice, as megaphone,
telephone and saxophone.

poly- a prefix meaning more than one, many, as polyan-
dry, the practice of having more than one husband.

-person *see* **-man**.

post- a prefix meaning after, as postpone, postscript and
post-war.

pre- a prefix meaning before, as precede, predict and pref-
ace.

pro- a prefix meaning **1** on or forth, as proceed and progress, **2** before, as prologue and prophet. **3** in favour of,
as pro-British and pro-hunting.

pseudo- a prefix meaning false, spurious or sham, as
pseudo-literary and pseudo-leather.

psych-, psycho- meaning mind, as psychiatry and psy-
chology.

re- a prefix meaning **1** back, as return, resign and retract,
2 again, as reconsider and retrial.

retro- a prefix indicating back, backwards, as retrograde,
retrospect and retrorocket.

semi- a prefix meaning half, as semicircle and semi-
detached.

-ship a suffix indicating a state or quality, as friendship, hardship and leadership

sub- a prefix meaning under, as submarine, submerge and subconscious.

super- a prefix meaning over, as supervise, supernatural and superfluous.

syn- a prefix meaning together, as synthesis and synonym

techno- a prefix meaning craft or skill, as technical and technology.

tele- a prefix meaning distance, as telephone, telescope and television.

-tor a prefix indicating a person, especially a person who does something, as actor, sponsor and victor.

trans- a prefix meaning across, as transaction, translate and trans-Atlantic.

-trix a prefix indicating a female equivalent, as proprietrix of proprietor, now not very common.

un- a prefix indicating **1** not, as unclean, untrue and unwise, **2** back, reversal, as in undo, unfasten and untie.

uni- a prefix meaning one, as in unicycle, unilateral and unity.

vice- a prefix meaning in place of, as vice-president and vice-chancellor.

-ward, -wards a suffix indicating direction, as homeward, seaward and outwards.

-ware a suffix meaning manufactured goods, as glassware and silverware.

-ways a suffix indicating manner, way or direction, as sideways.

-wise a suffix indicating **1** manner, way, or direction as clockwise, lengthwise and otherwise, **2** with reference to, as careerwise, **3** clever, sensible, as streetwise.

-work a suffix indicating **1** material from which something is made, as ironwork and woodwork, **2** a job or activity, as farmwork, housework and needlework.

Eponyms

An **eponym** refers to a person after whom something is named. The name of the thing in question can also be referred to as an eponym, or it can be said to be **eponymous**, eponymous being the adjective from eponym. English has several eponymous words. Some examples are listed below together with their derivations:

Bailey bridge, a type of temporary military bridge that can be assembled very quickly, called after Sir Donald **Bailey** (1901–85), the English engineer who invented it.

Bowie knife, a type of hunting knife with a long curving blade, called after the American soldier and adventurer, James **Bowie** (1799–1836), who made it popular.

cardigan, a knitted jacket fastened with buttons called after the Earl of **Cardigan** (1797–1868) who was fond of wearing such a garment and was the British cavalry officer who led the unsuccessful Charge of the Light Brigade during the Crimean War (1854).

Celsius the temperature scale, called after the Swedish astronomer, Anders **Celsius** (1701–44).

freesia, a type of sweet-smelling flower, called after the German physician, Friedrich Heinrich Theodor **Freese** (died 1876).

garibaldi, a type of biscuit with a layer of currants in it, called after Giuseppe **Garibaldi** (1807–1882), an Italian soldier patriot who is said to have enjoyed such biscuits.

Granny Smith, a variety of hard green apple, called after the Australian gardener, Maria Ann Smith, known as **Granny Smith** (died 1870), who first grew the apple in Sydney in the 1860s.

greengage, a type of greenish plum, called after Sir William **Gage** who introduced it into Britain from France (1777–1864).

leotard, a one-piece, close-fitting garment worn by acrobats and dancers, called after the French acrobat, Jules **Leotard** (1842–70), who introduced the costume as a circus garment.

mackintosh, a type of raincoat, especially one made of rubberized cloth, called after the Scottish chemist, Charles **Mackintosh** (1766–1843), who patented it in the early 1820s.

praline, a type of confectionery made from nuts and sugar, is called after Count Plessis-**Praslin** (1598–1675), a French field marshal, whose chef is said to have been the first person to make the sweet.

plimsoll, a type of light rubber-soled canvas shoe, called after the English shipping reform leader, Samuel **Plimsoll** (1824–98). The shoe is so named because the upper edge of the rubber was thought to resemble the **Plimsoll** Line, the set of markings on the side of a ship which indicate the levels to which the ship may be safely loaded. The Plimsoll Line became law in 1876.

salmonella, the bacteria that causes some diseases such as food poisoning, called after Daniel Elmer **Salmon** (1850–1914), the American veterinary surgeon who identified it.

sandwich, a snack consisting of two pieces of buttered bread with a filling, called after the Earl of **Sandwich**

(1718–92) who was such a compulsive gambler that he would not leave the gaming tables to eat, but had some cold beef between two slices of bread brought to him.

saxophone, a type of keyed brass instrument often used in jazz music, called after Adolphe **Sax** (1814–94), the Belgium instrument-maker who invented it.

shrapnel, an explosive projectile that contains bullets or fragments of metal and a charge that is exploded before impact, called after the British army officer, Henry **Shrapnel** (1761–1842), who invented it.

stetson, a type of wide-brimmed, high-crowned felt hat, called after its designer, the American hat-maker, John Batterson **Stetson** (1830–1906).

trilby, a type of soft felt hat with an indented crown, called after *Trilby*, the dramatized version of the novel by the English writer, George du Maurier. The heroine of the play, Trilby O'Ferrall, wore such a hat.

wellington, a waterproof rubber boot that extends to the knee, called after the Duke of **Wellington** (1769–1852), who defeated Napoleon at Waterloo (1815).

Homographs, Homonyms and Homophones

Homographs

A homograph is a word that is spelt the same as another word but has a different meaning and pronunciation. Some examples are:

bow, pronounced to rhyme with how, a verb meaning to bend the head or body as a sign of respect or in greeting, etc, as in 'The visitors bowed to the emperor' and 'The mourners bowed their heads as the coffin was lowered into the grave'.

bow, pronounced to rhyme with low, a noun meaning a looped knot, a ribbon tied in this way', as in 'She tied her hair in a bow and 'She wears blue bows in her hair'.

lead, pronounced leed, a verb meaning to show the way, as in 'The guide will lead you down the mountain'.

lead, pronounced led, a noun meaning a type of greyish metal, as in 'They are going to remove any water pipes made from lead'.

row, pronounced to rhyme with low, a noun meaning a number of people or things arranged in a line', as in 'The princess sat in the front row'.

row, pronounced to rhyme with how, a noun meaning a quarrel, a disagreement, as in 'He has had a row with his neighbour over repairs to the garden wall'.

slough, pronounced to rhyme with rough, a verb meaning to cast off, as in 'The snake had sloughed off its old skin'.

slough, pronounced to rhyme with how, a noun meaning a swamp, as in 'Get bogged down in a slough' and 'in the Slough of Despond'.

sow, pronounced to rhyme with low, a verb meaning to scatter seeds in the earth, as in 'In the spring the gardener sowed some flower seeds in the front garden'.

sow, pronounced to rhyme with how, a noun meaning a female pig, as in 'The sow is in the pigsty with her piglets'.

Homonyms

A homonym is a word that has the same spelling and the same pronunciation as another word but has a different meaning from it. Examples include:

bill, a noun meaning a written statement of money owed, as in 'You must pay the bill for the conversion work immediately', or a written or printed advertisement, as in 'We were asked to deliver handbills advertising the play'.

bill, a noun meaning a bird's beak, as in 'The seagull has injured its bill'.

fair, an adjective meaning attractive, as in 'fair young women'; light in colour, as in 'She has fair hair'; fine, not raining, as in 'I hope it keeps fair'; just, free from prejudice, as in 'We felt that the referee came to a fair decision'.

fair, a noun meaning a market held regularly in the same place, often with stalls, entertainments and rides (now often simply applying to an event with entertainments and rides without the market), as in 'He won a coconut at the fair'; a trade exhibition, as in 'the Frankfurt Book Fair'.

pulse, a noun meaning the throbbing caused by the contractions of the heart, as in 'The patient has a weak pulse'.

pulse, a noun meaning the edible seeds of any of various crops of the pea family, as lentils, peas and beans, as in 'Vegetarians eat a lot of food made with pulses'.

row, a verb, pronounced to rhyme with low, meaning to propel a boat by means of oars, as in 'He plans to row across the Atlantic single-handed'.

row, a noun, pronounced to rhyme with low, meaning a number of people or things arranged in a line, as in 'We tried to get into the front row to watch the procession'

Homophones

A homophone is a word that is pronounced in the same way as another but is spelt in a different way and has a different meaning. Examples include:

aisle, a noun meaning a passage between rows of seats in a church, theatre, cinema etc, as in 'The bride walked down the aisle on her father's arm'.

isle, a noun meaning an island, as in 'the Isle of Wight'.

alter, a verb meaning to change, as in 'They have had to alter their plans'.

altar, a noun meaning in the Christian church, the table on which the bread and wine are consecrated for Communion and which serves as the centre of worship, as in 'The priest moved to the altar, from where he dispensed Communion', 'There is a holy painting above the altar'; or 'a raised structure on which sacrifices are made or incense burned in worship', as in 'The Druids made human sacrifices on the altar of their gods'.

ail, a verb meaning to be ill, as in 'The old woman is ailing'; or to be the matter, to be wrong, as in 'What ails you?'

ale, a noun meaning a kind of beer, as in 'a pint of foaming ale'.

blew, a verb, the past tense of the verb to blow, as in 'They blew the trumpets loudly'.

blue, a noun and adjective meaning a colour of the shade of a clear sky, as in 'She wore a blue dress'.

boar, a noun meaning a male pig, as in 'a dish made with wild boar'.

bore, a verb meaning to make tired and uninterested, as in 'The audience was obviously bored by the rather academic lecture'.

bore, a verb, the past tense of the verb to bear, as in 'They bore their troubles lightly'.

cereal, a noun meaning a plant yielding grain suitable for food, as in 'countries which grow cereal crops' and a prepared food made with grain, as in 'We often have cereal for breakfast'.

serial, a noun meaning a story or television play which is published or appears in regular parts, as in 'the final instalment of the magazine serial which she was following'.

cite, a verb meaning to quote or mention by way of example or proof, as in 'The lawyer cited a previous case to try and get his client off'.

sight, a noun meaning the act of seeing, as in 'They recognized him at first sight'.

site, a noun meaning a location, place, as in 'They have found a site for the new factory'.

feat, a noun meaning a notable act or deed, as in 'The old man received an award for his courageous feat'.

feet, a noun, the plural form of foot, as in 'The child got her feet wet from wading in the puddle'.

none, a pronoun meaning not any, as in 'They are demanding money but we have none'.

nun, a noun meaning a woman who joins a religious order and takes of poverty, chastity and obedience, as in 'She gave up the world to become a nun'.

know, a verb meaning to have understanding or knowledge of, as in 'He is the only one who knows the true facts of the situation', and 'to be acquainted with', as in 'I met her once but I don't really know her'.

no, an adjective meaning not any, as in 'We have no food left'.

rite, a noun meaning a ceremonial act or words, as in 'rites involving witchcraft'.

right, an adjective meaning correct, as in 'Very few people gave the right answer to the question'.

write a verb meaning to form readable characters, as in 'He writes regularly for the newspapers'.

stare, a verb and noun meaning to look fixedly and a fixed gaze, as in 'She stared at him in disbelief when he told her the news' and 'He has the stare of a basilisk'.

stair, a noun meaning a series of flights of stairs, as in 'The old lady is too feeble to climb the stairs to her bedroom'.

Euphemism

Euphemism is a term given to an expression that is a milder, more pleasant, less direct way of saying something that might be thought to be too harsh or direct. English has a great many euphemisms, many of these referring to specific areas of life. Euphemisms range from the high-flown, to the coy, to slang. Some examples of euphemisms, and of the areas in which they tend to occurs, are listed below:

euphemisms for die or be dead: be in the arms of Jesus, be laid to rest, be with one's maker, be no longer with us, be with the Lord, be written out of the script, bite the dust, cash in one's chips, croak, depart this life, go to a better place, go the way of all flesh, go to one's long home, go to the happy hunting grounds, have been taken by the grim reaper, have bought it, have breathed one's last, have gone to a better place, kick the bucket, meet one's end, pass away, pay the supreme sacrifice, pop off, push up the daisies, rest in peace, shuffle off this mortal coil, slip one's rope, turn up one's toes.

euphemisms for old: getting on a bit, not as young as one was, not in the first flush of youth, in the sunset years, in the twilight years, of advanced years, so many years young (as in '90 years young').

euphemisms for suicide: do away with oneself, die by one's own hand, end it all, make away with oneself, take one's own life, take the easy way out, top oneself.

euphemisms for to dismiss: declare (someone) redundant, deselect, dispense with (someone's) services, give early retirement to, give (someone) a golden handshake, give (someone) his/her marching orders, let (someone) go, not to renew (someone's) contract, to rationalize staff.

euphemisms for drunk: blotto, feeling no pain, happy, half-cut, legless, merry, one over the eight, plastered, three sheets to the wind, tiddly, tipsy, tired and emotional, squiffy, well-oiled.

euphemisms for naked: in a state of nature, in one's birthday suit, in the buff, in the nuddy, in the raw, starkers, without a stitch, wearing only a smile.

euphemisms for pregnant: awaiting the patter of tiny feet, expecting, expecting a happy event, in a delicate condition, in an interesting condition, in the club, in the family way, in the pudding club, up the pole, up the spout, with a bun in the oven.

euphemisms for to have sexual intercourse: be intimate with, do it, get one's end away, go to bed with, have it off with, make love, make out, sleep with, score.

euphemisms for sexual intercourse: hanky panky, intimacy, nookie, roll in the hay, rumpy pumpy/rumpty pumpty.

euphemisms for to go to the toilet: answer the call of nature, freshen up, go somewhere, pay a visit, powder one's nose, spend a penny, take a slash, wash one's hands.

toilet

euphemisms for toilet: bathroom, bog, can, john, karzy, powder room, rest room, the facilities, the conveniences, the geography of the house, the little boys' room/the little girls' room, the littlest room, the smallest room, the plumbing, wash room.

euphemisms and political correctness: Many of the expressions advocated by the politically correct movement for viewing physical and mental disabilities in a more positive light are in fact euphemisms. These include 'aurally challenged' for 'deaf', 'optically challenged' for 'blind', and 'uniquely abled' for 'physically disabled'.

Irregular Verbs and Nouns

Irregular verbs

Irregular verbs are verbs that do not conform to the usual pattern of the addition of -*ed* to the past tense and past participle. They fall into several categories.

One category concerns those which have the same form in the past tense and past participle forms as the infinitive and do not end in -*ed*, like regular verbs. These include:

infinitive	past tense	past participle
bet	bet	bet
burst	burst	burst
cast	cast	cast
cost	cost	cost
cut	cut	cut
hit	hit	hit
hurt	hurt	hurt
let	let	let
put	put	put
set	set	set
shed	shed	shed
shut	shut	shut
slit	slit	slit
split	split	split
spread	spread	spread

Some irregular verbs have two past tenses and two past participles which are the same, as in:

irregular verbs

infinitive	past tense	past participle
burn	burned, burnt	burned, burnt,
dream	dreamed, dreamt	dreamed, dreamt,
dwell	dwelled, dwelt	dwelled, dwelt,
hang	hanged, hung,	hanged, hung
kneel	kneeled, knelt,	kneeled, knelt
lean	leaned, leant	learned, learnt
leap	leaped, leapt,	leaped, leapt
learn	learned, learnt	learned, learnt
light	lighted, lit	lighted, lit
smell	smelled, smelt	smelled, smelt
speed	speeded, sped	speeded, sped
spill	spilled, spilt	spilled, spilt
spoil	spoiled, spoilt	spoiled, spoilt
weave	weaved, woven	weaved, woven
wet	wetted, wet	wetted, wet,

Some irregular verbs have past tenses that do not end in -*ed* and have the same form as the past participle. These include:

infinitive	past tense	past participle
bend	bent	bent
bleed	bled	bled
breed	bred	bred
build	built	built
cling	clung	clung
dig	dug	dug
feel	felt	felt
fight	fought	fought
find	found	found

flee	fled	fled,
fling	flung	flung
get	got	got
grind	ground	ground
hear	heard	heard
hold	held	held
keep	kept	kept
lay	laid	laid
lead	led	led
leave	left	left
lend	lent	lent
lose	lost	lost
make	made	made
mean	meant	meant
meet	met	met
pay	paid	paid
rend	rent	rent
say	said	said
seek	sought	sought
sell	sold	sold
send	sent	sent
shine	shone	shone
shoe	shod	shod
sit	sat	sat
sleep	slept	slept
slide	slid	slid
sling	slung	slung
slink	slunk	slunk
spend	spent	spent
stand	stood	stood
stick	stuck	stuck

irregular verbs

sting	stung	stung
strike	struck	struck
string	strung	strung
sweep	swept	swept
swing	swung	swung
teach	taught	taught
tell	told	told
think	thought	thought
understand	understood	understood
weep	wept	wept
win	won	won
wring	wrung	wrung

Some irregular verbs have regular past tense forms but two possible past participles, one of which is regular. These include:

infinitive	past tense	past participle
mow	mowed	mowed, mown
prove	proved	proved, proven
sew	sewed	sewn, sewed
show	showed	showed, shown
sow	sowed	sowed, sown
swell	swelled	swelled, swollen

Some irregular verbs have past tenses and past participles that are different from each other and different from the infinitive. These include:

infinitive	past tense	past participle
arise	arose	arisen
awake	awoke	awoken

bear	bore	borne
begin	began	begun
bid	bade	bidden
bite	bit	bitten
blow	blew	blown
break	broke	broken
choose	chose	chosen
do	did	done
draw	drew	drawn
drink	drank	drunk
drive	drove	driven
eat	ate	eaten
fall	fell	fallen
fly	flew	flown
forbear	forbore	forborne
forbid	forbade	forbidden
forgive	forgave	forgiven
forget	forgot	forgotten
forsake	forsook	forsaken
freeze	froze	frozen
forswear	forswore	foresworn
give	gave	given
go	went	gone
grow	grew	grown
hew	hewed	hewn
hide	hid	hidden
know	knew	known
lie	lay	lain
ride	rode	ridden
ring	rang	rung
saw	sawed	sawn
see	saw	seen

Irregular plural nouns

rise	rose	risen
shake	shook	shaken
shrink	shrank	shrunk
slay	slew	slain
speak	spoke	spoken
spring	sprang	sprung
steal	stole	stolen
stink	stank	stunk
strew	strewed	strewn
stride	strode	stridden
strive	strove	striven
swear	swore	sworn
swim	swam	swum
take	took	taken
tear	tore	torn
throw	threw	thrown
tread	trod	trodden
wake	woken	woke
wear	wore	worn
write	written	wrote

Irregular plural nouns

Irregular plurals refer to the plural form of nouns that do not form their plural in the regular way. Most nouns in English add -s to the singular form to form the plural form, as in *boy* to *boys*.

Some add -es to the singular form to form the plural, as in *church* to *churches*. Nouns ending in a consonant followed by -y have -ies as a regular plural ending. Thus *fairy* becomes *fairies* and *berry* becomes *berries*. The foregoing are all examples of *regular plurals*.

Irregular plurals include words that are different in form from the singular forms and do not simply add an ending. These include *men* from *man*, *women* from *woman* and *mice* from *mouse*.

Some irregular plurals are formed by changing the vowel of the singular forms, as in *feet* from *foot*, *geese* from *goose* and *teeth* from *tooth*.

Some irregular plural forms are formed by adding *-en*, as *oxen* from *ox* and *children* from *child*.

Some nouns ending in *-f* form plurals in *-ves*, as in *loaf* to *loaves*, *half* to *halves*, *wife* to *wives* and *wolf* to *wolves*, but some have alternative endings, as *hoof* to either *hoofs* or *hooves*, and some form regular plurals unchanged, as *roof* to *roofs*.

Some irregular plural forms are the original foreign plural forms of words adopted into English, for example *stimuli* from *stimulus*, *phenomena* from *phenomenon*, *criteria* from *criterion*, *larvae* from *larva*. In modern usage there is a growing tendency to anglicize the plural forms of foreign words. Many of these coexist with the plural form, for example *thesauruses* and *thesauri*, *formulas* and *formulae*, *gateaus* and *gateaux* and *indexes* and *indices*. Sometimes the anglicized plural formed according to the regular English rules differs slightly in meaning from the irregular foreign plural. Thus, *indexes* usually applies to guides in books and *indices* is usually used in mathematics.

Some nouns have irregular plurals in that the plural form and the singular form are the same. These include *sheep*, *grouse* (the game-bird) and *salmon*. Also, some

Irregular plural nouns

nouns have a regular plural and an irregular plural form. Thus, *brother* has the plural forms *brothers* and *brethren*, although *brethren* is now mainly used in a religious context and is archaic in general English.